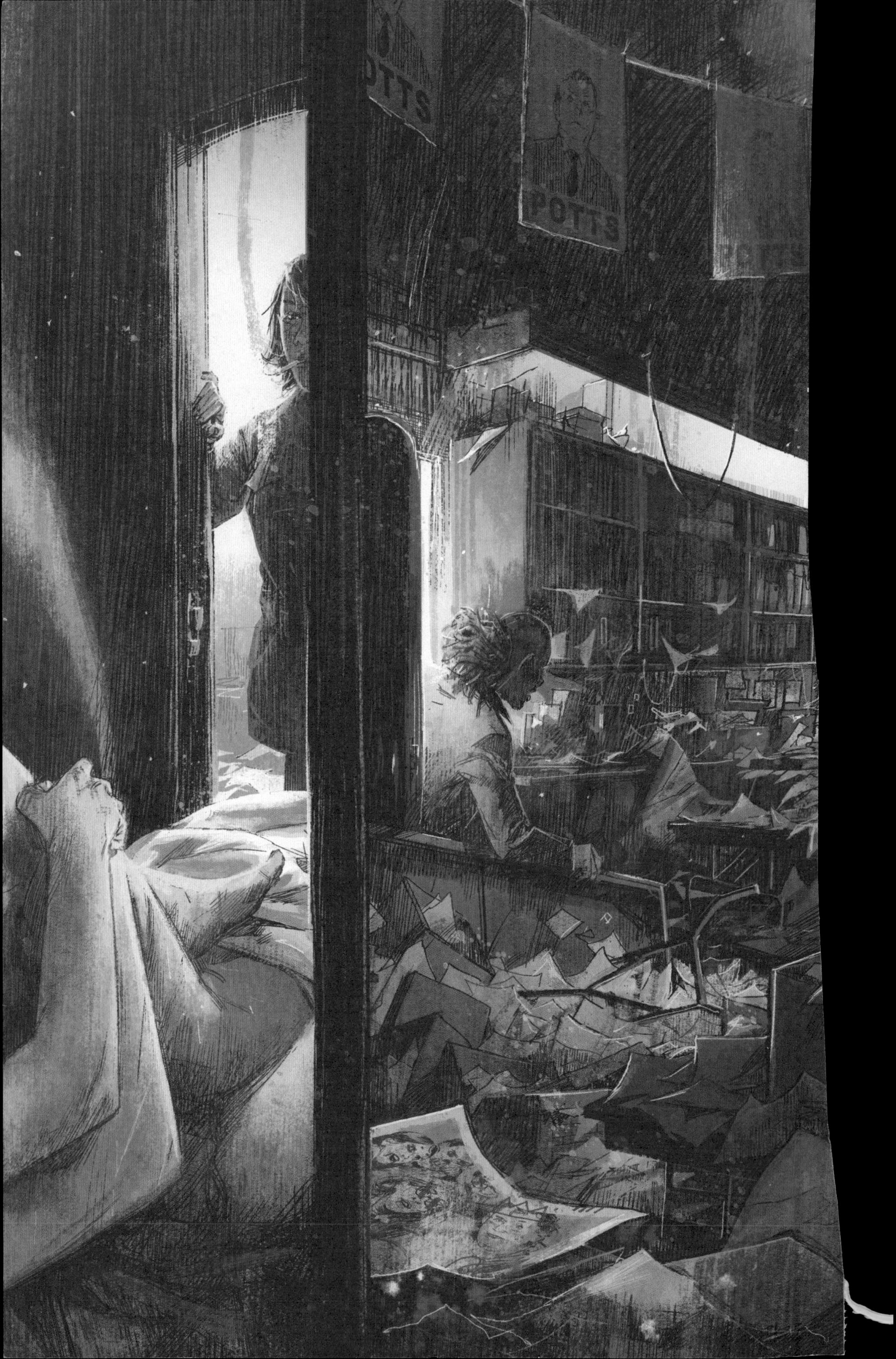
POTTS
POTTS

THE BUNKER

VOLUME 4

Written by
Joshua Hale Fialkov

Illustrated and Lettered by
Joe Infurnari

Colored by
Gonzalo Duarte

Edited by
James Lucas Jones and Robin Herrera

Designed by
Jason Storey

PUBLISHED BY ONI PRESS, INC.

Publisher, Joe Nozemack
Editor In Chief, James Lucas Jones
V.P. of Marketing & Sales, Andrew McIntire
Sales Manager, David Dissanayake
Publicity Coordinator, Rachel Reed
Director of Design & Production, Troy Look
Graphic Designer, Hilary Thompson
Digital Prepress Technician, Angie Dobson
Managing Editor, Ari Yarwood
Senior Editor, Charlie Chu
Editor, Robin Herrera
Administrative Assistant, Alissa Sallah
Director of Logistics, Brad Rooks
Logistics Associate, Jung Lee

VOLUME 4

This volume collects issues 15-19 of the Oni Press series *The Bunker*

ONIPRESS.COM
FACEBOOK.COM/ONIPRESS • TWITTER.COM/ONIPRESS
ONIPRESS.TUMBLR.COM • INSTAGRAM.COM/ONIPRESS
THEFIALKOV.COM/@JOSHFIALKOV • JOEINFURNARI.COM/@INFURNARI

FIRST EDITION:
MAY 2017

LIBRARY OF CONGRESS CONTROL NUMBER:
2016958673

ISBN 978-1-62010-401-9
eISBN 978-1-62010-402-6

10 8 6 4 2 1 3 5 7 9

PRINTED IN CHINA

CHAPTER
15

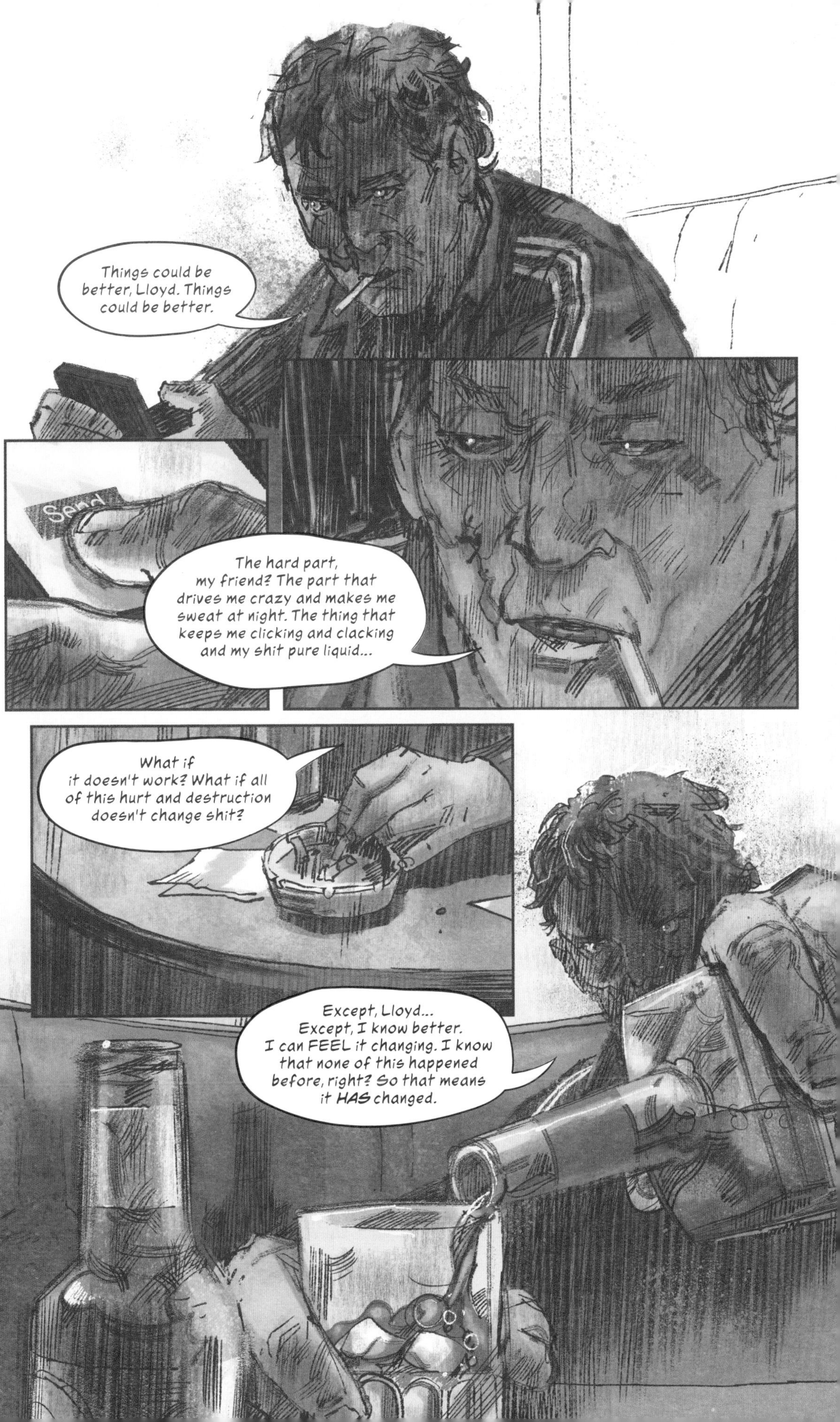
Things could be better, Lloyd. Things could be better.
Send
The hard part, my friend? The part that drives me crazy and makes me sweat at night. The thing that keeps me clicking and clacking and my shit pure liquid...
What if it doesn't work? What if all of this hurt and destruction doesn't change shit?
Except, Lloyd... Except, I know better. I can FEEL it changing. I know that none of this happened before, right? So that means it HAS changed.

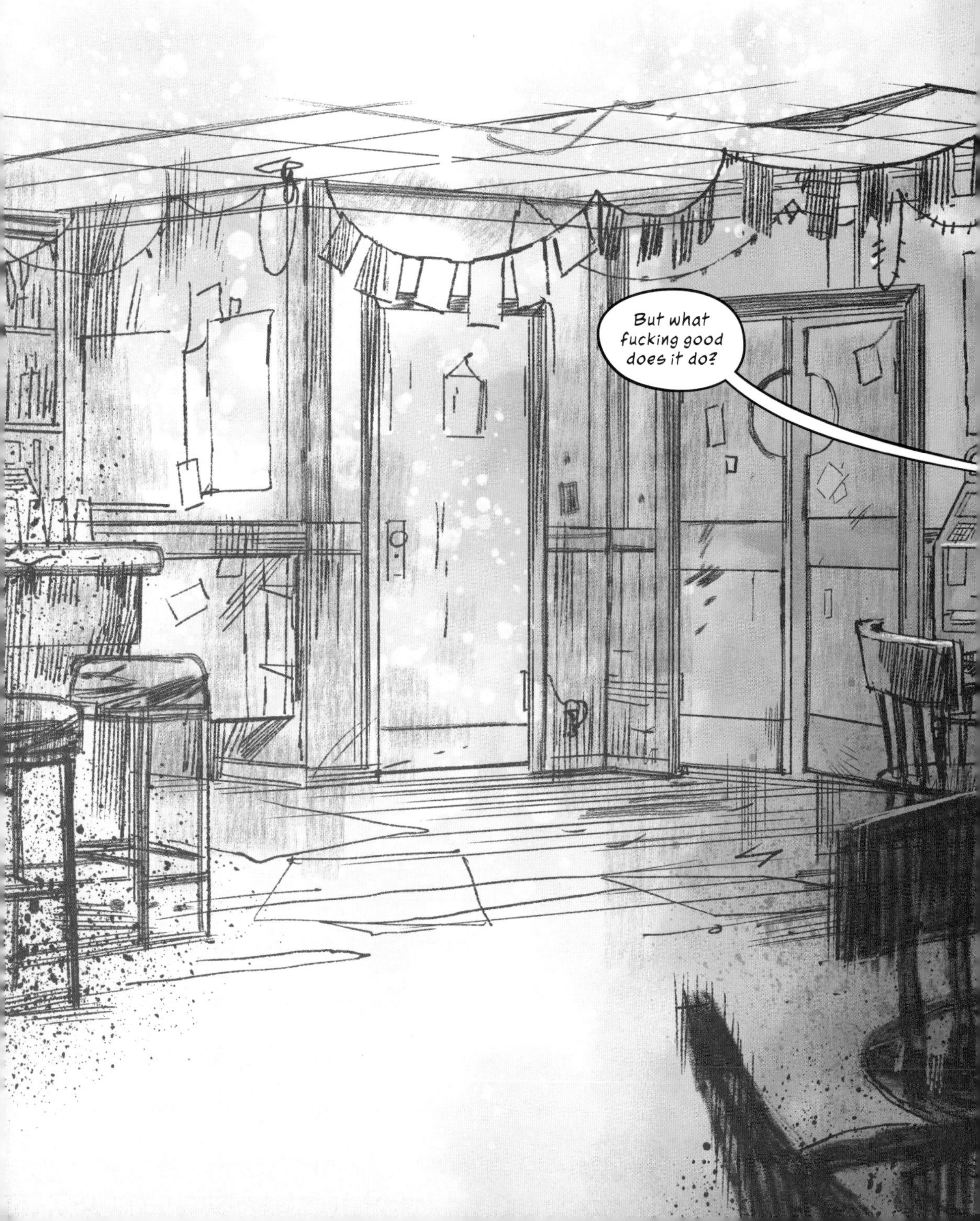
But what fucking good does it do?

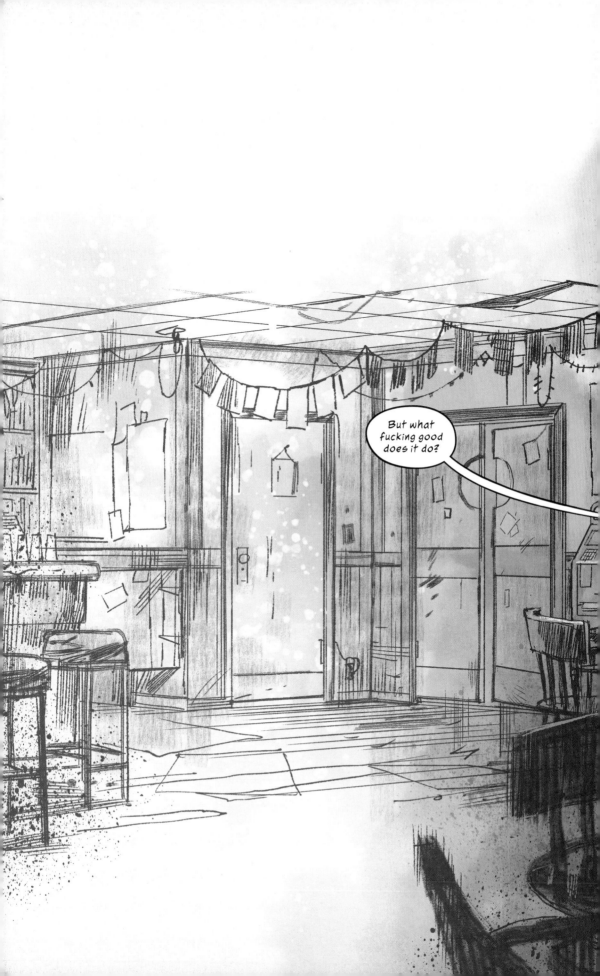

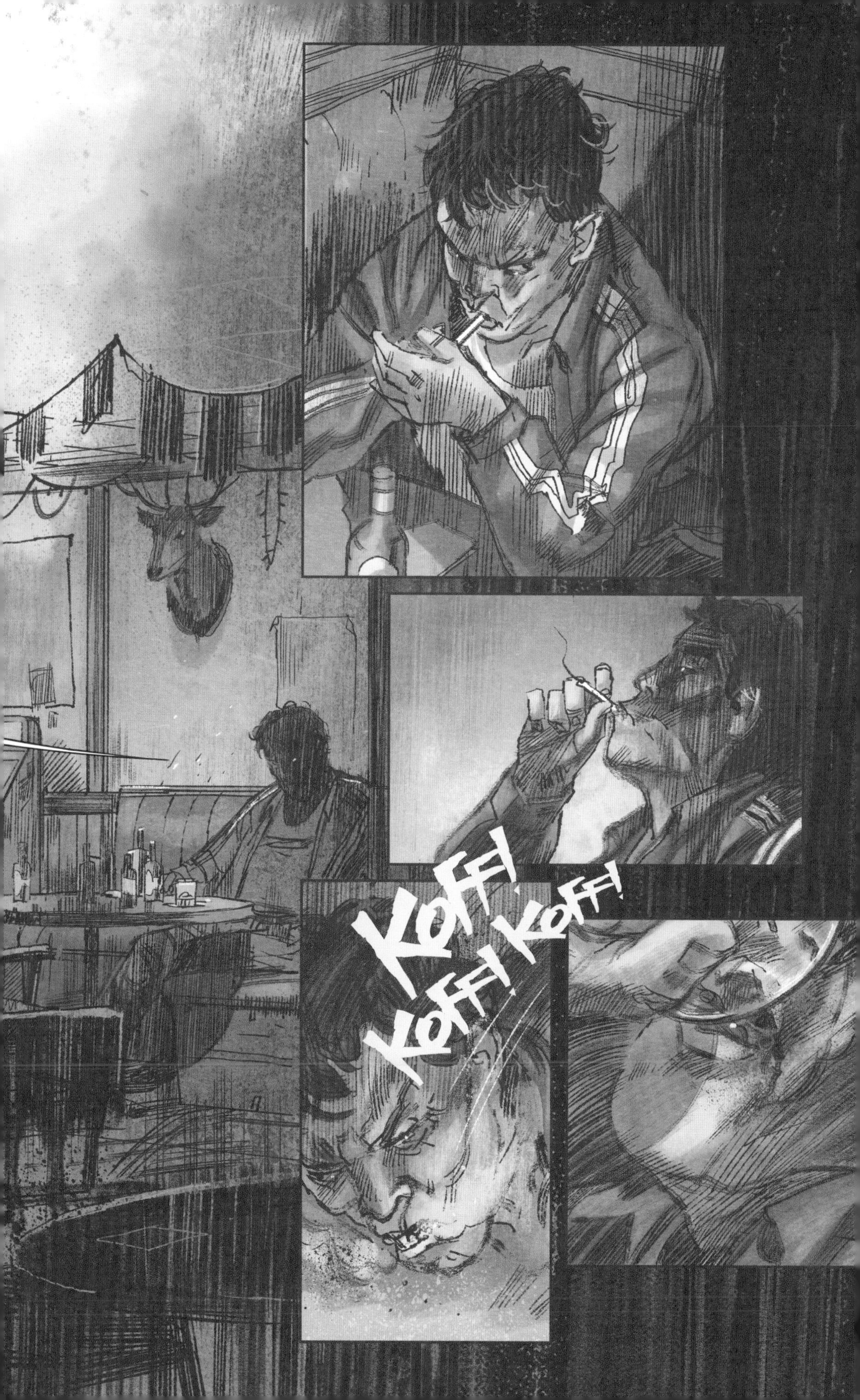
KOFF!
KOFF!
KOFF!

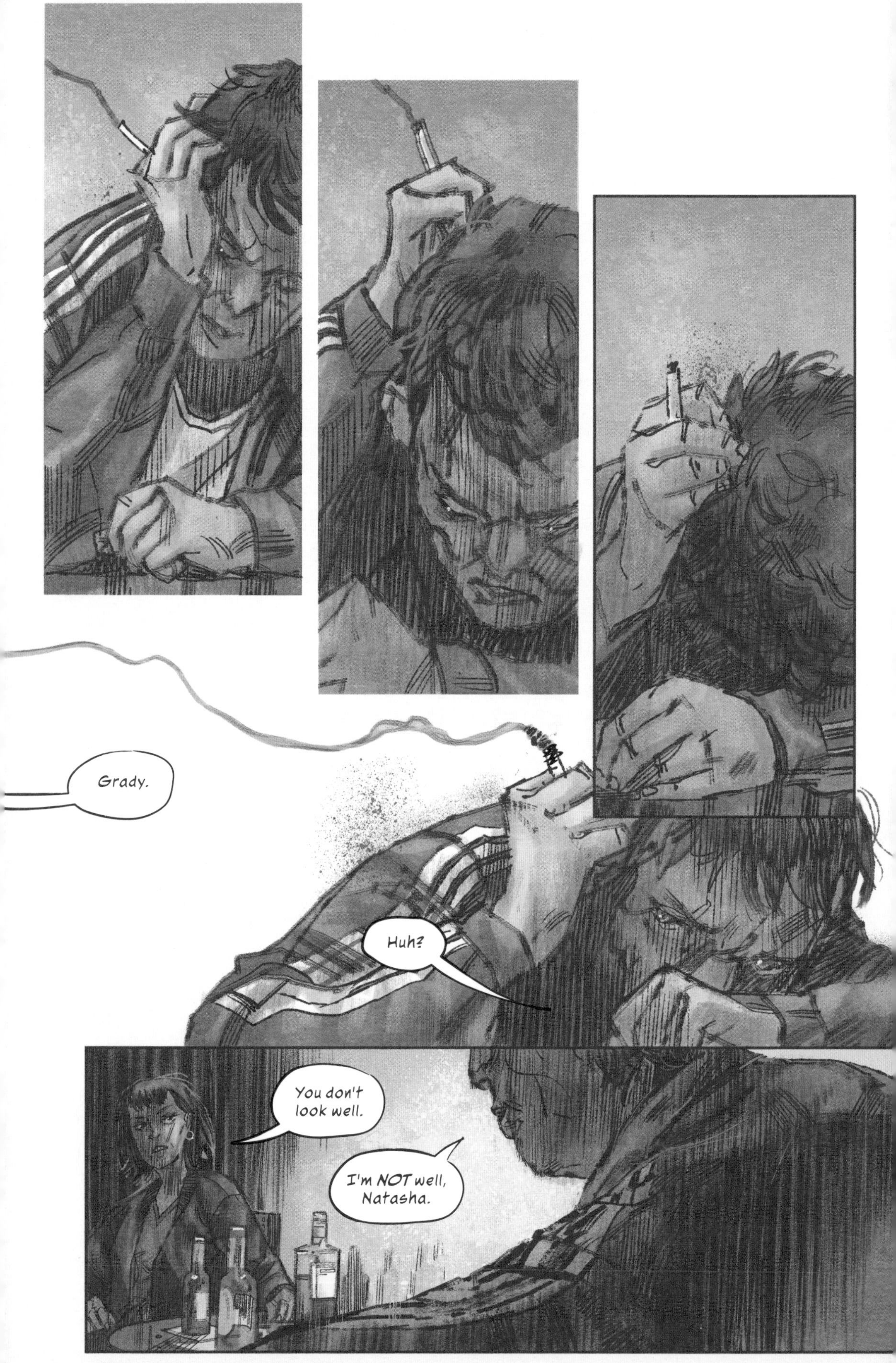
Grady.
Huh?
You don't look well.
I'm NOT well, Natasha.

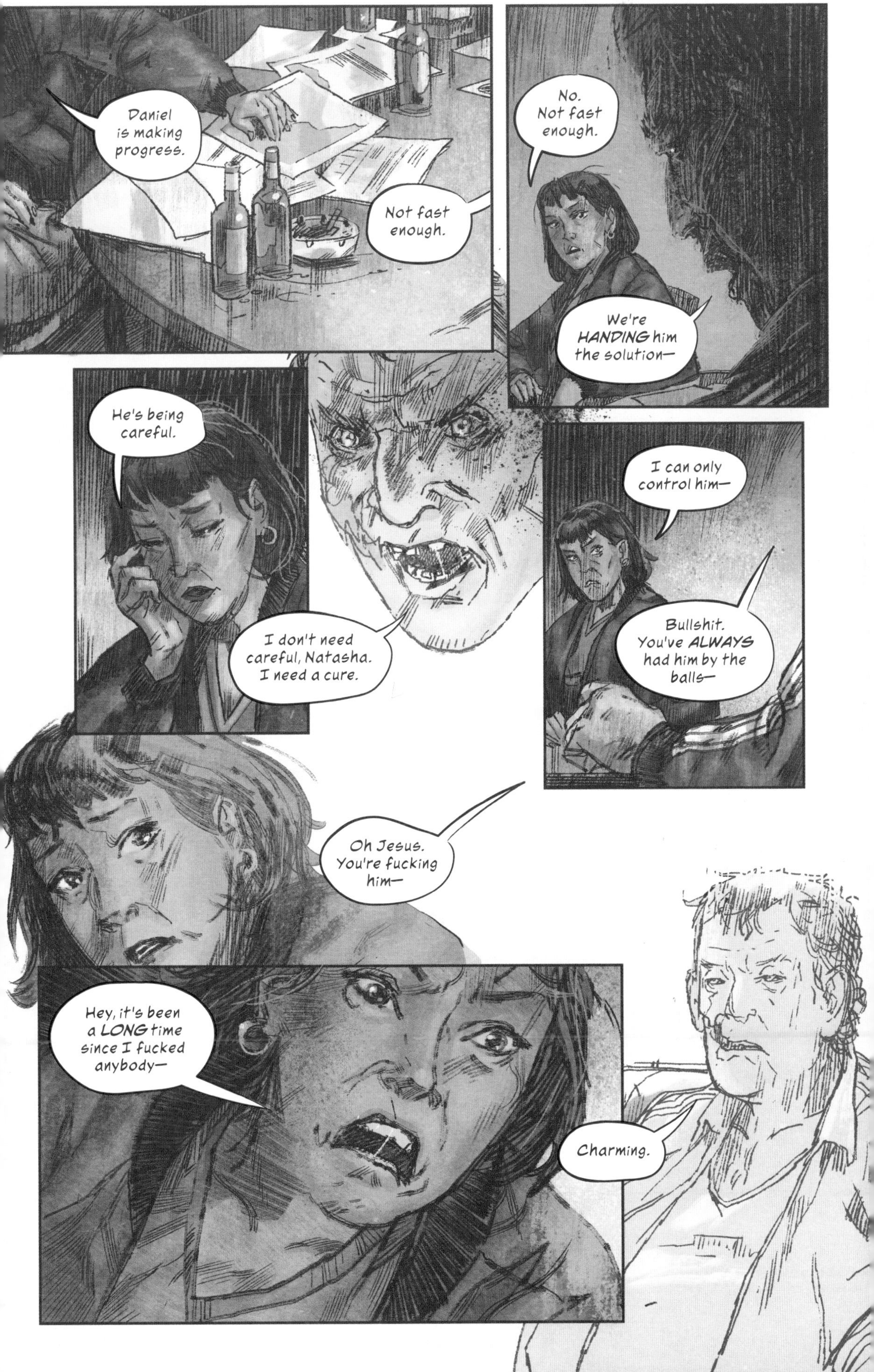
Daniel is making progress.
Not fast enough.
No. Not fast enough.
We're HANDING him the solution—
He's being careful.
I don't need careful, Natasha. I need a cure.
I can only control him—
Bullshit. You've ALWAYS had him by the balls—
Oh Jesus. You're fucking him—
Hey, it's been a LONG time since I fucked anybody—
Charming.

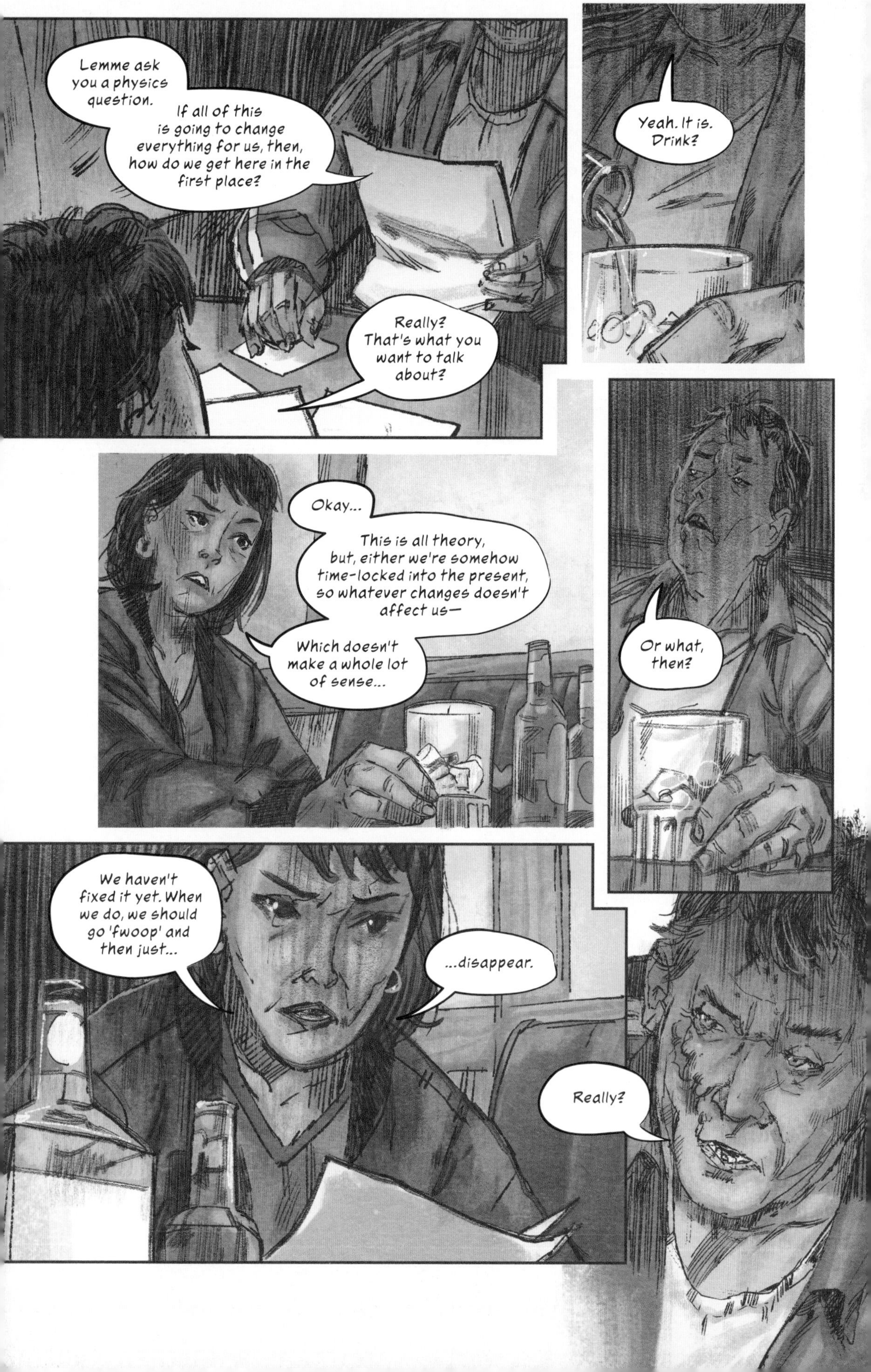
Lemme ask you a physics question.
If all of this is going to change everything for us, then, how do we get here in the first place?
Really? That's what you want to talk about?
Yeah. It is. Drink?
Okay...
This is all theory, but, either we're somehow time-locked into the present, so whatever changes doesn't affect us—
Which doesn't make a whole lot of sense...
Or what, then?
We haven't fixed it yet. When we do, we should go 'fwoop' and then just...
...disappear.
Really?

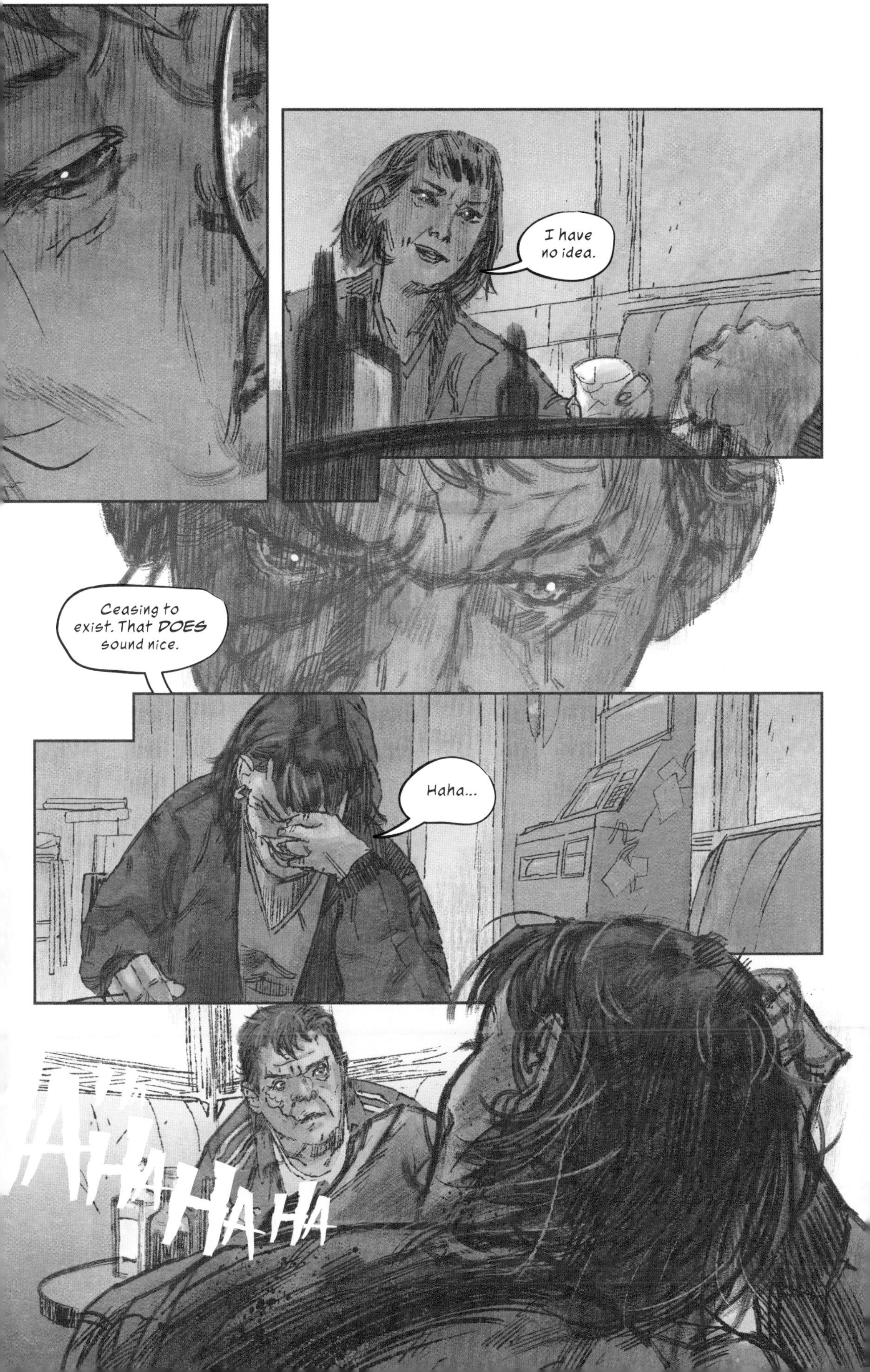
I have no idea.
Ceasing to exist. That DOES sound nice.
Haha...
HA HA HAHAHAHA

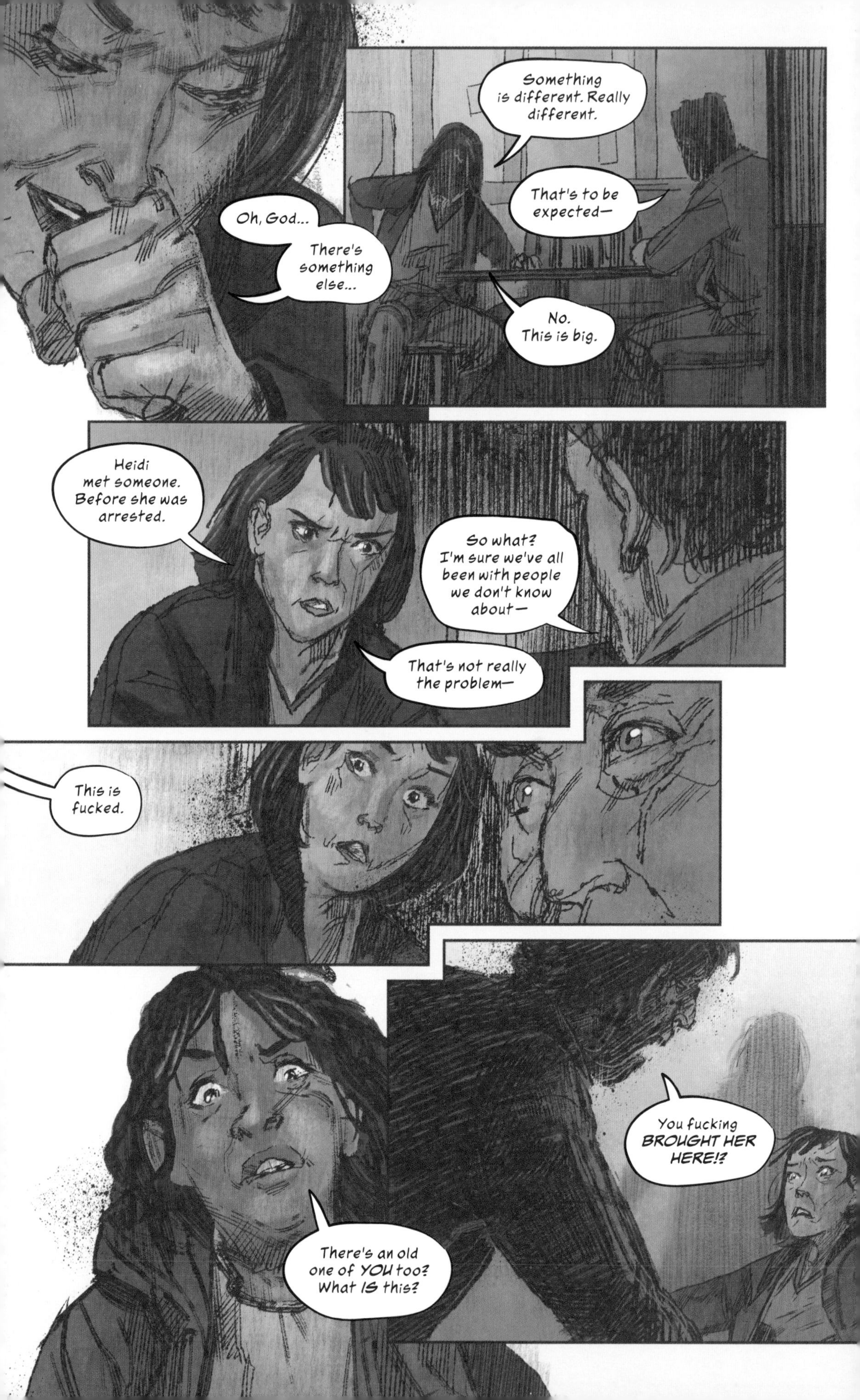
Something is different. Really different.
That's to be expected—
Oh, God...
There's something else...
No. This is big.
Heidi met someone. Before she was arrested.
So what? I'm sure we've all been with people we don't know about—
That's not really the problem—
This is fucked.
You fucking BROUGHT HER HERE!?
There's an old one of YOU too? What IS this?

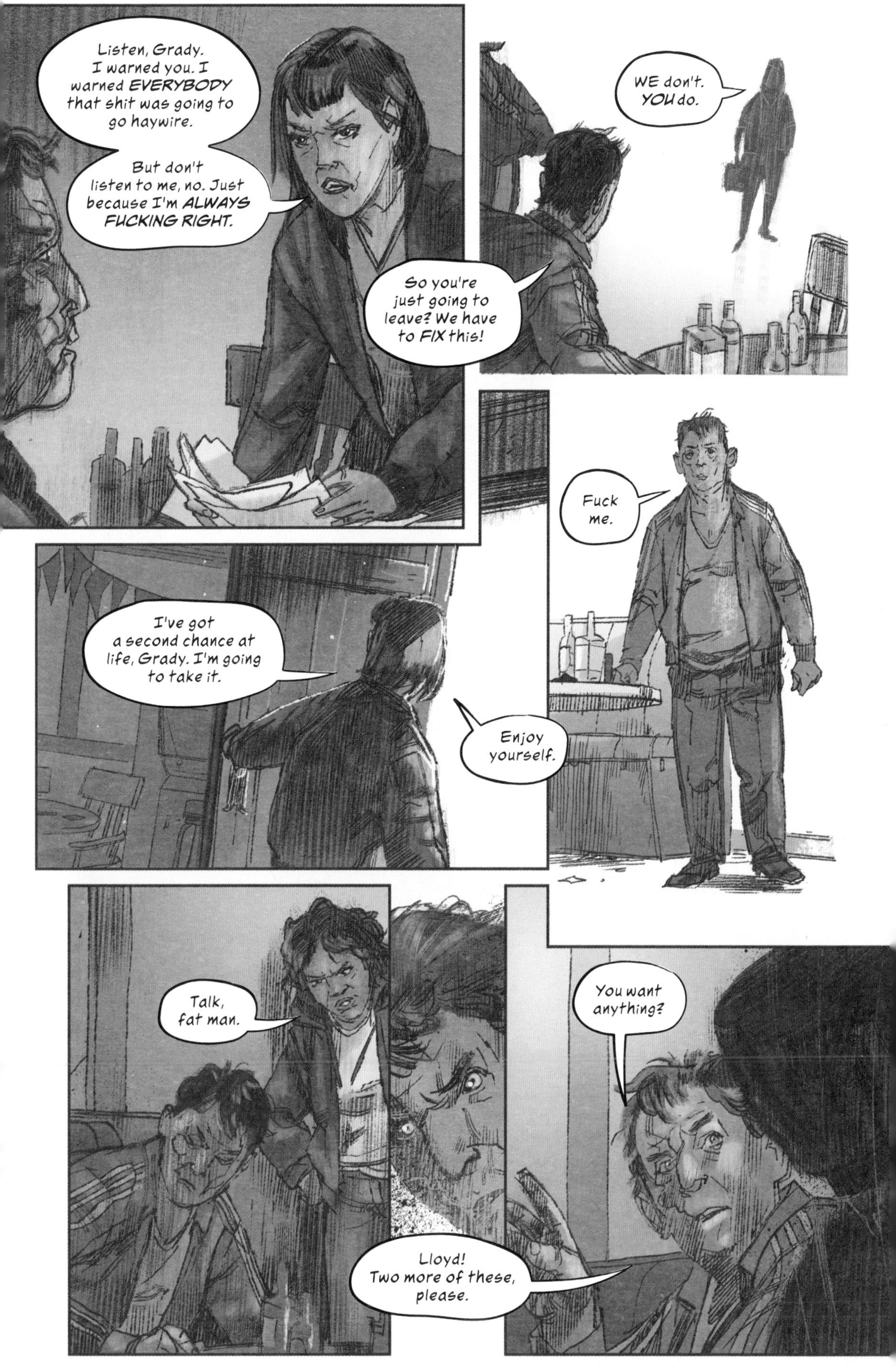
Listen, Grady. I warned you. I warned EVERYBODY that shit was going to go haywire.
But don't listen to me, no. Just because I'm ALWAYS FUCKING RIGHT.
So you're just going to leave? We have to FIX this!
WE don't. YOU do.
Fuck me.
I've got a second chance at life, Grady. I'm going to take it.
Enjoy yourself.
Talk, fat man.
You want anything?
Lloyd! Two more of these, please.

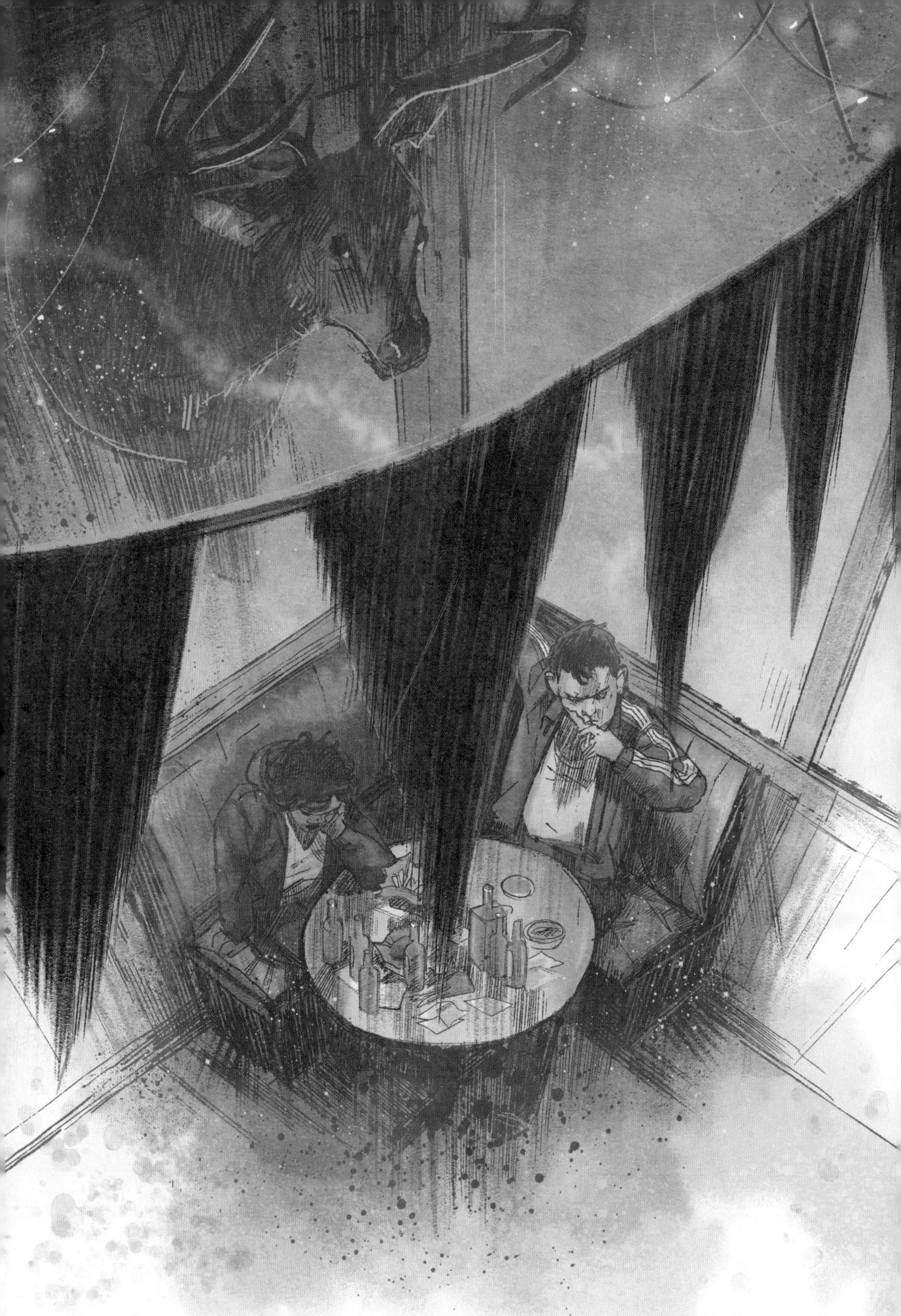

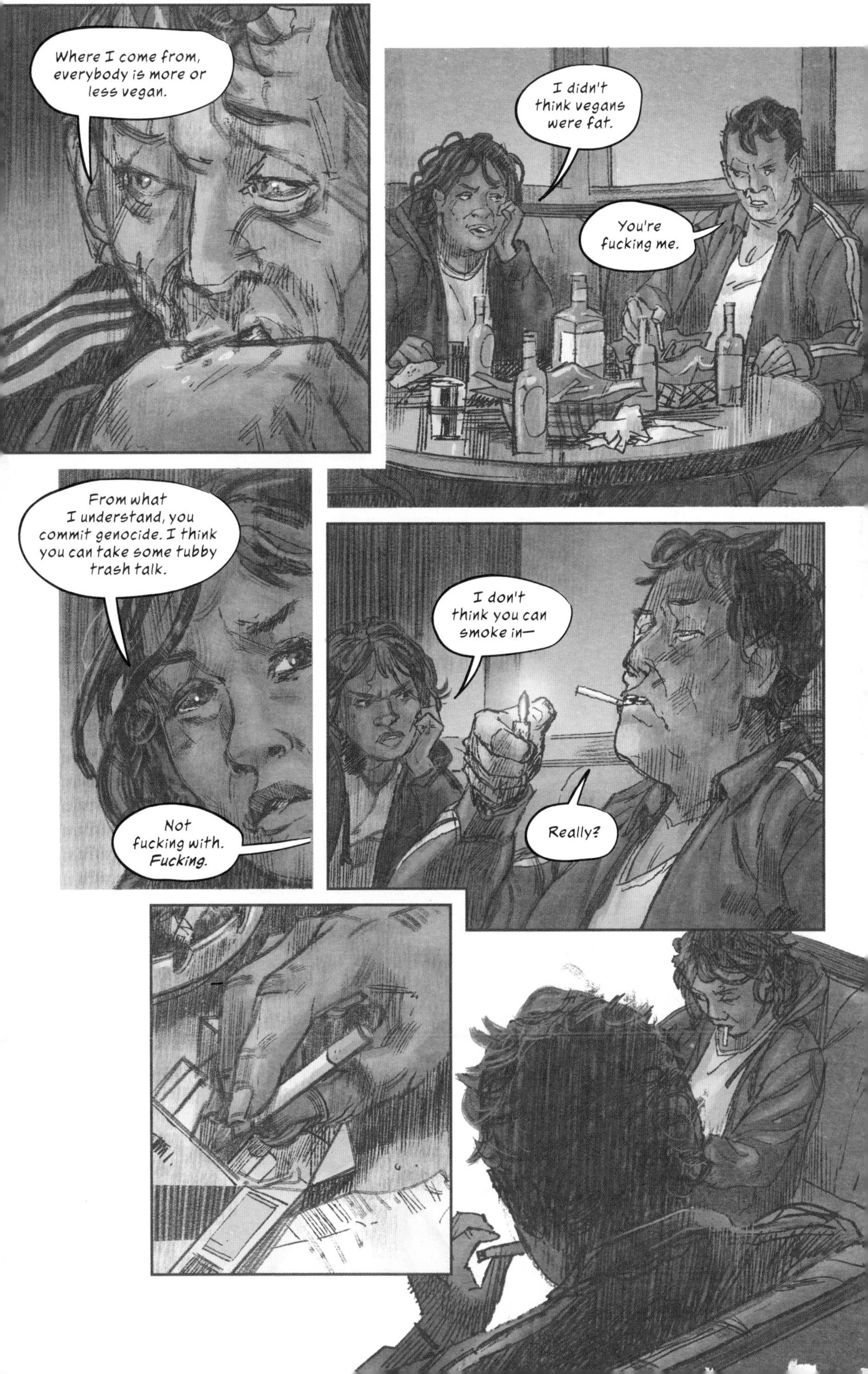
Where I come from, everybody is more or less vegan.
I didn't think vegans were fat.
You're fucking me.
From what I understand, you commit genocide. I think you can take some tubby trash talk.
Not fucking with. Fucking.
I don't think you can smoke in—
Really?

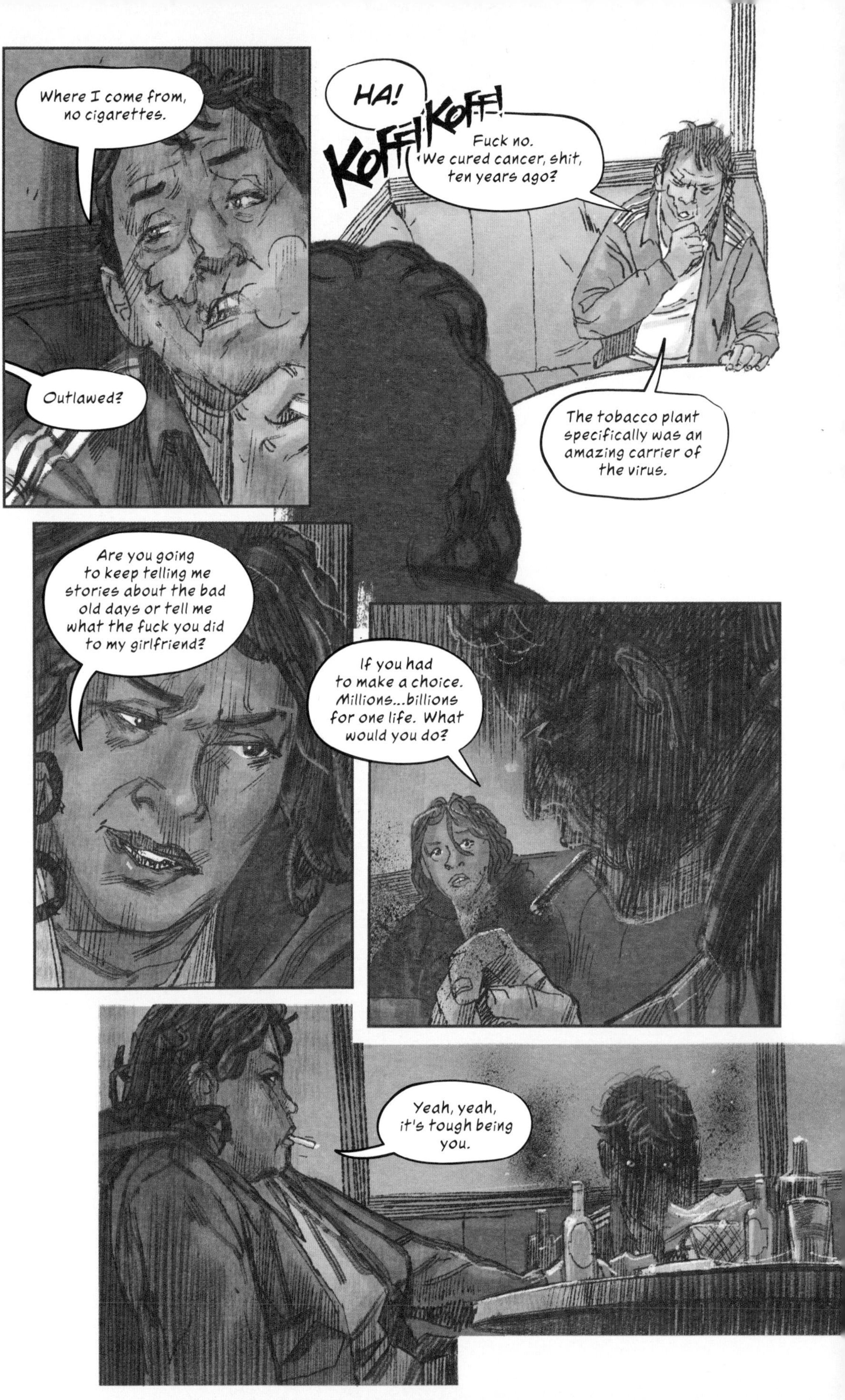
Where I come from, no cigarettes.
Outlawed?
HA!
KOFF! KOFF!
Fuck no. We cured cancer, shit, ten years ago?
The tobacco plant specifically was an amazing carrier of the virus.
Are you going to keep telling me stories about the bad old days or tell me what the fuck you did to my girlfriend?
If you had to make a choice. Millions...billions for one life. What would you do?
Yeah, yeah, it's tough being you.

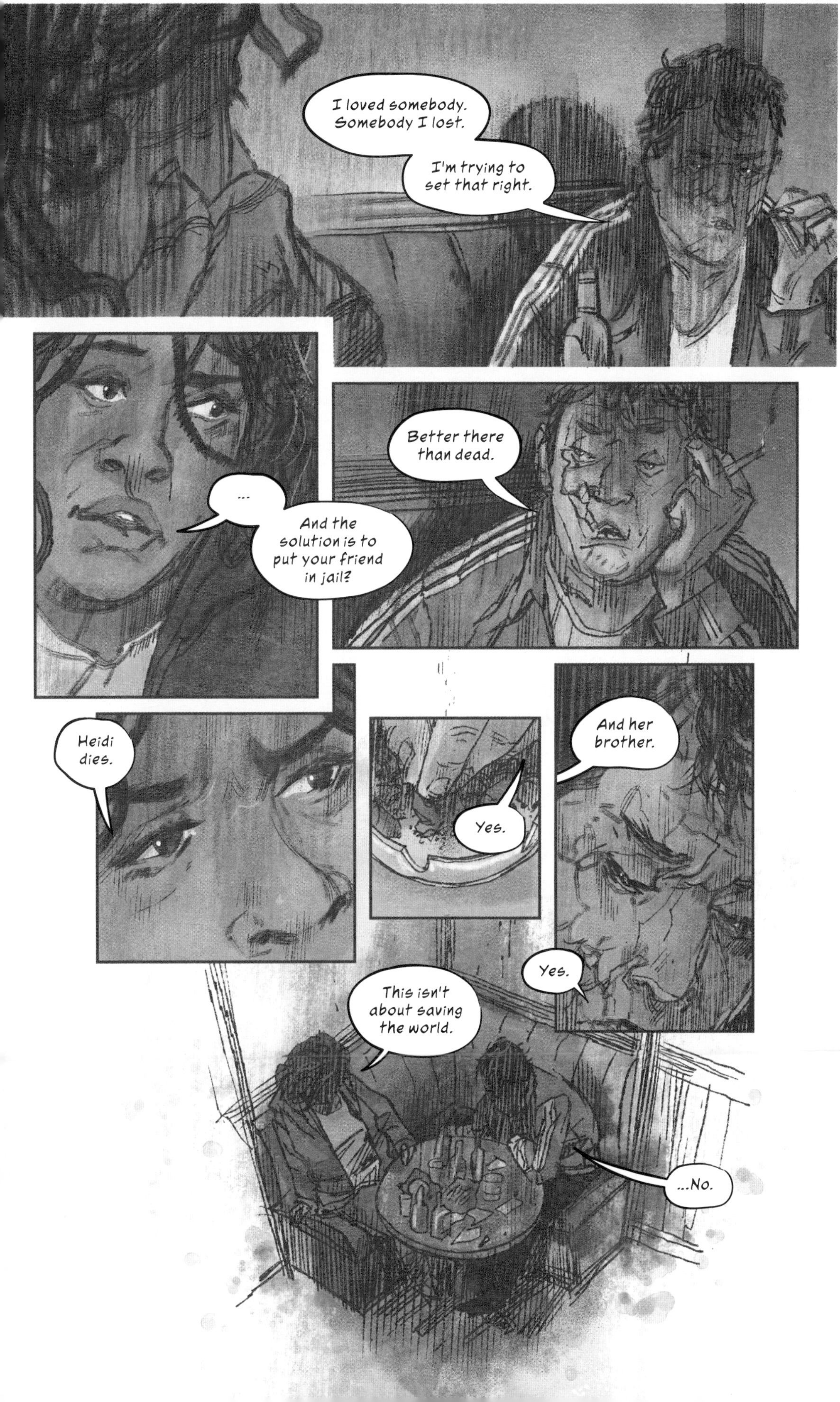
I loved somebody. Somebody I lost.
I'm trying to set that right.
...
And the solution is to put your friend in jail?
Better there than dead.
Heidi dies.
Yes.
And her brother.
Yes.
This isn't about saving the world.
...No.

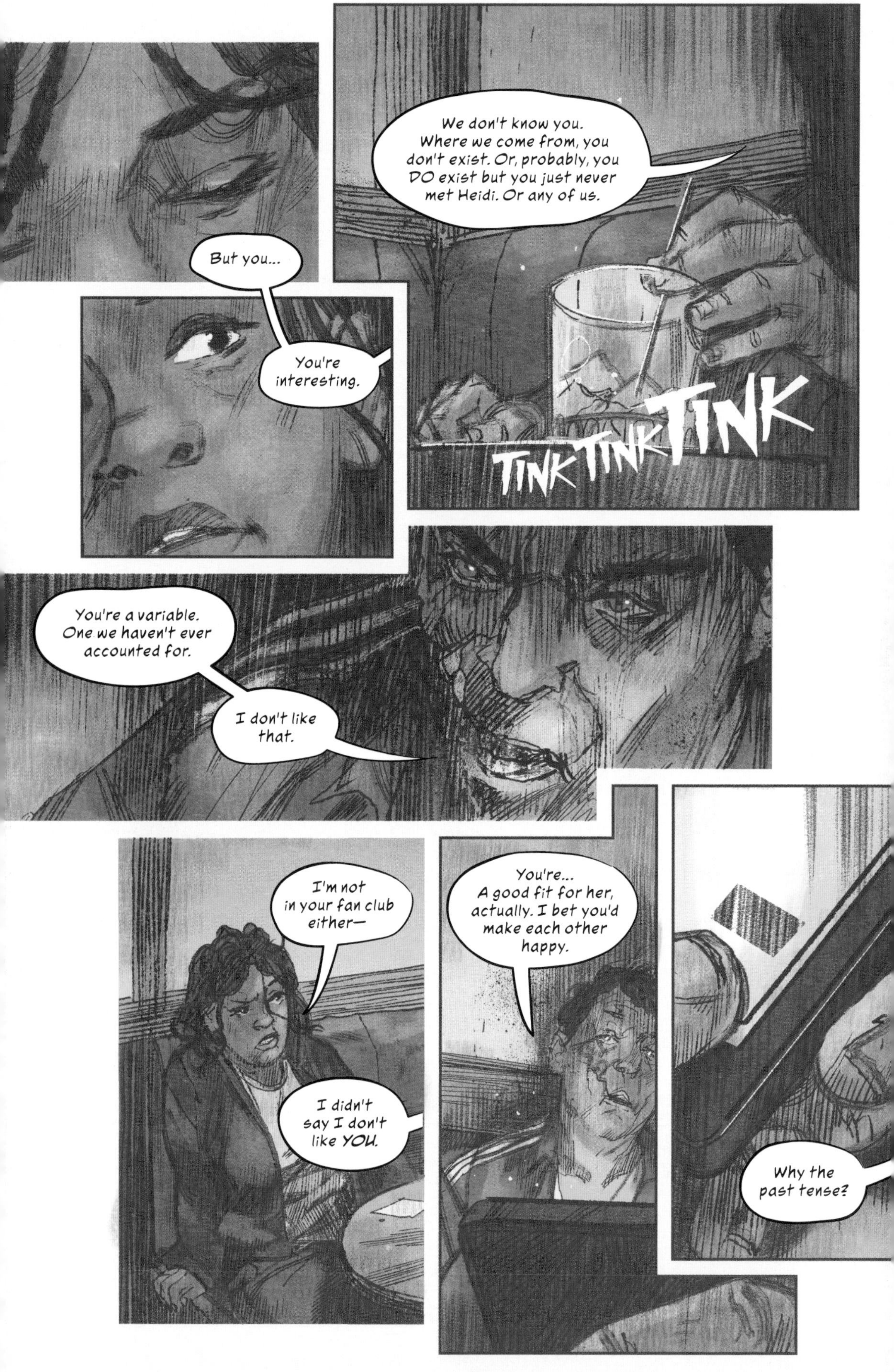
We don't know you. Where we come from, you don't exist. Or, probably, you DO exist but you just never met Heidi. Or any of us.
But you...
You're interesting.
TINK TINK TINK
You're a variable. One we haven't ever accounted for.
I don't like that.
I'm not in your fan club either—
I didn't say I don't like YOU.
You're... A good fit for her, actually. I bet you'd make each other happy.
Why the past tense?

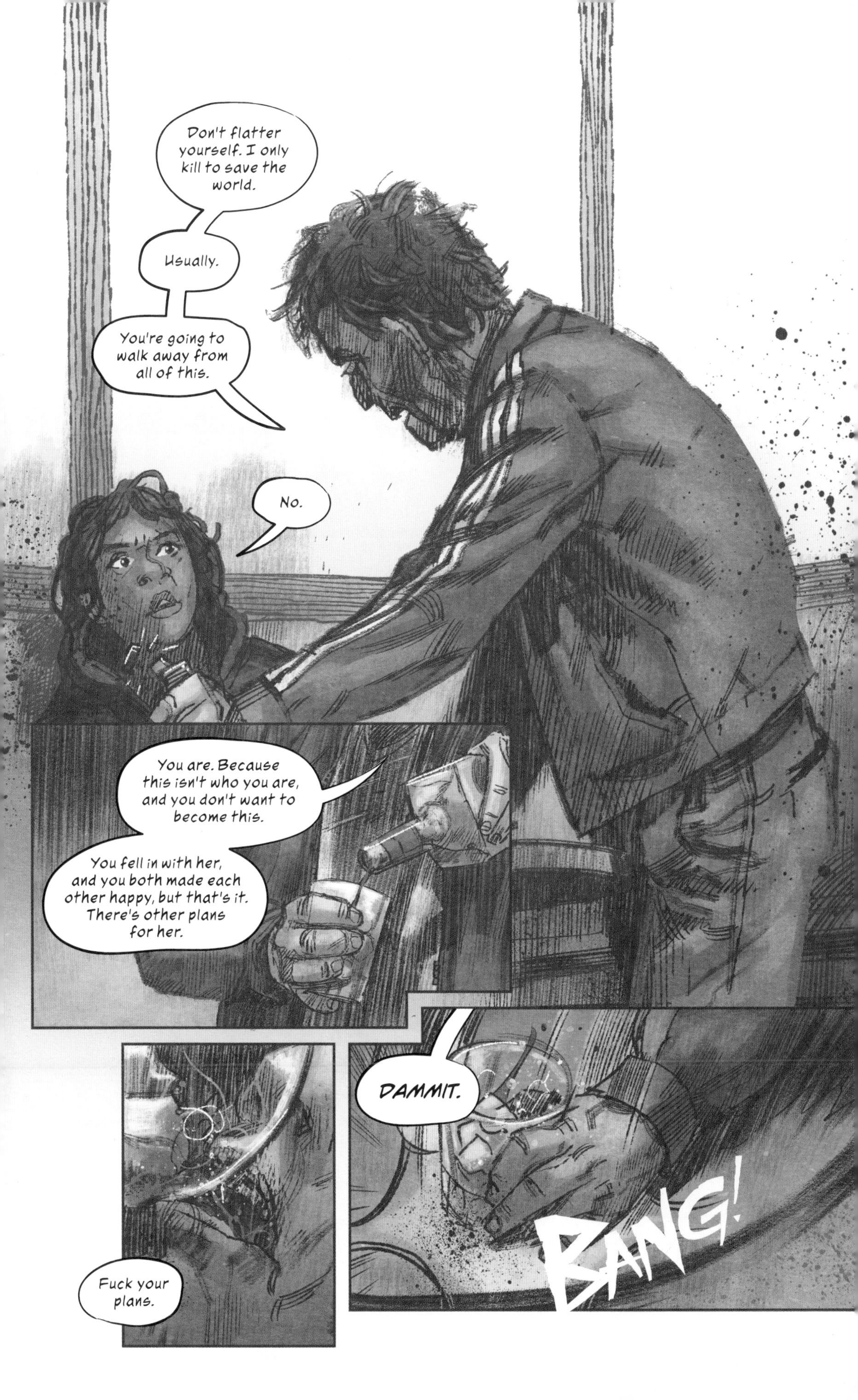
Don't flatter yourself. I only kill to save the world.
Usually.
You're going to walk away from all of this.
No.
You are. Because this isn't who you are, and you don't want to become this.
You fell in with her, and you both made each other happy, but that's it. There's other plans for her.
Fuck your plans.
DAMMIT.
BANG!

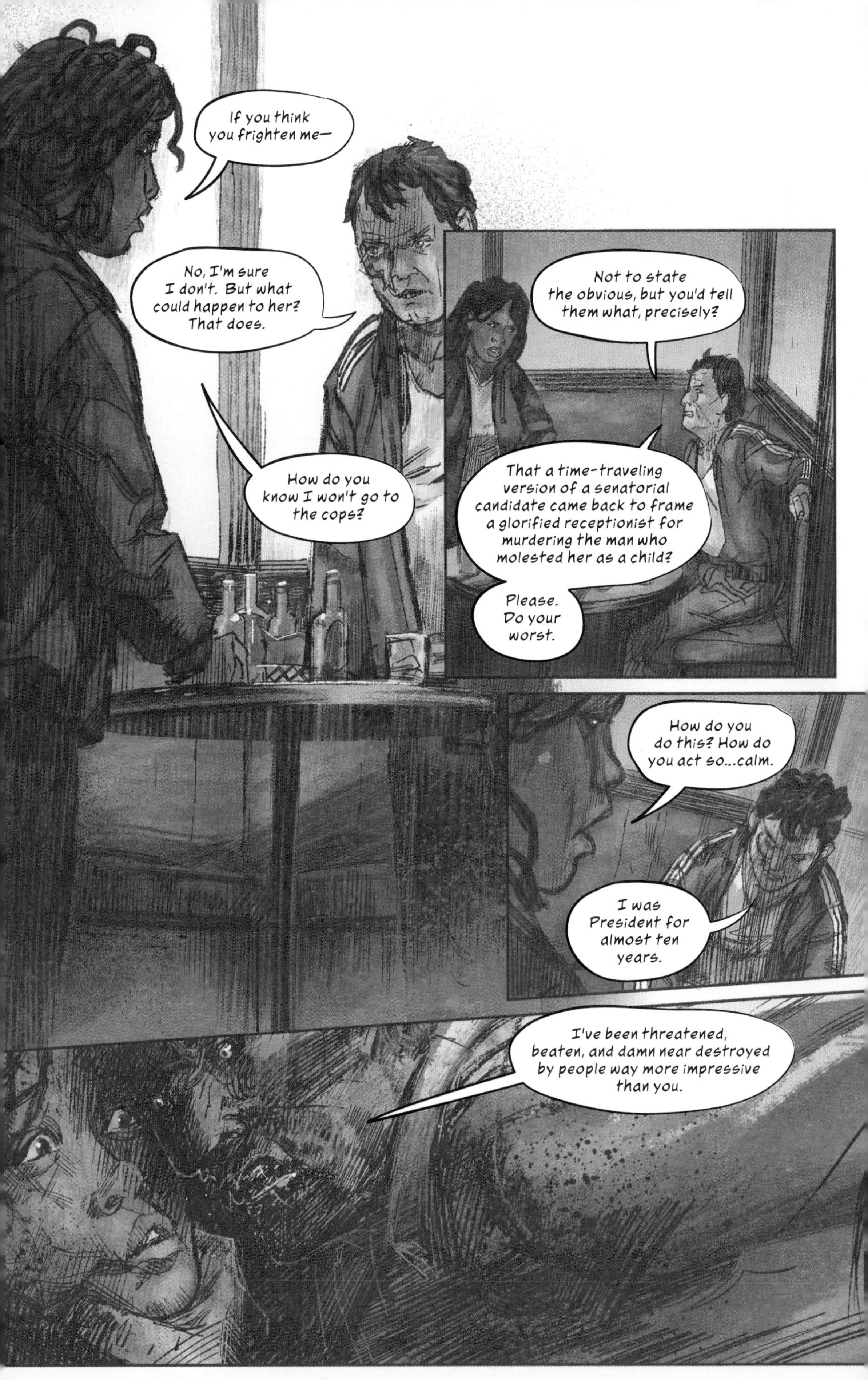
If you think you frighten me—
No, I'm sure I don't. But what could happen to her? That does.
How do you know I won't go to the cops?
Not to state the obvious, but you'd tell them what, precisely?
That a time-traveling version of a senatorial candidate came back to frame a glorified receptionist for murdering the man who molested her as a child?
Please. Do your worst.
How do you do this? How do you act so...calm.
I was President for almost ten years.
I've been threatened, beaten, and damn near destroyed by people way more impressive than you.

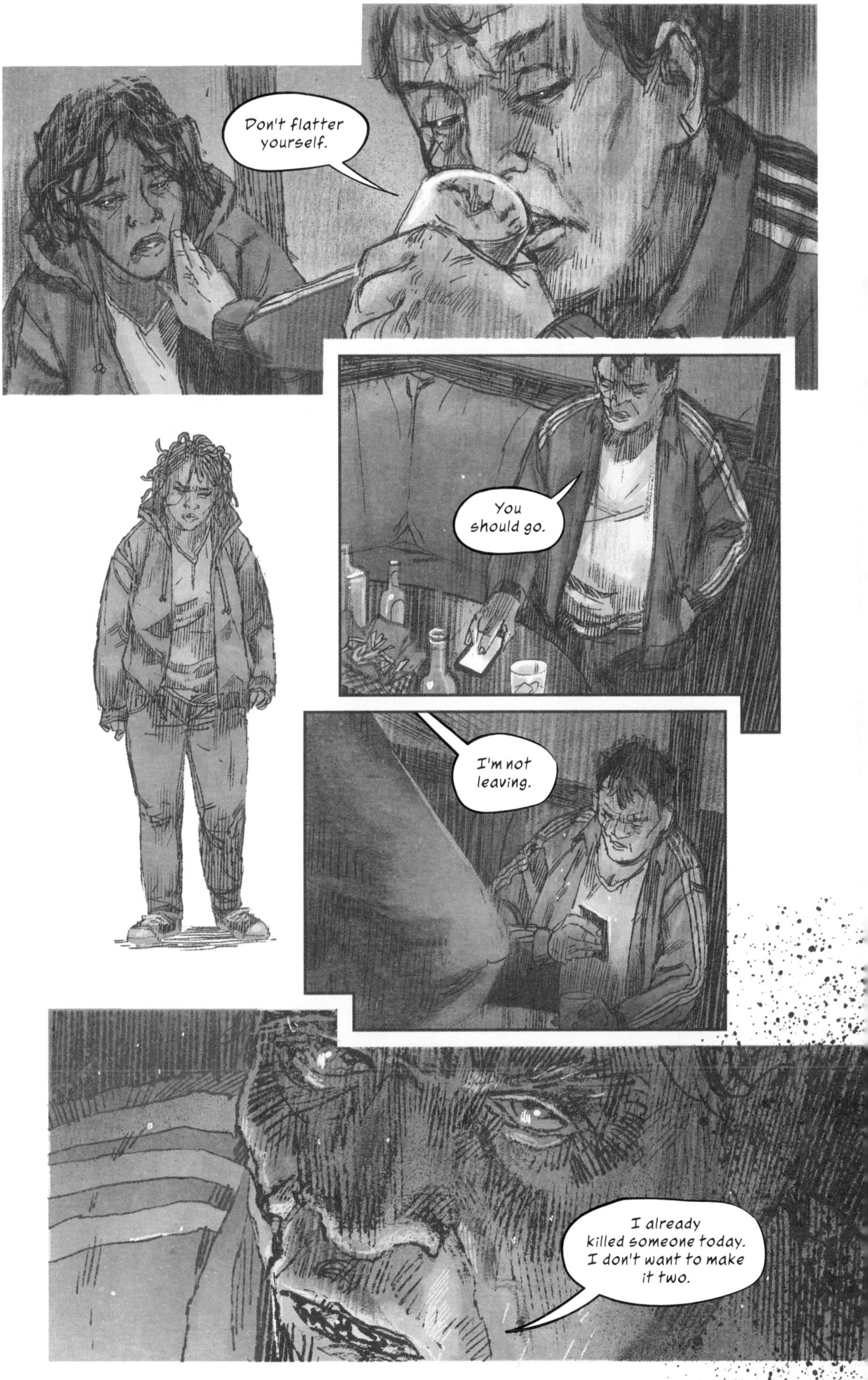
Don't flatter yourself.
You should go.
I'm not leaving.
I already killed someone today. I don't want to make it two.

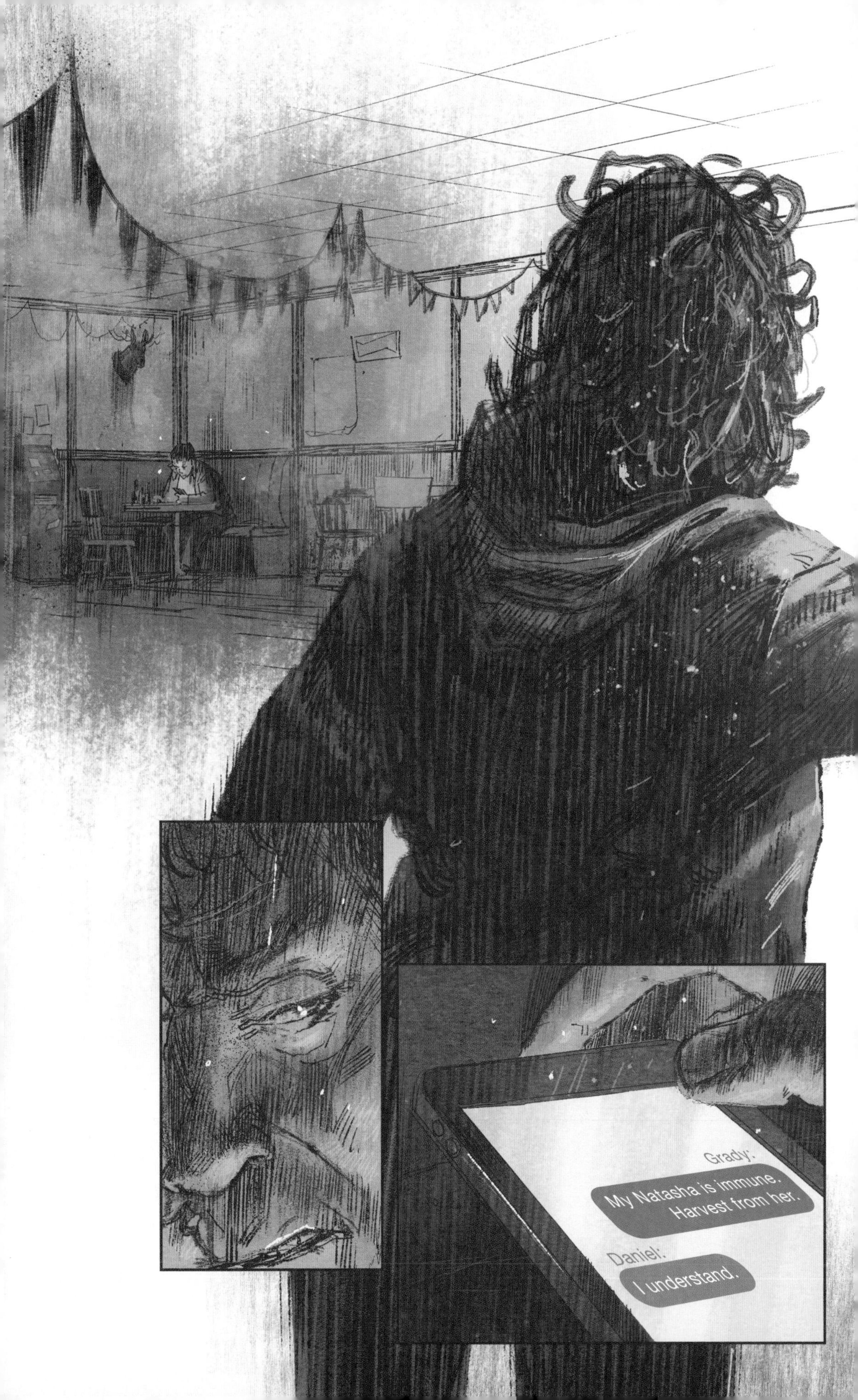
Grady:
My Natasha is immune. Harvest from her.
Daniel:
I understand.

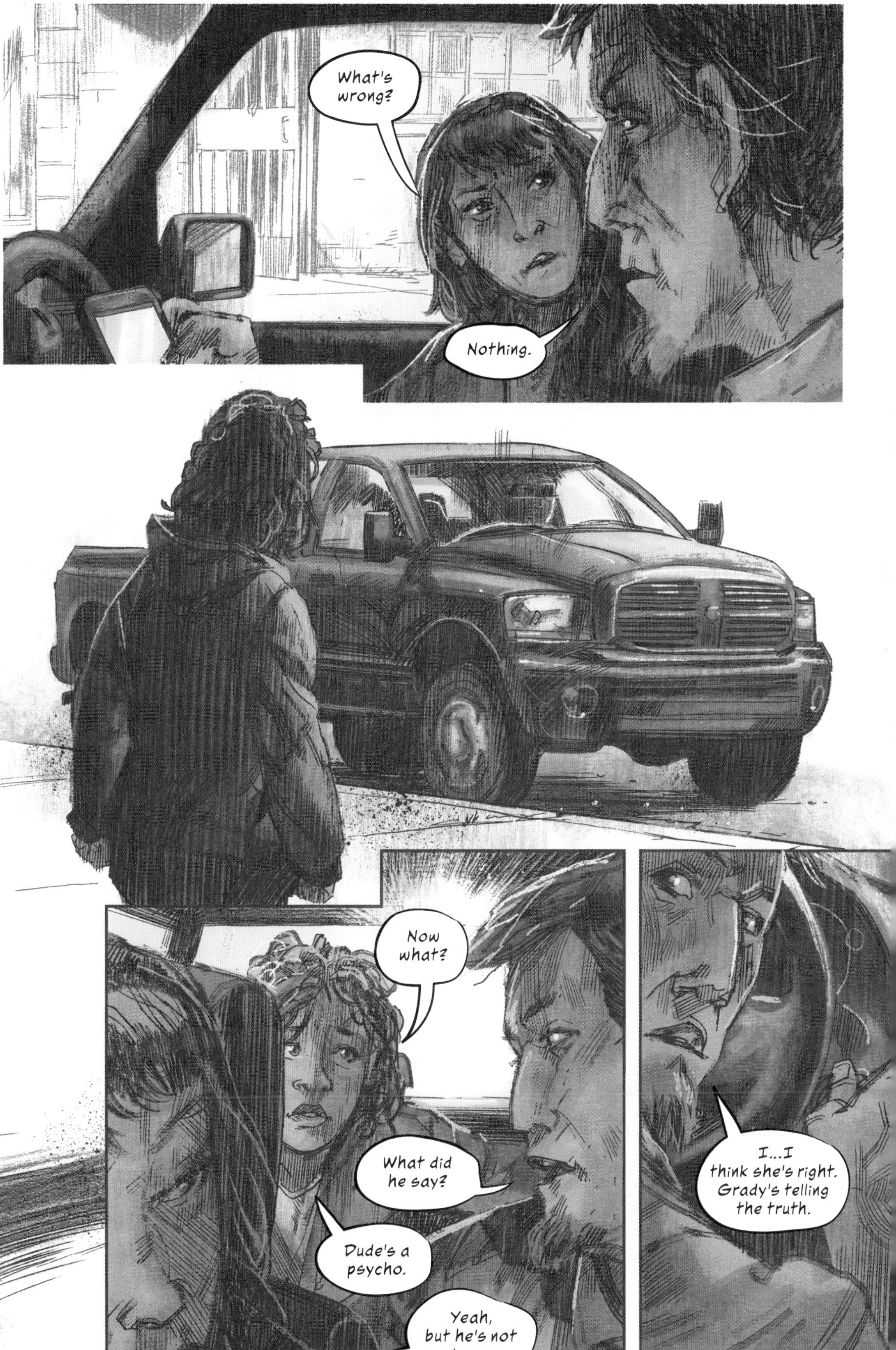
What's wrong?
Nothing.
Now what?
What did he say?
Dude's a psycho.
Yeah, but he's not lying.
I...I think she's right. Grady's telling the truth.

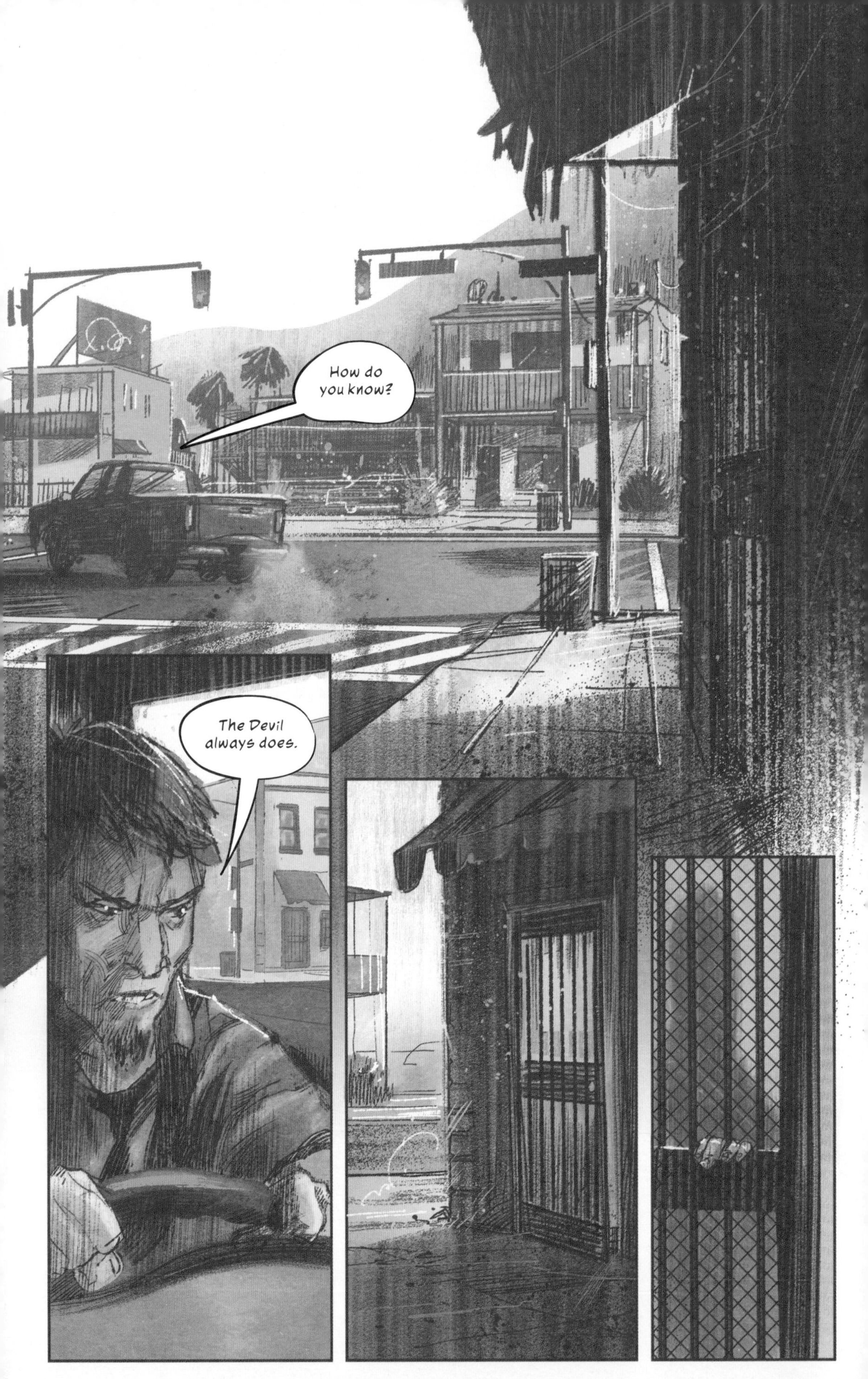
How do you know?
The Devil always does.

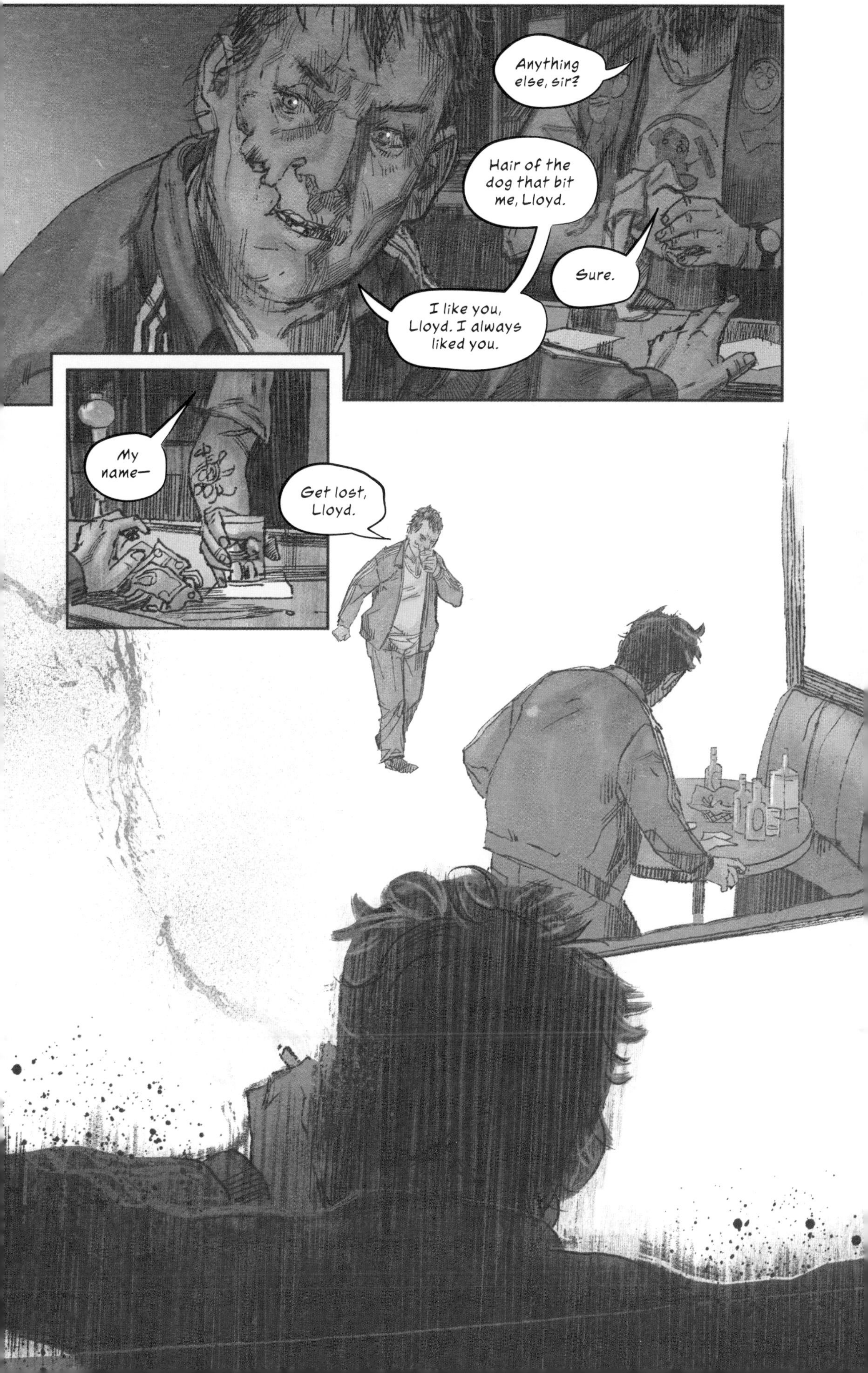

Anything else, sir?
Hair of the dog that bit me, Lloyd.
Sure.
I like you, Lloyd. I always liked you.
My name—
Get lost, Lloyd.

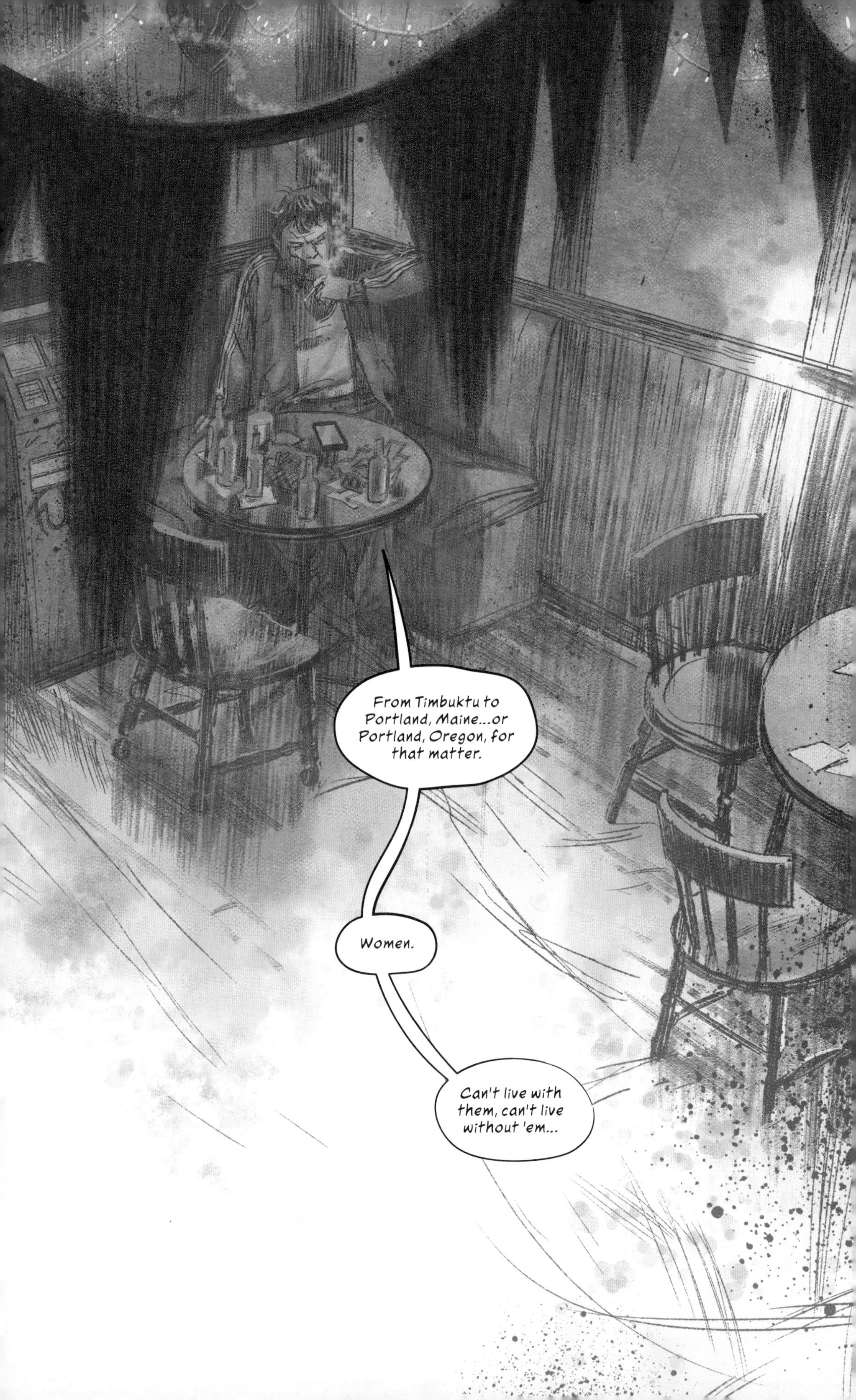
From Timbuktu to Portland, Maine...or Portland, Oregon, for that matter.
Women.
Can't live with them, can't live without 'em...

CHAPTER
16

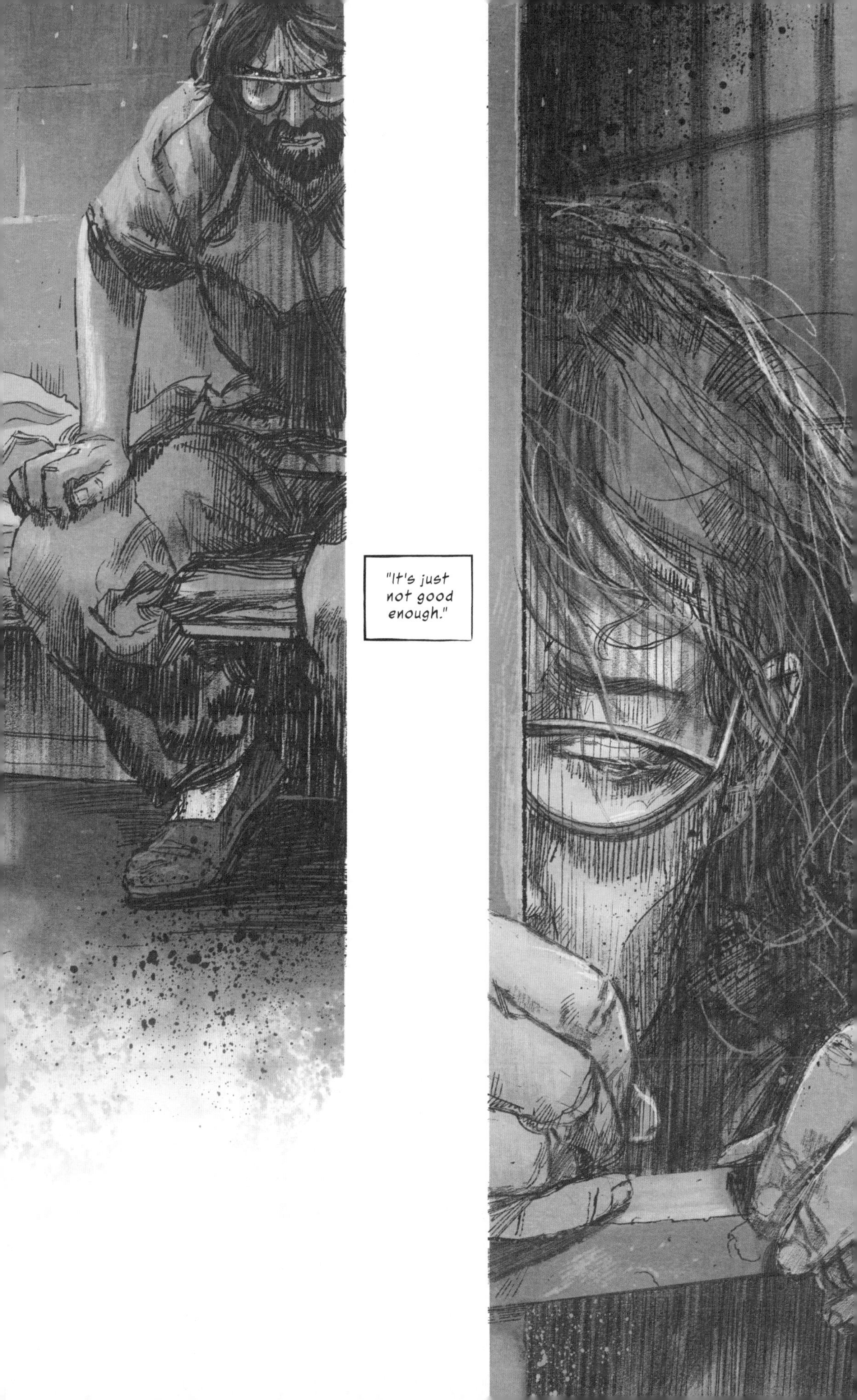
"It's just not good enough."

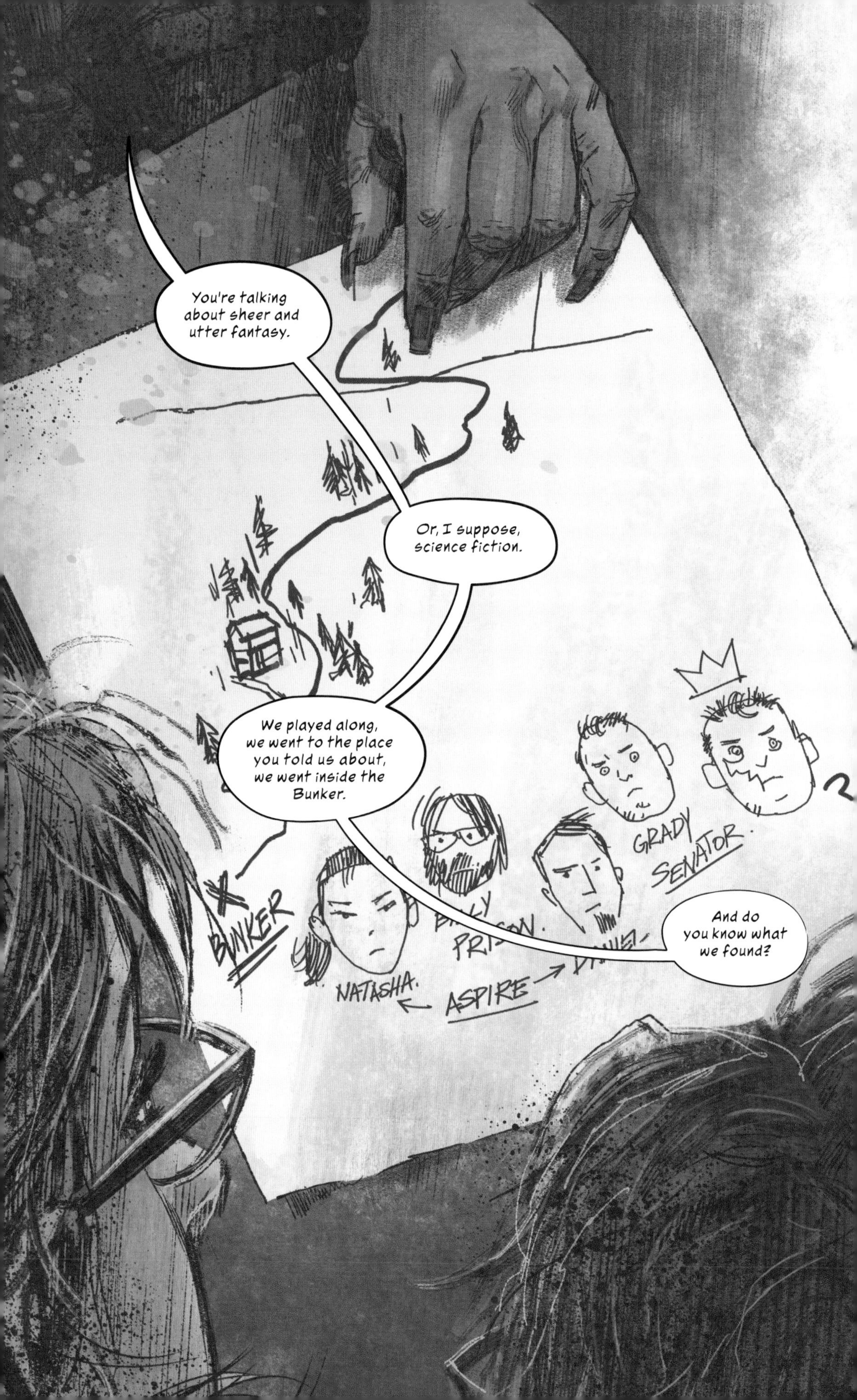
You're talking about sheer and utter fantasy.
Or, I suppose, science fiction.
We played along, we went to the place you told us about, we went inside the Bunker.
And do you know what we found?
BUNKER
NATASHA.
ASPIRE
GRADY
SENATOR

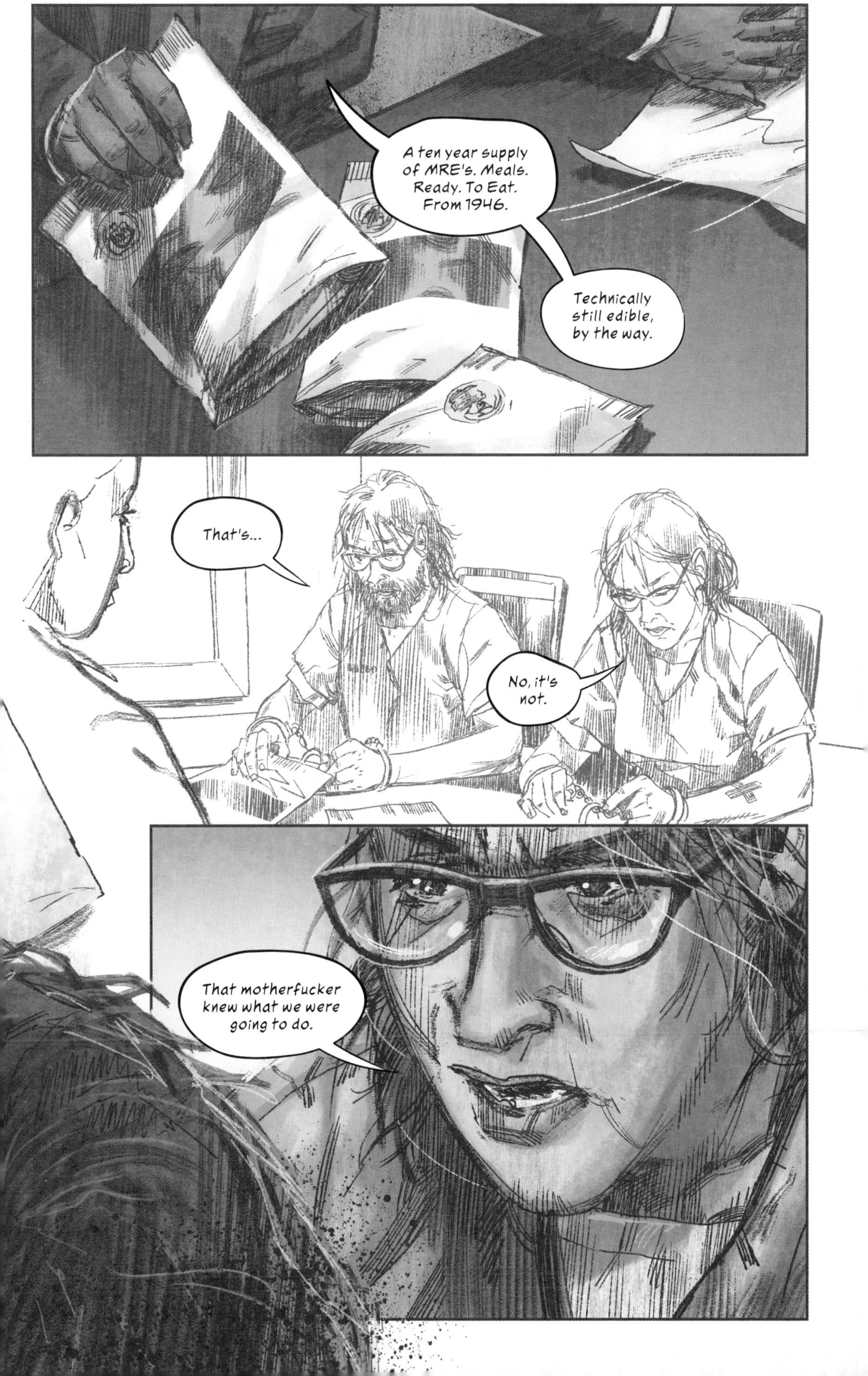
A ten year supply of MRE's. Meals. Ready. To Eat. From 1946.
Technically still edible, by the way.
That's...
No, it's not.
That motherfucker knew what we were going to do.

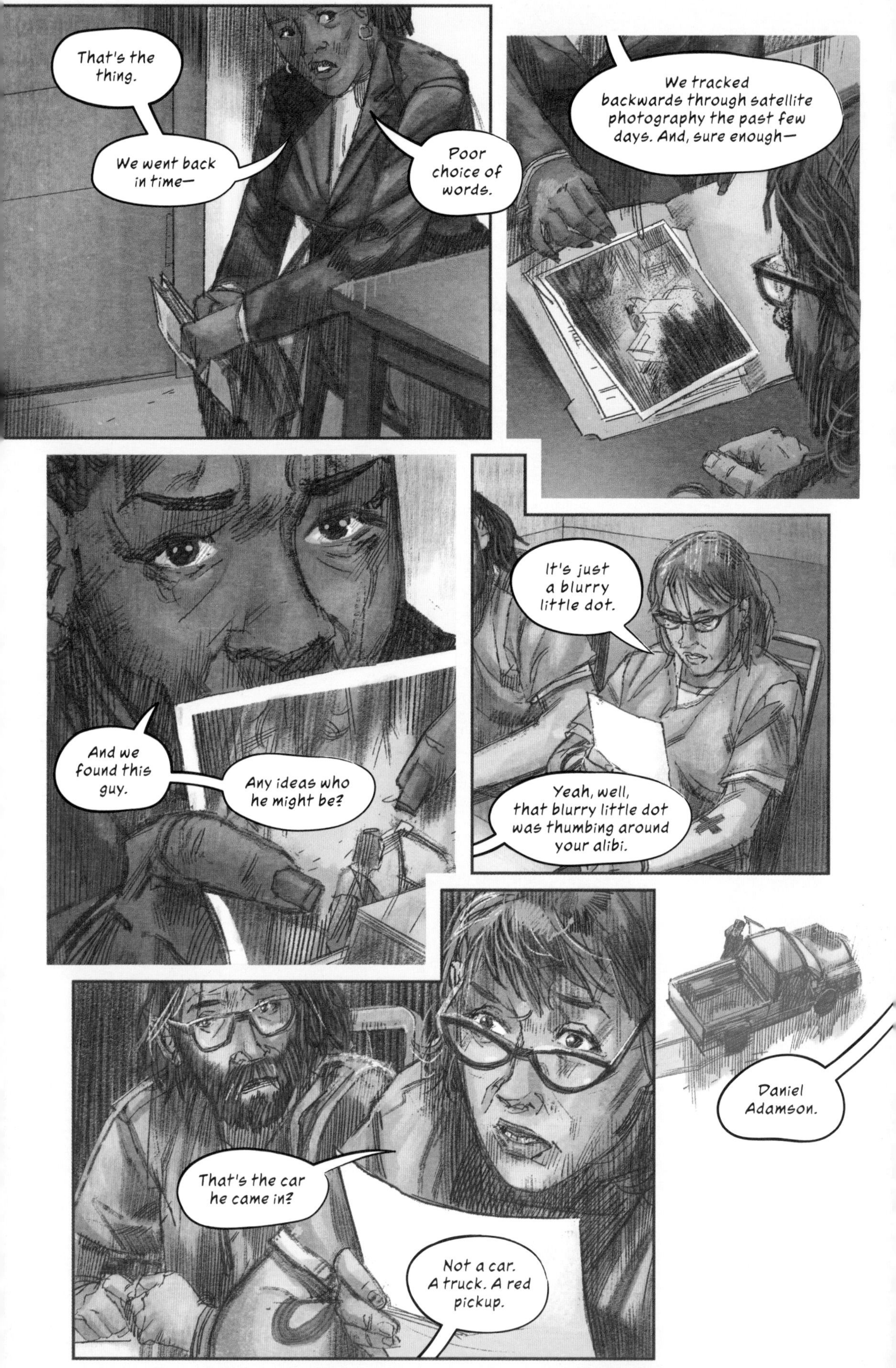
That's the thing.
We went back in time—
Poor choice of words.
We tracked backwards through satellite photography the past few days. And, sure enough—
And we found this guy.
Any ideas who he might be?
It's just a blurry little dot.
Yeah, well, that blurry little dot was thumbing around your alibi.
That's the car he came in?
Not a car. A truck. A red pickup.
Daniel Adamson.

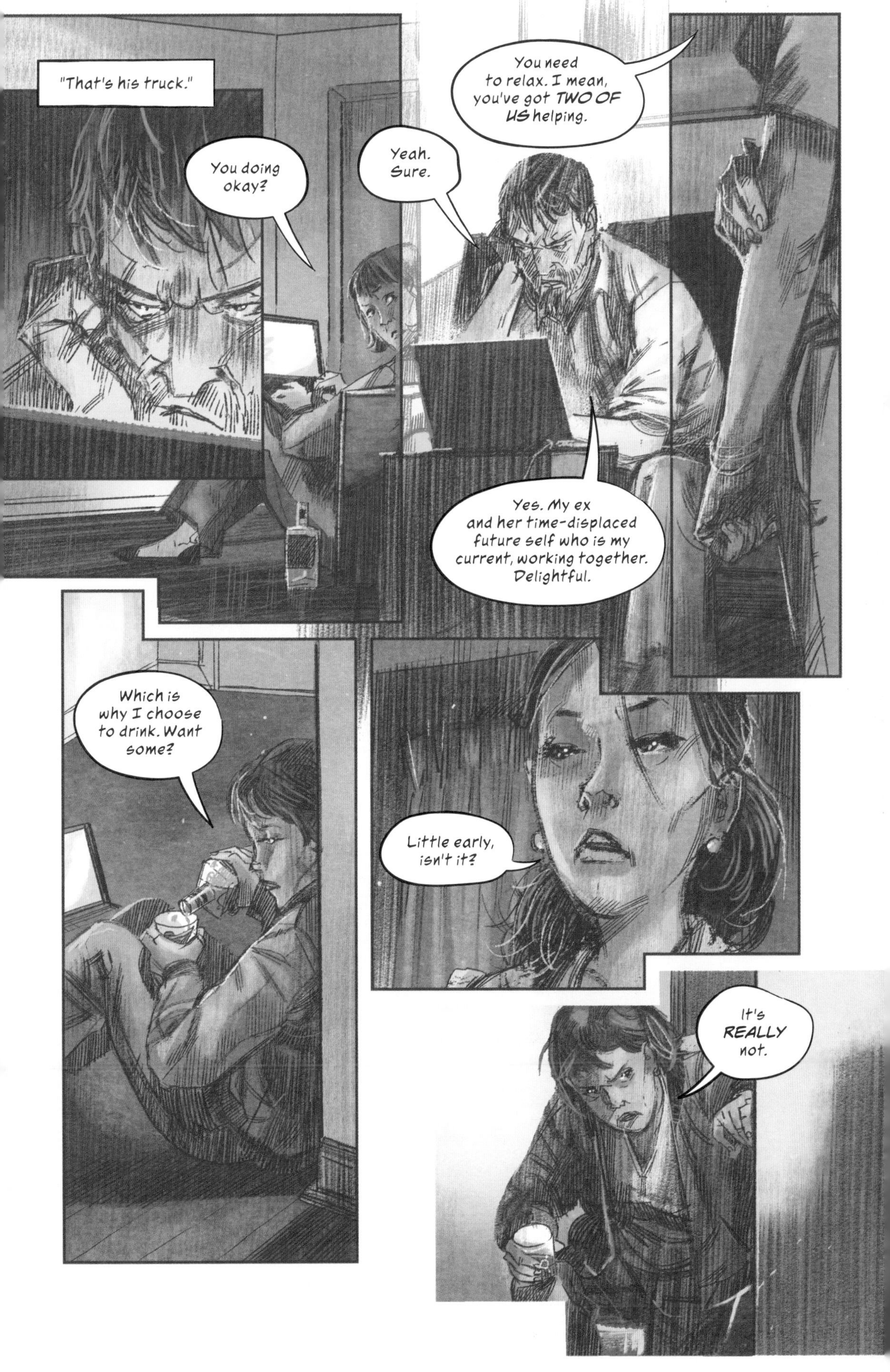
"That's his truck."
You doing okay?
Yeah. Sure.
You need to relax. I mean, you've got TWO OF US helping.
Yes. My ex and her time-displaced future self who is my current, working together. Delightful.
Which is why I choose to drink. Want some?
Little early, isn't it?
It's REALLY not.

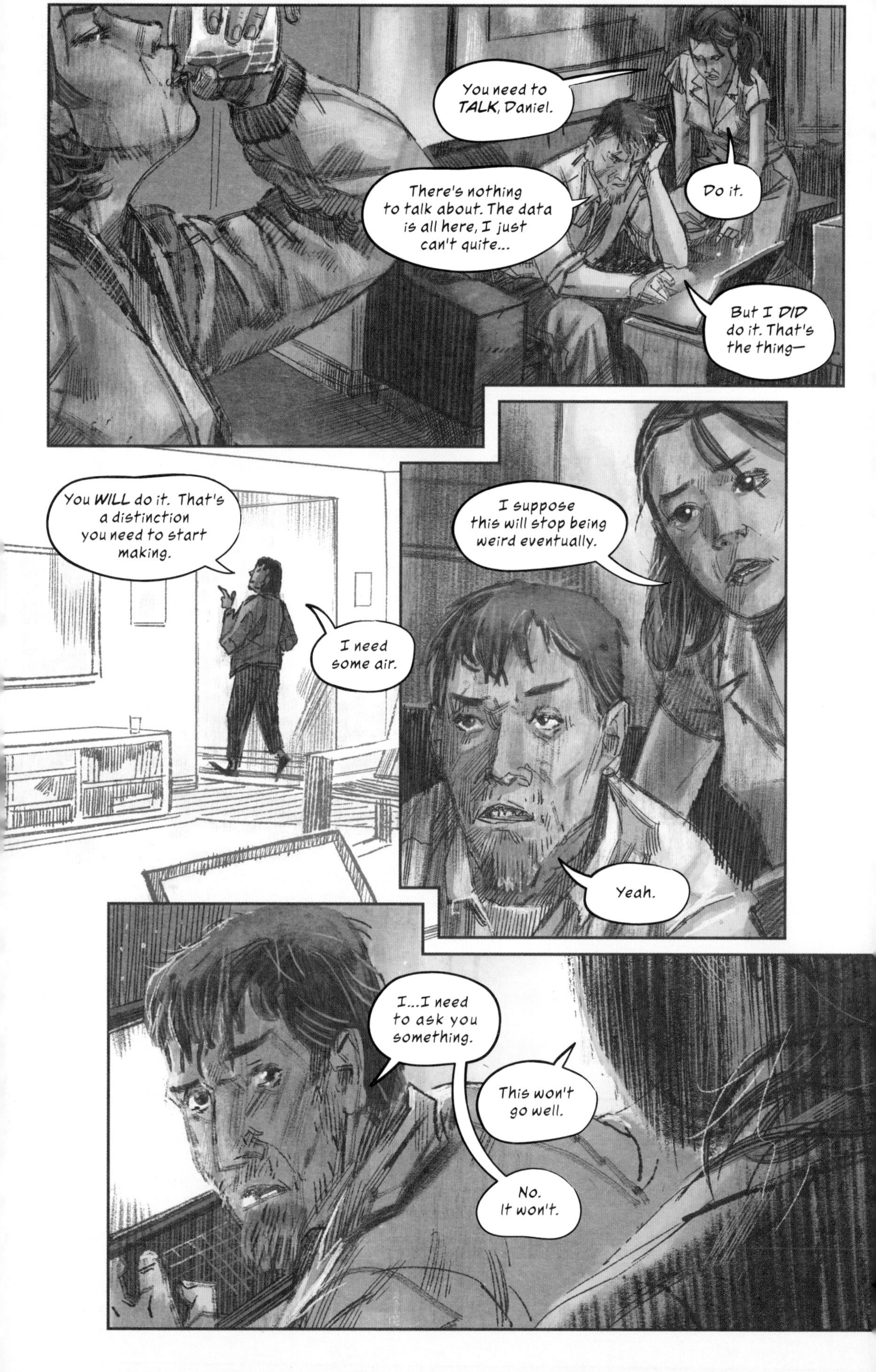
You need to TALK, Daniel.
There's nothing to talk about. The data is all here, I just can't quite...
Do it.
But I DID do it. That's the thing—
You WILL do it. That's a distinction you need to start making.
I need some air.
I suppose this will stop being weird eventually.
Yeah.
I...I need to ask you something.
This won't go well.
No. It won't.

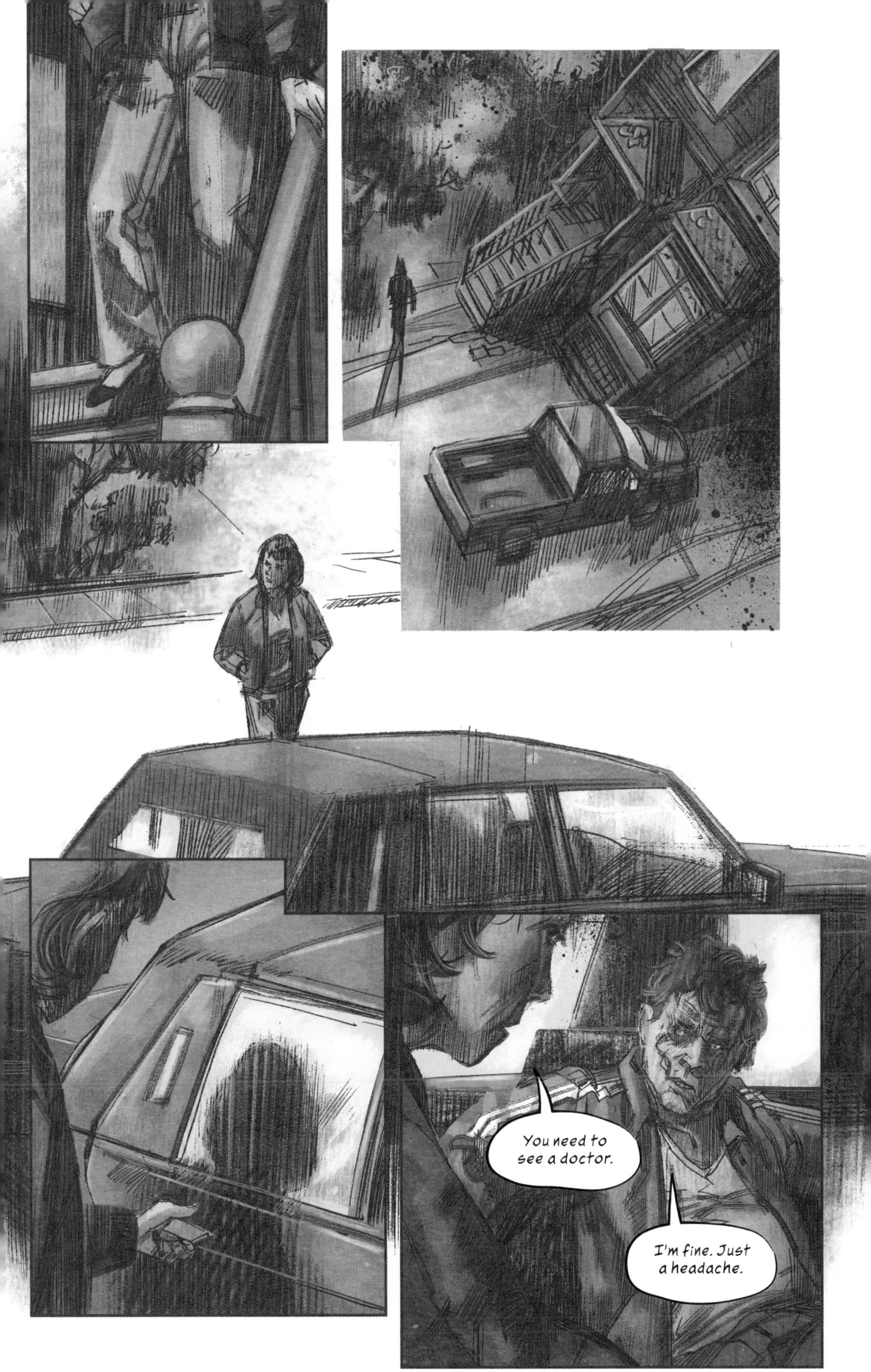
You need to see a doctor.
I'm fine. Just a headache.

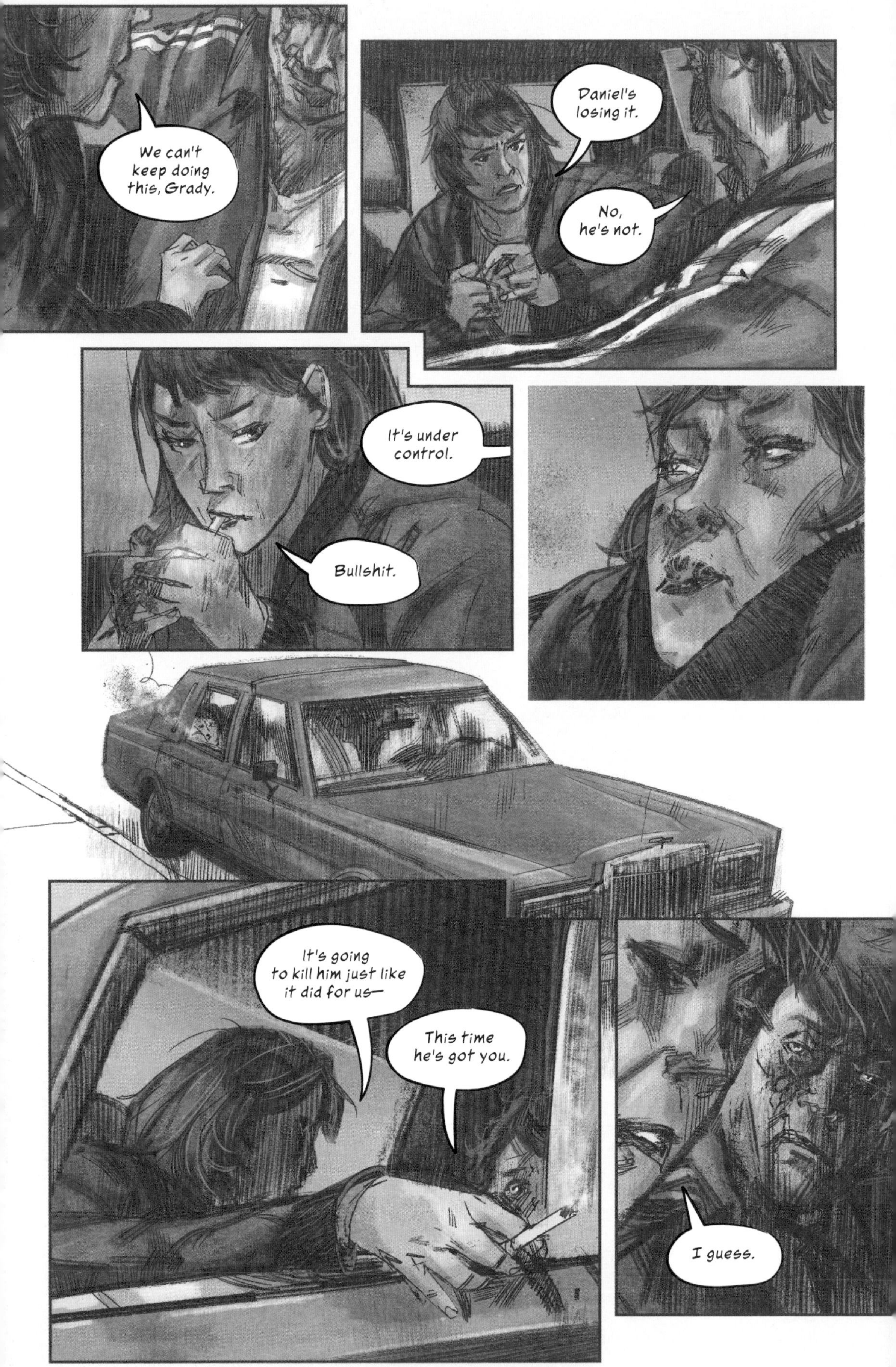
We can't keep doing this, Grady.
Daniel's losing it.
No, he's not.
It's under control.
Bullshit.
It's going to kill him just like it did for us—
This time he's got you.
I guess.

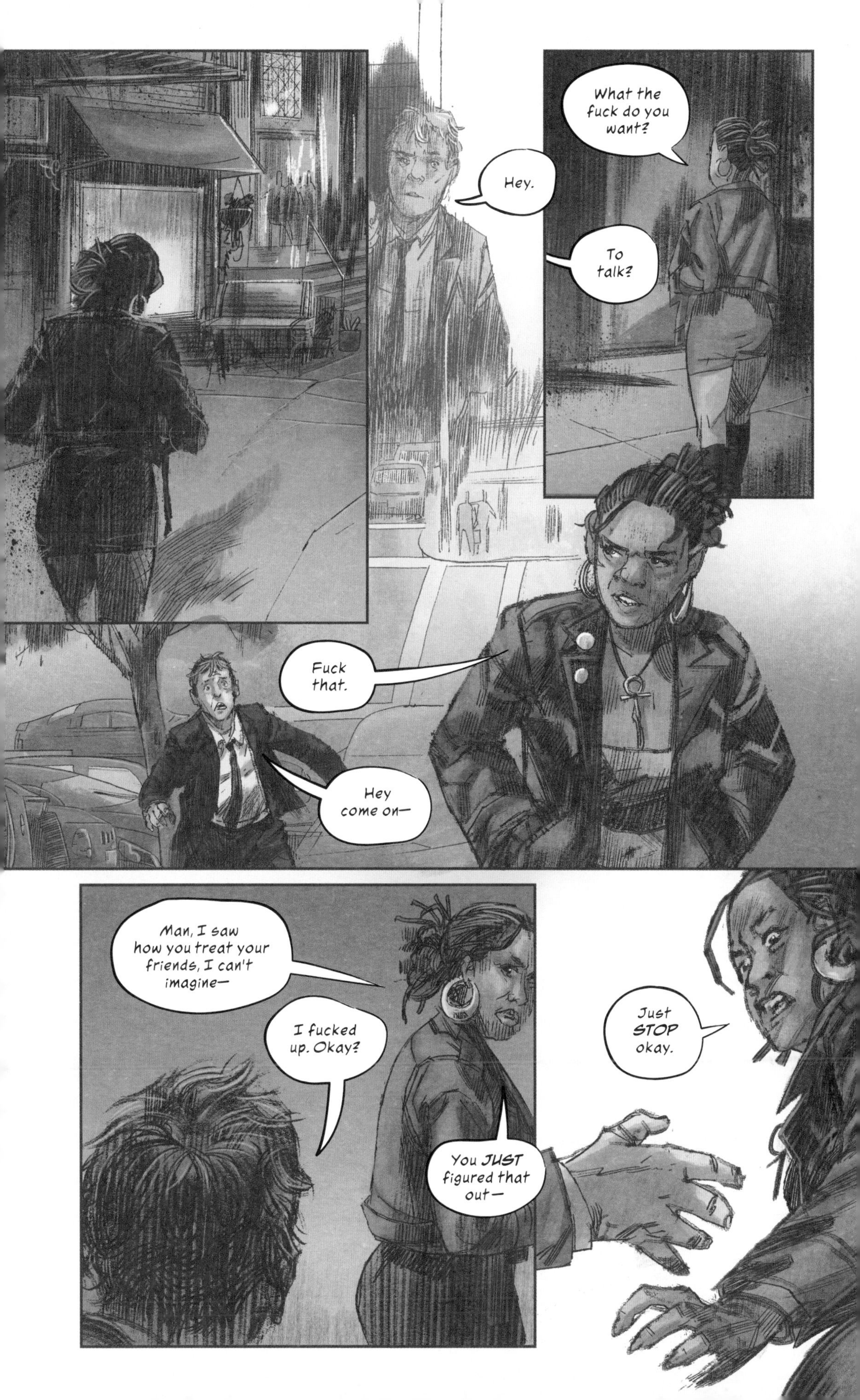

Hey.
What the fuck do you want?
To talk?
Fuck that.
Hey come on—
Man, I saw how you treat your friends, I can't imagine—
I fucked up. Okay?
You JUST figured that out—
Just STOP okay.

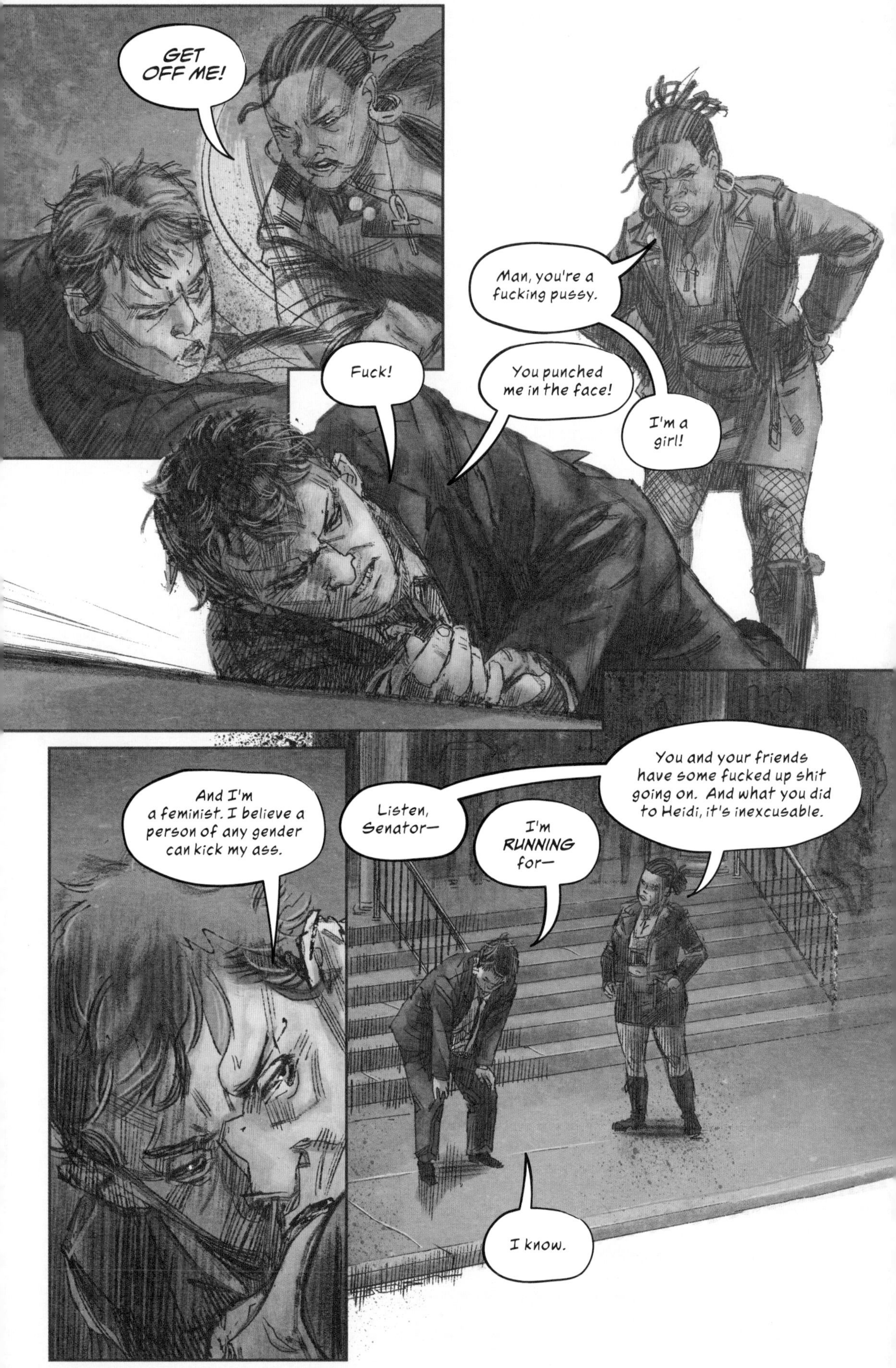
GET OFF ME!
Man, you're a fucking pussy.
Fuck!
You punched me in the face!
I'm a girl!
And I'm a feminist. I believe a person of any gender can kick my ass.
Listen, Senator—
I'm RUNNING for—
You and your friends have some fucked up shit going on. And what you did to Heidi, it's inexcusable.
I know.

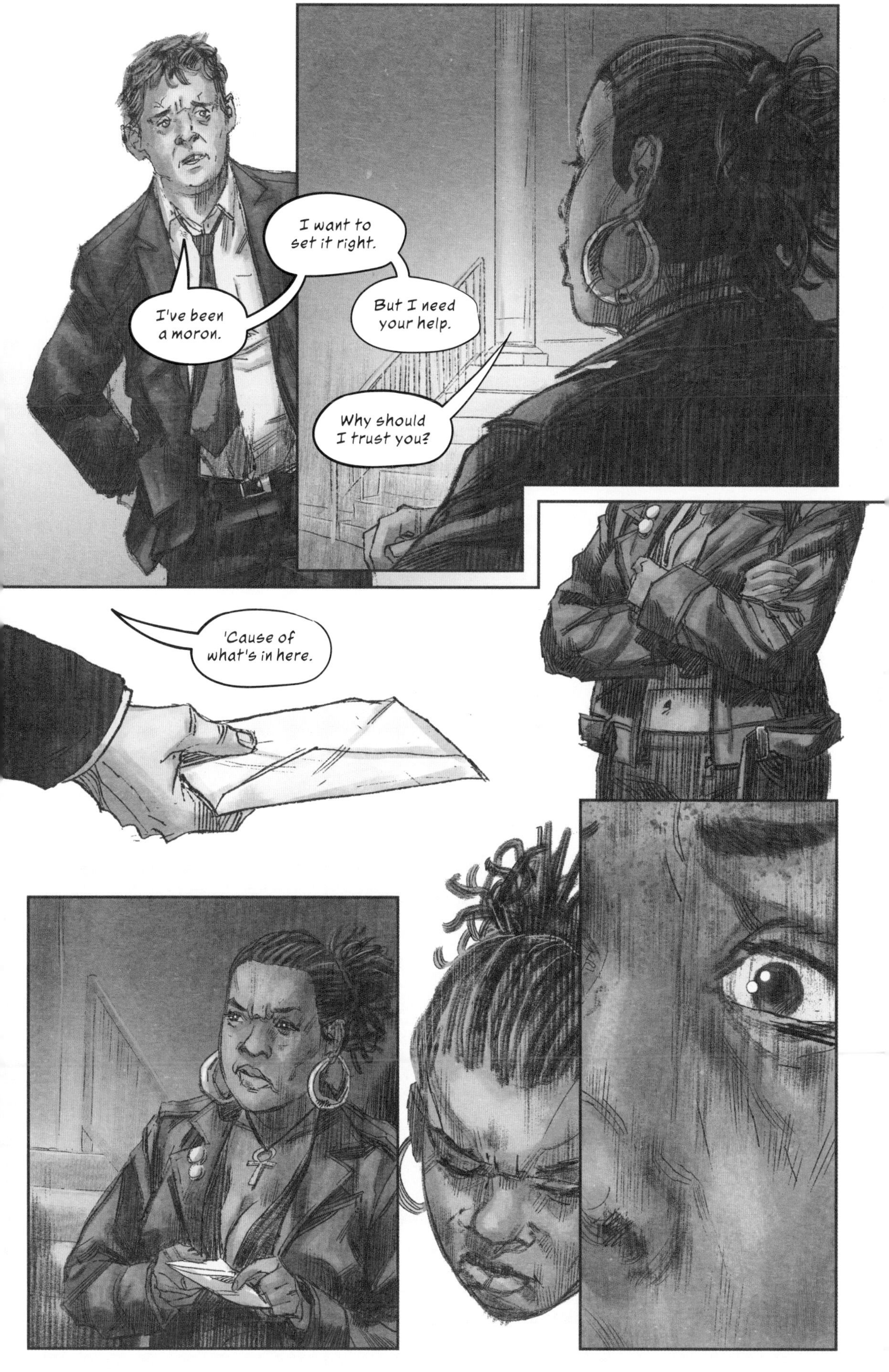
I've been a moron.
I want to set it right.
But I need your help.
Why should I trust you?
'Cause of what's in here.

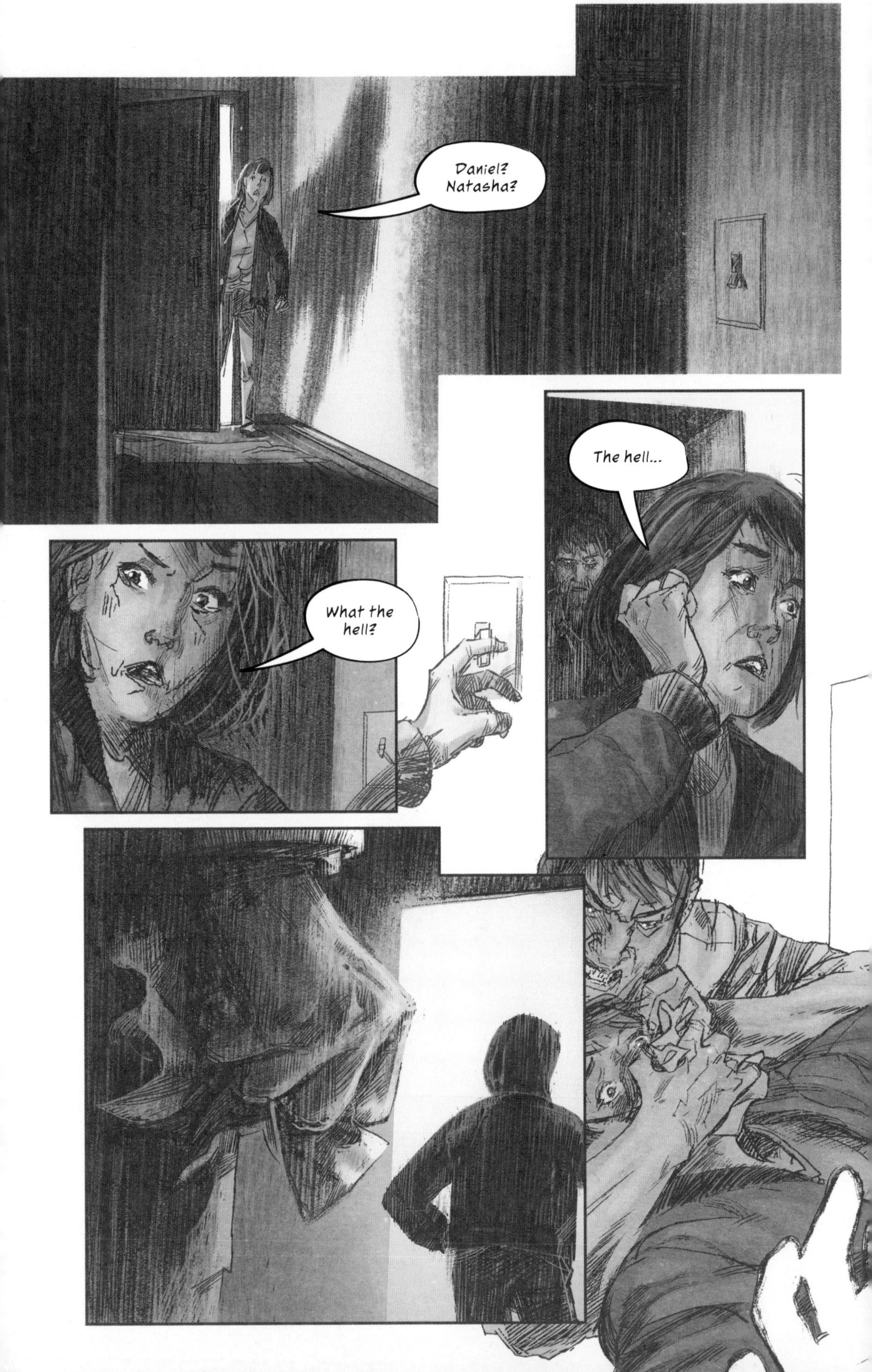
Daniel? Natasha?
What the hell?
The hell...

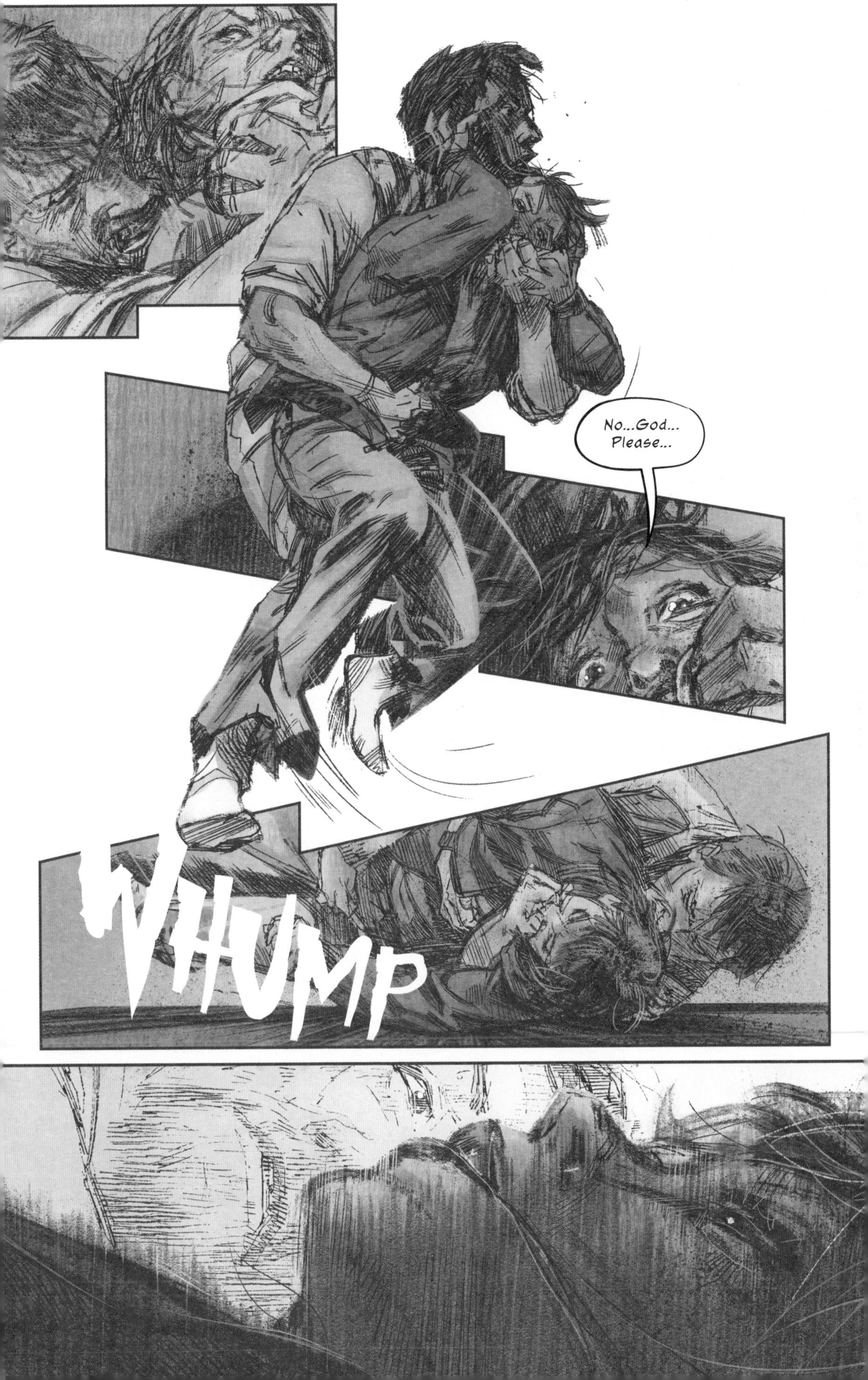
No...God... Please...
WHUMP

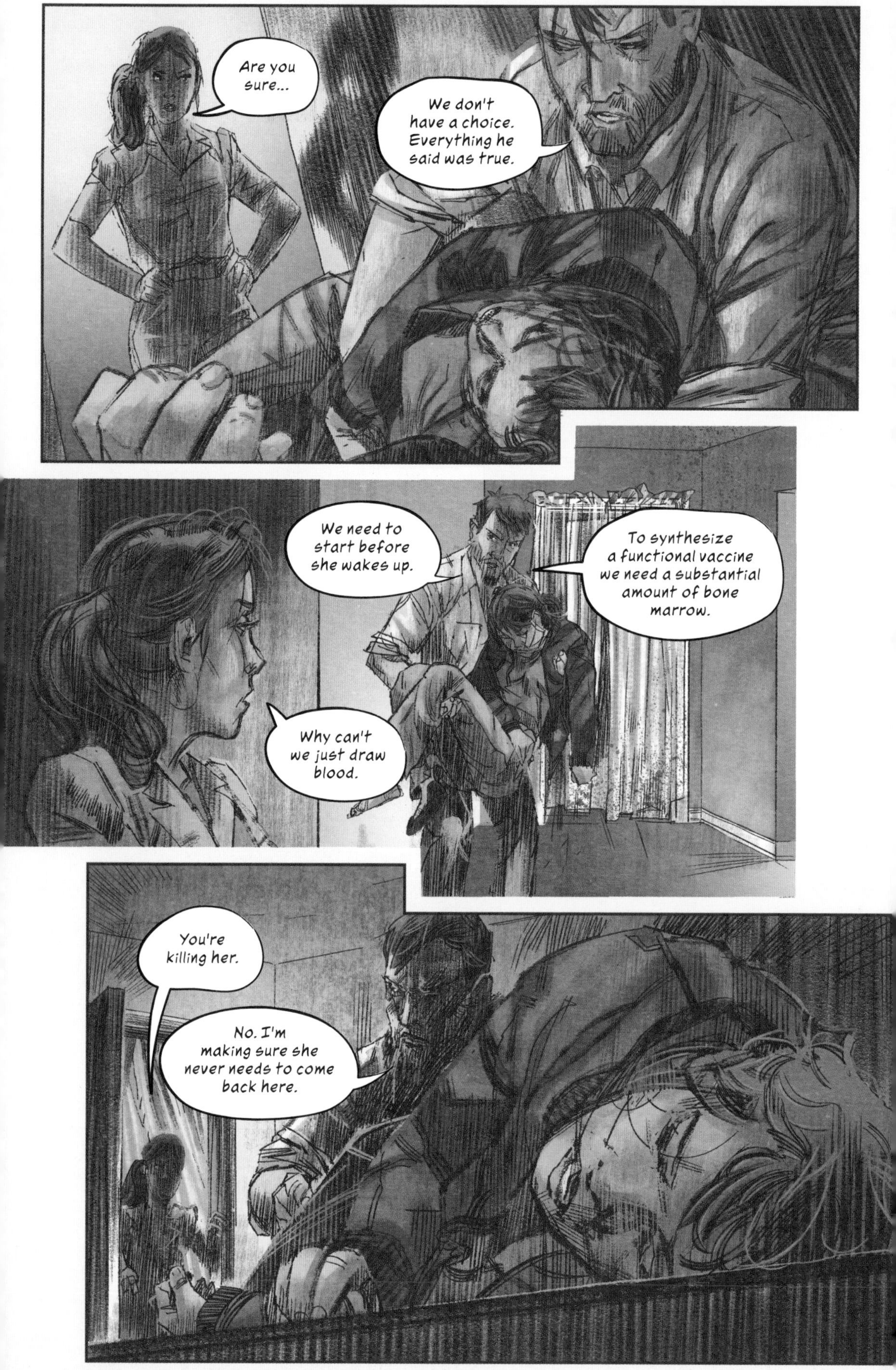
Are you sure...
We don't have a choice. Everything he said was true.
We need to start before she wakes up.
To synthesize a functional vaccine we need a substantial amount of bone marrow.
Why can't we just draw blood.
You're killing her.
No. I'm making sure she never needs to come back here.

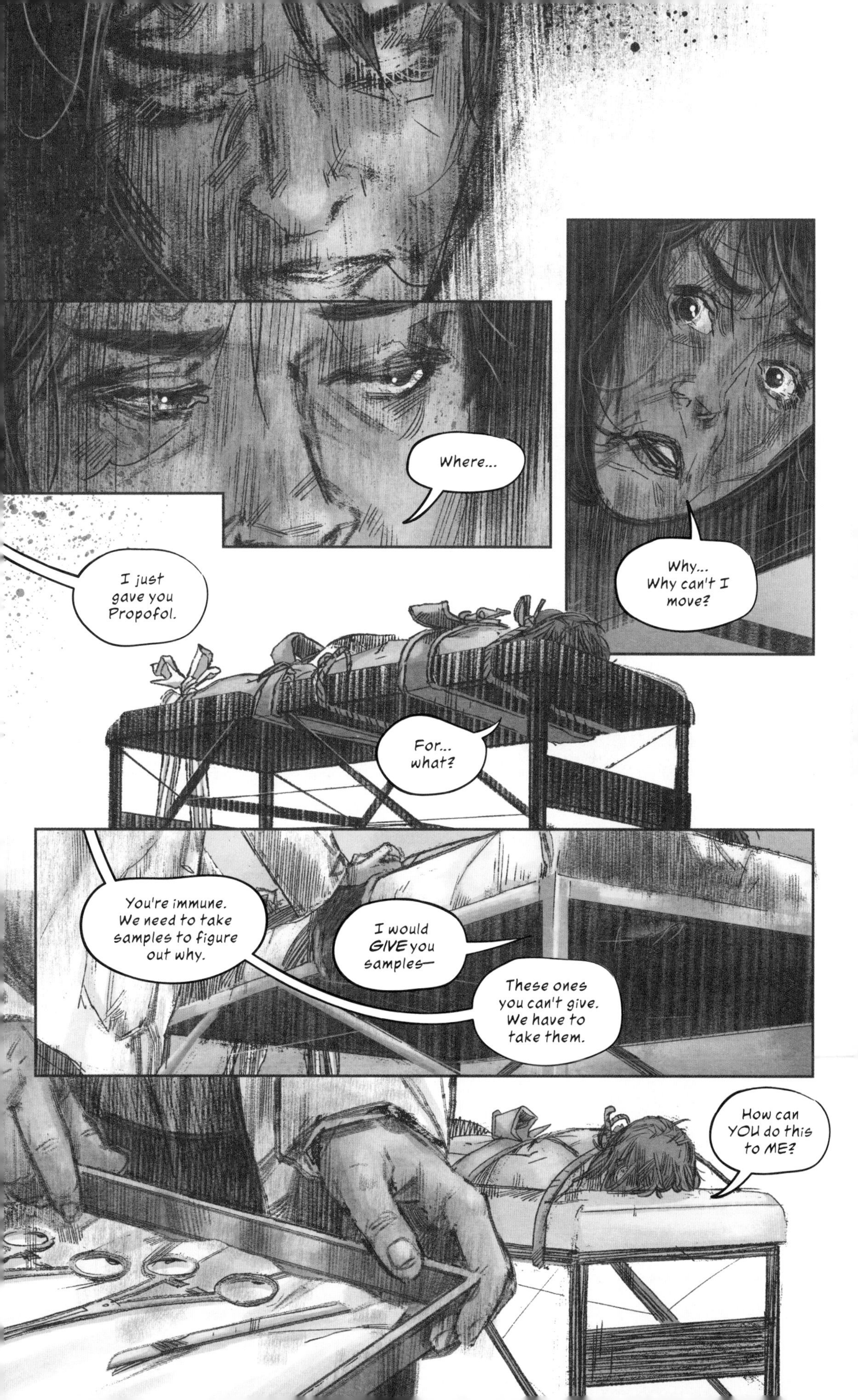
Where...
Why... Why can't I move?
I just gave you Propofol.
For... what?
You're immune. We need to take samples to figure out why.
I would GIVE you samples—
These ones you can't give. We have to take them.
How can YOU do this to ME?

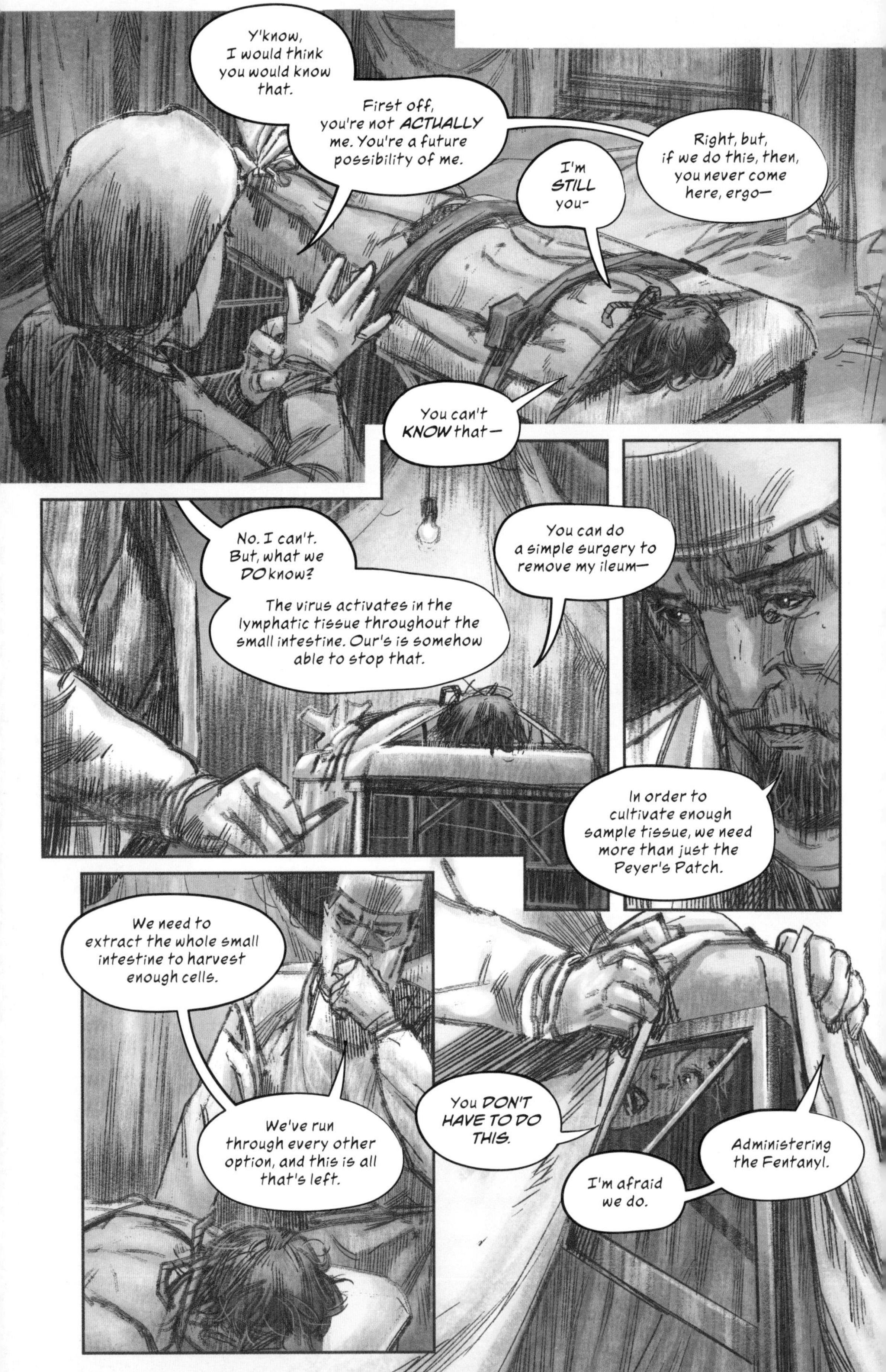
Y'know, I would think you would know that.
First off, you're not ACTUALLY me. You're a future possibility of me.
I'm STILL you-
Right, but, if we do this, then, you never come here, ergo—
You can't KNOW that—
No. I can't. But, what we DO know?
The virus activates in the lymphatic tissue throughout the small intestine. Our's is somehow able to stop that.
You can do a simple surgery to remove my ileum—
In order to cultivate enough sample tissue, we need more than just the Peyer's Patch.
We need to extract the whole small intestine to harvest enough cells.
We've run through every other option, and this is all that's left.
You DON'T HAVE TO DO THIS.
I'm afraid we do.
Administering the Fentanyl.

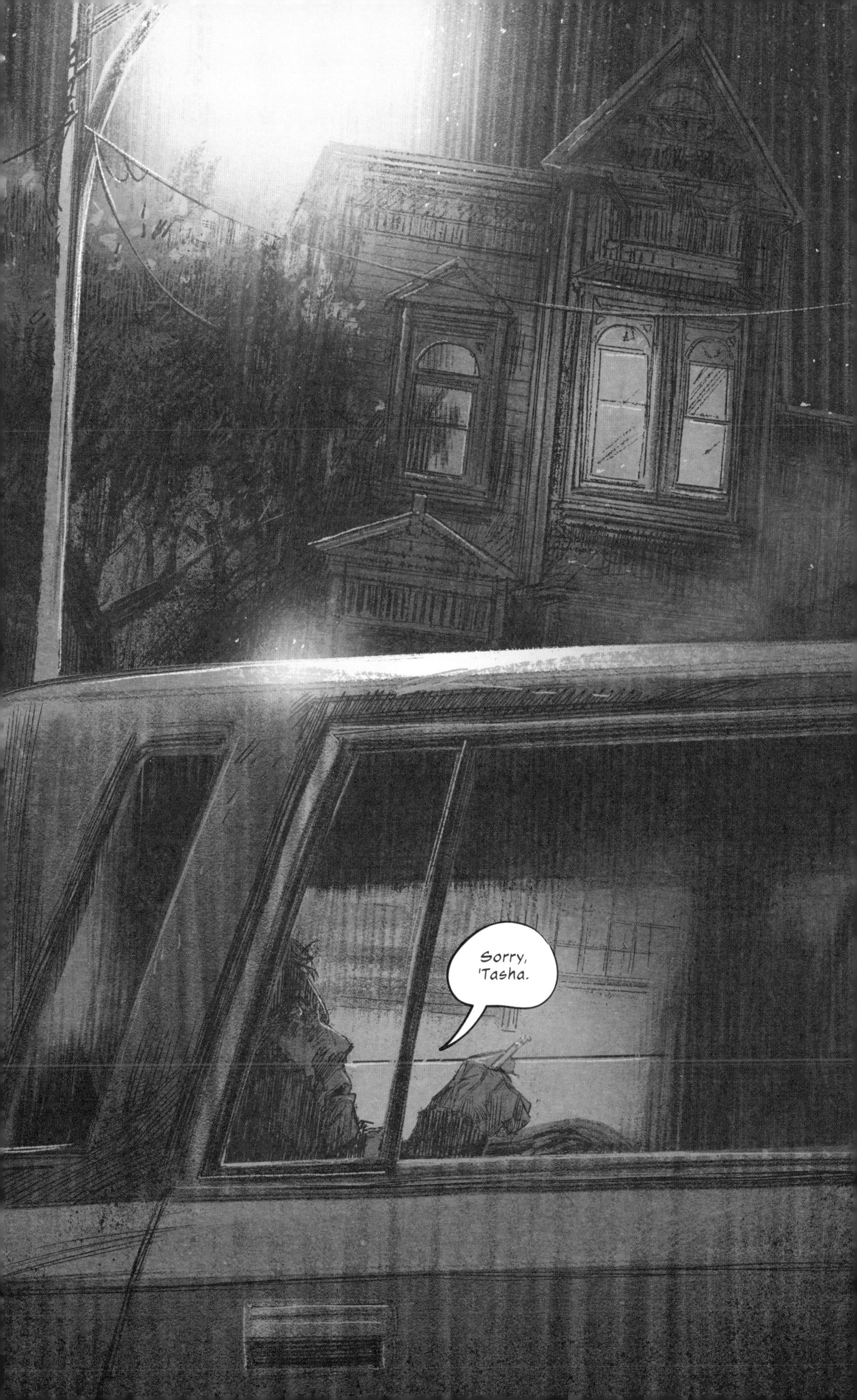
Sorry, 'Tasha.

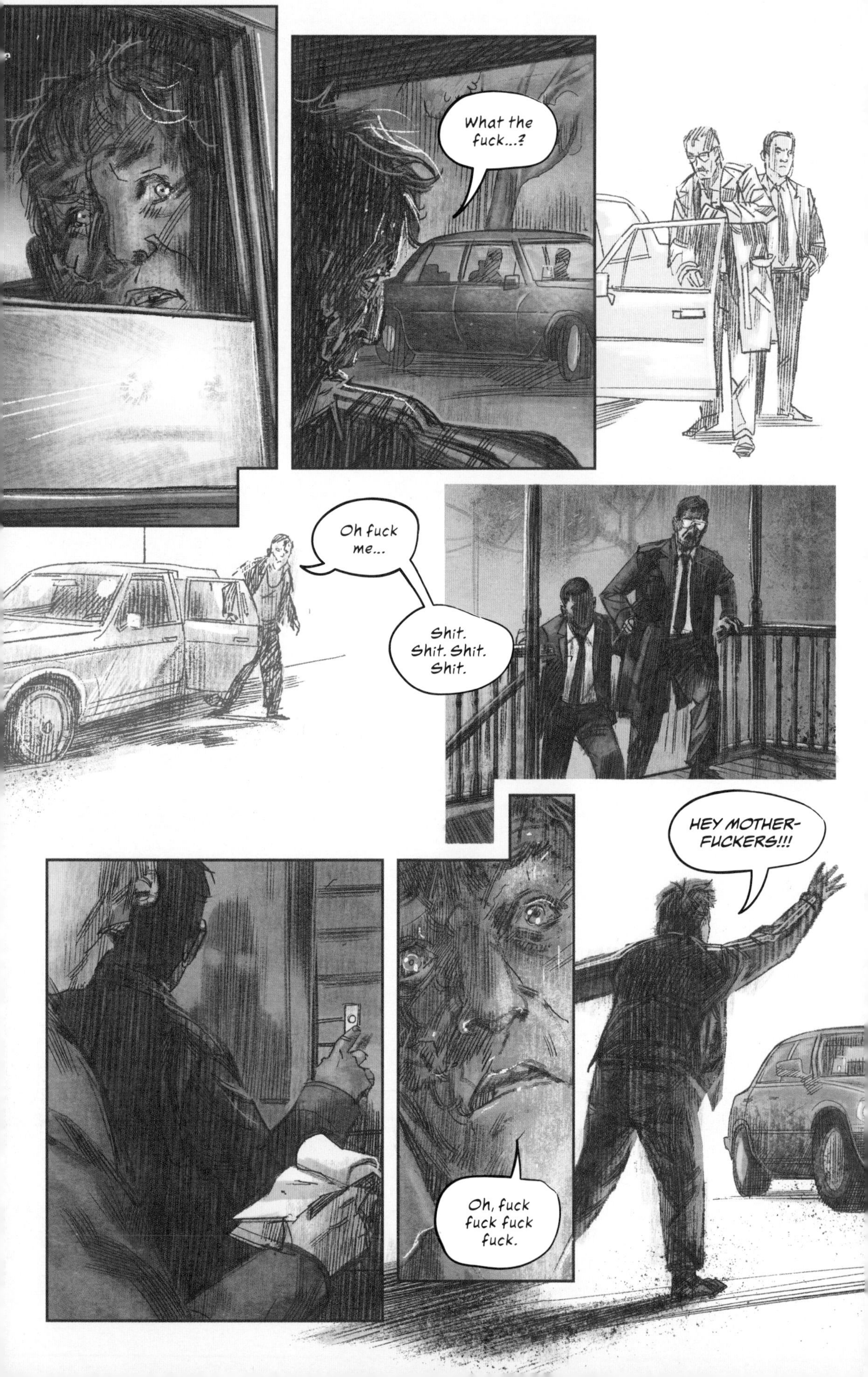
What the fuck...?
Oh fuck me...
Shit. Shit. Shit. Shit.
HEY MOTHER-FUCKERS!!!
Oh, fuck fuck fuck fuck.

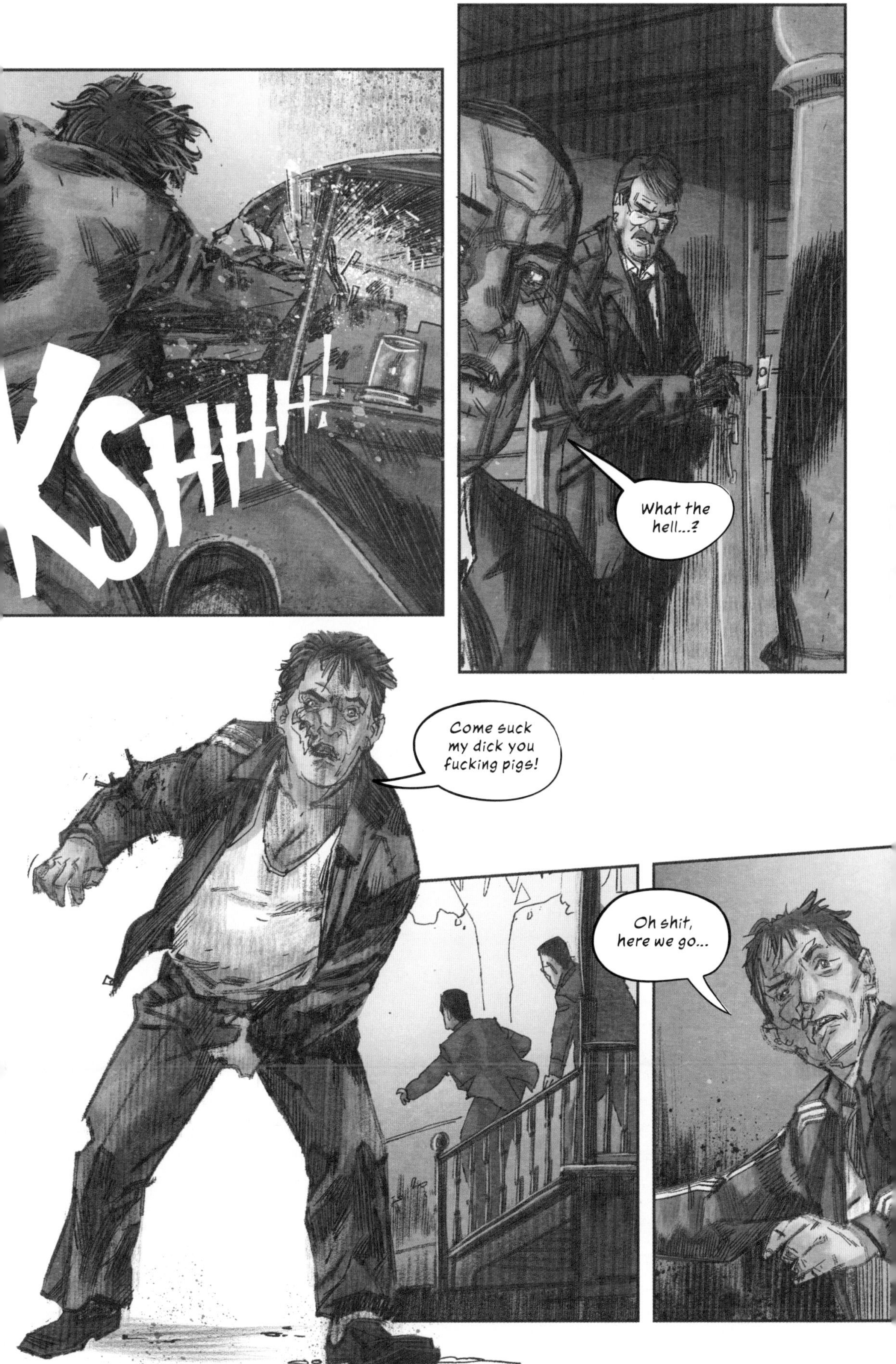
KSHHH!
What the hell...?
Come suck my dick you fucking pigs!
Oh shit, here we go...

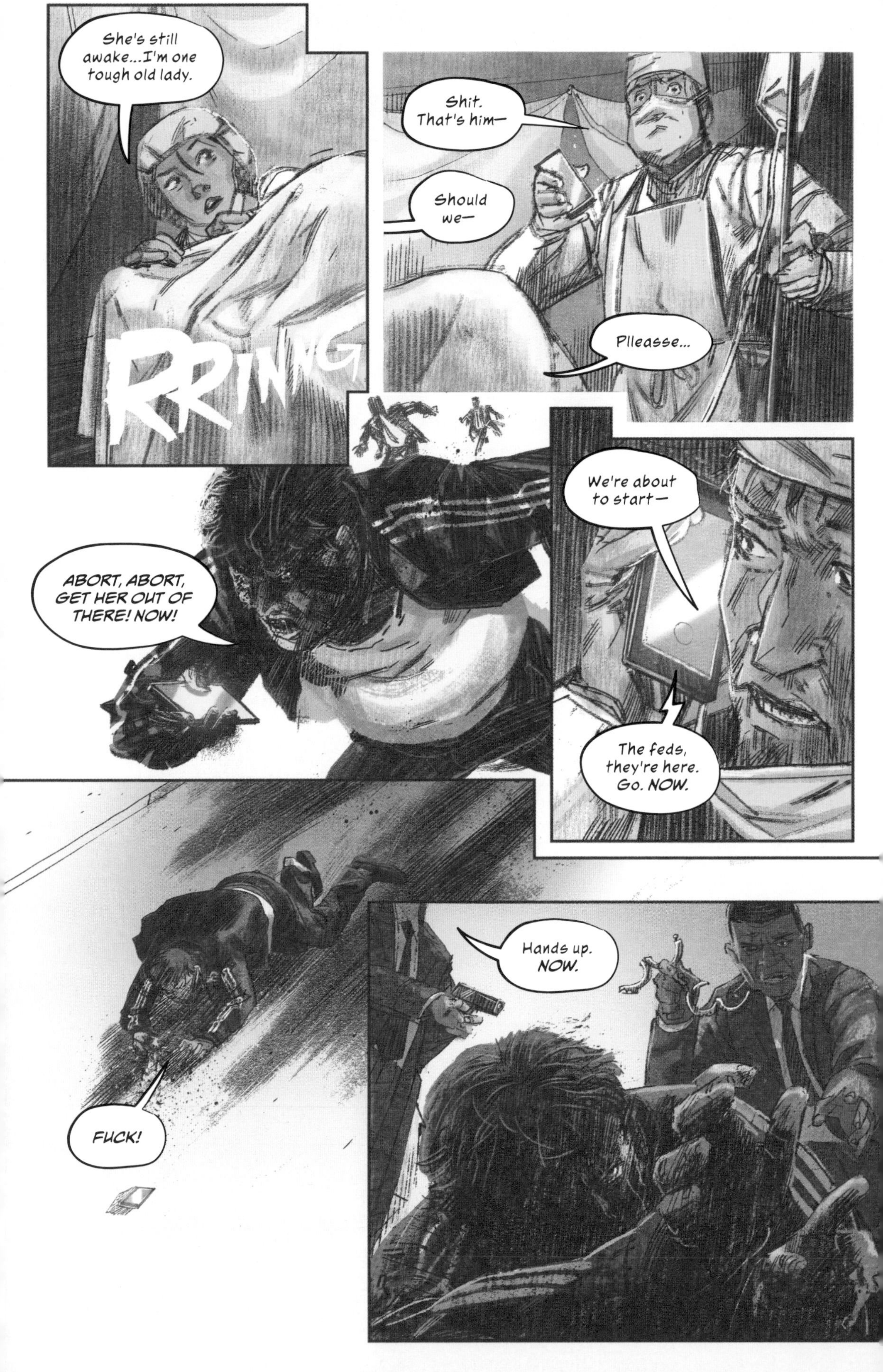
She's still awake...I'm one tough old lady.
RRING
Shit. That's him—
Should we—
Plleasse...
ABORT, ABORT, GET HER OUT OF THERE! NOW!
We're about to start—
The feds, they're here. Go. NOW.
FUCK!
Hands up. NOW.

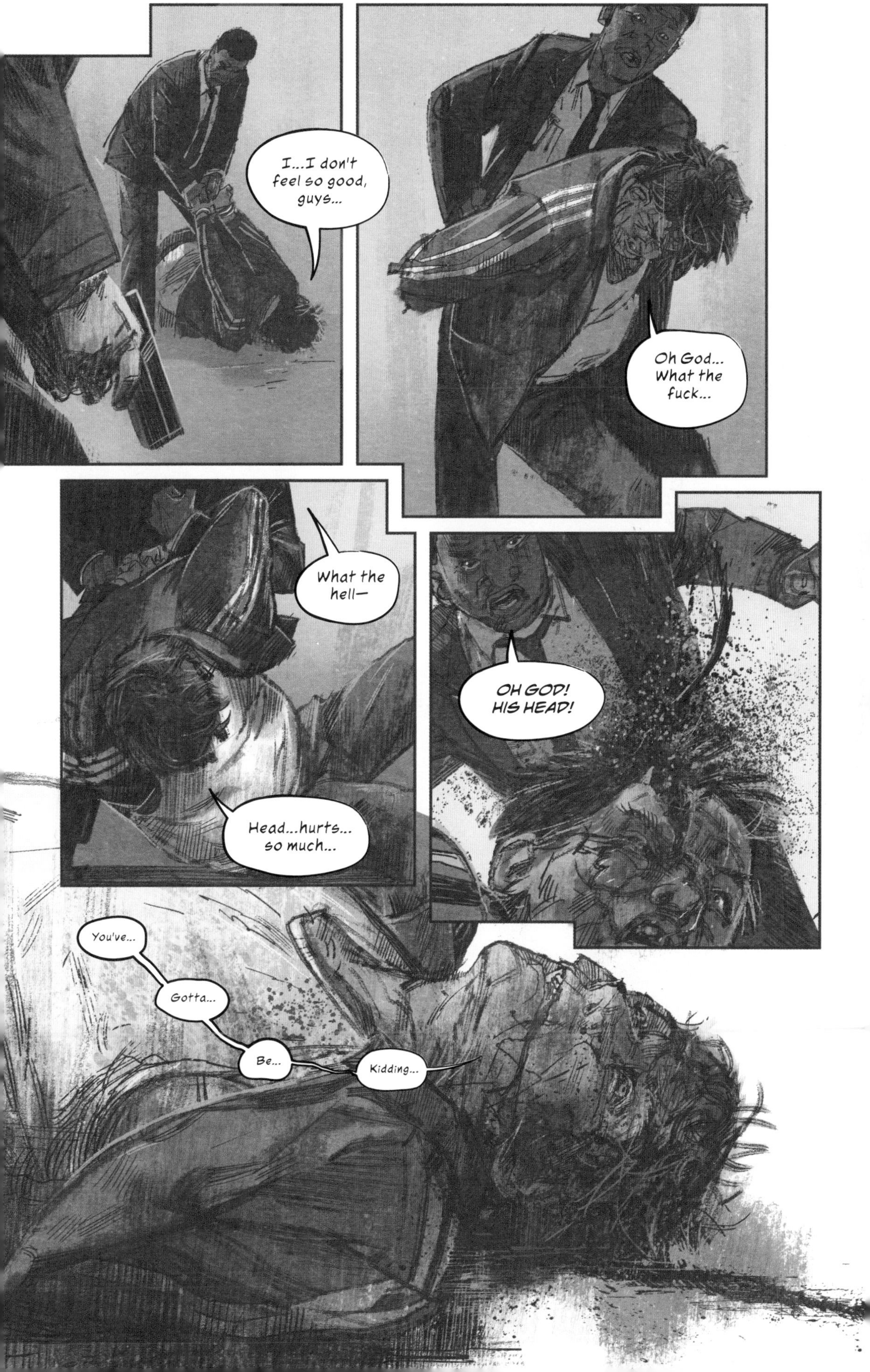
I...I don't feel so good, guys...
Oh God... What the fuck...
What the hell—
Head...hurts... so much...
OH GOD! HIS HEAD!
You've...
Gotta...
Be...
Kidding...

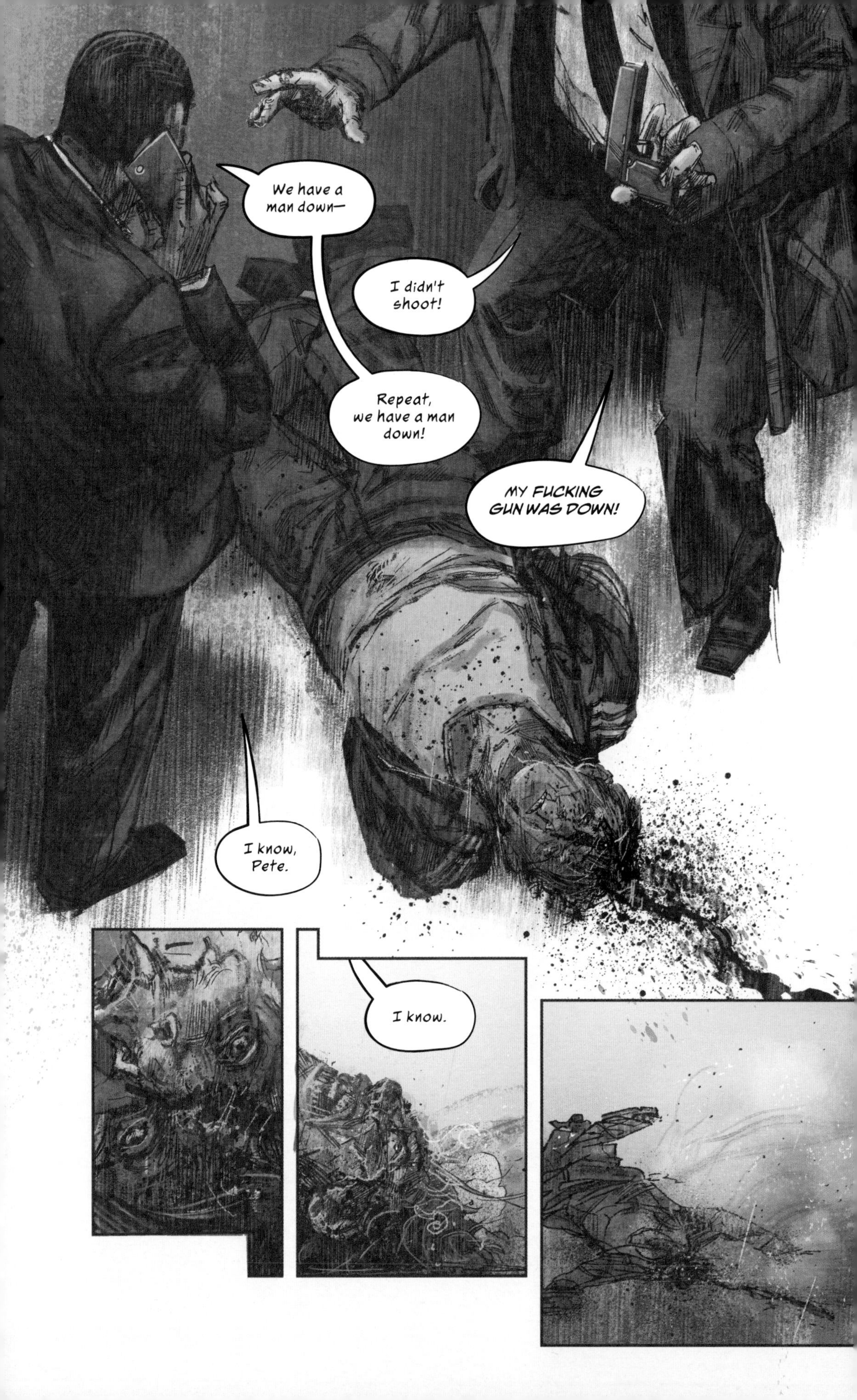
We have a man down—
I didn't shoot!
Repeat, we have a man down!
MY FUCKING GUN WAS DOWN!
I know, Pete.
I know.

CHAPTER 17

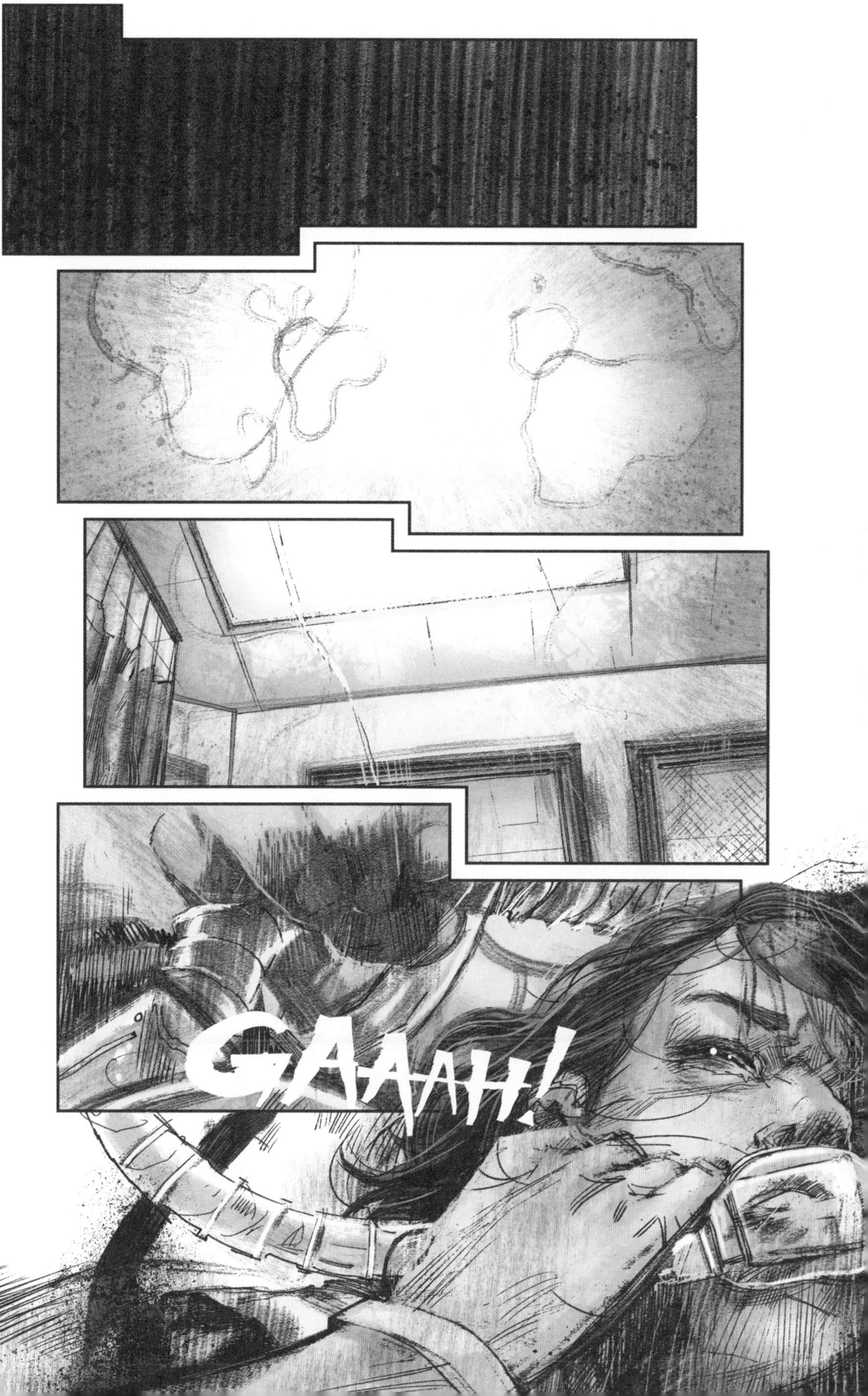
GAAAH!

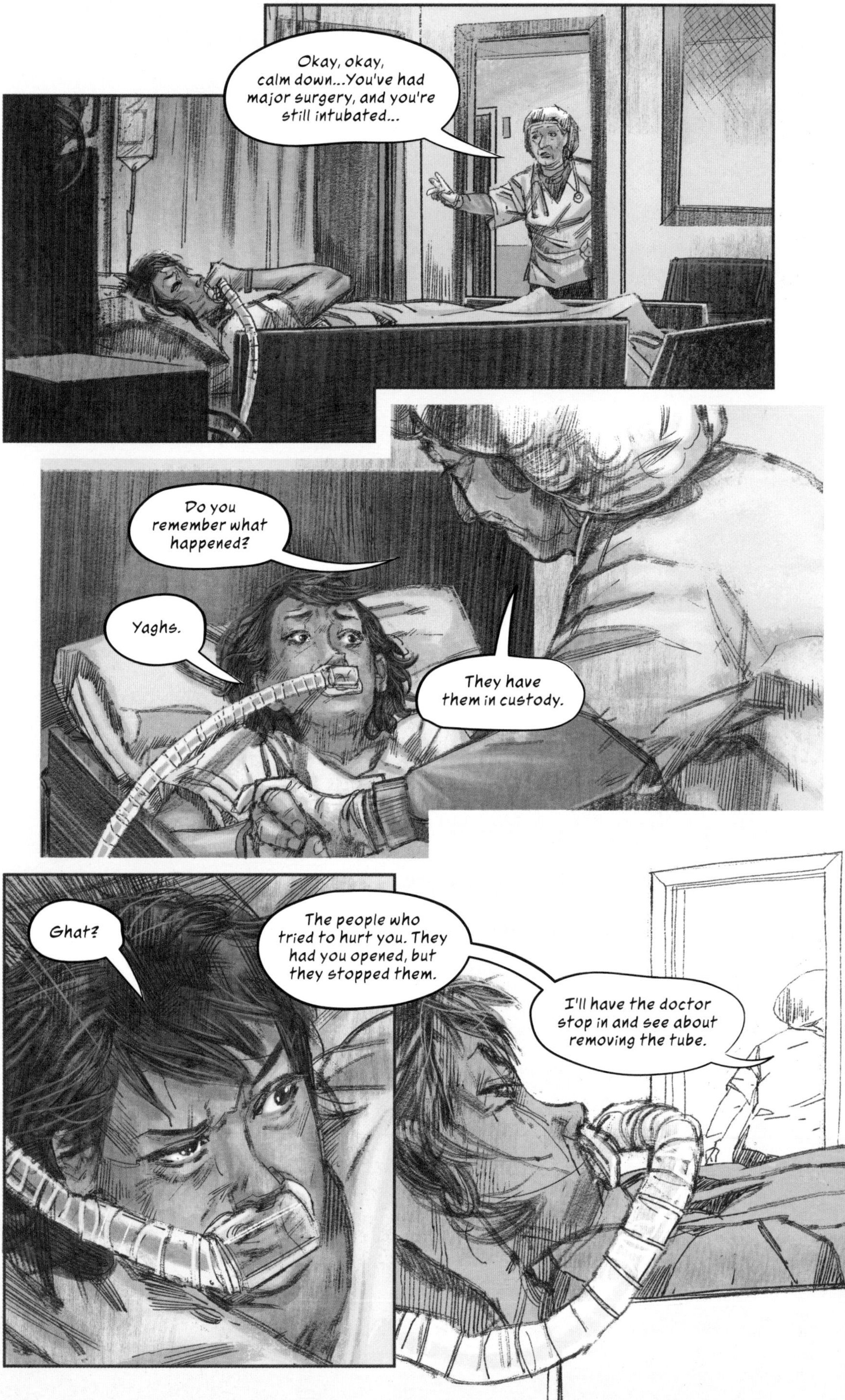
Okay, okay, calm down...You've had major surgery, and you're still intubated...
Do you remember what happened?
Yaghs.
They have them in custody.
Ghat?
The people who tried to hurt you. They had you opened, but they stopped them.
I'll have the doctor stop in and see about removing the tube.

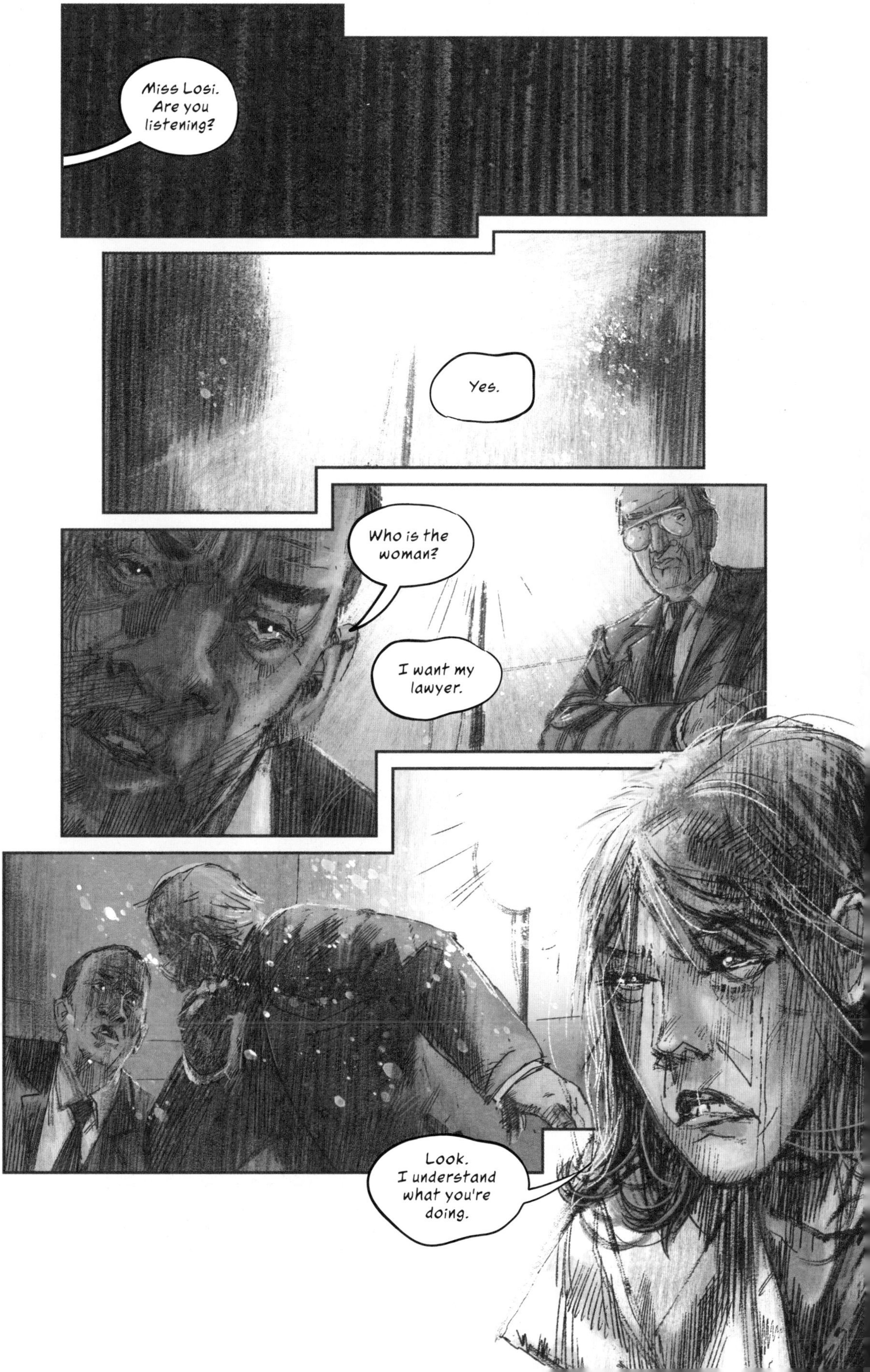
Miss Losi. Are you listening?
Yes.
Who is the woman?
I want my lawyer.
Look. I understand what you're doing.

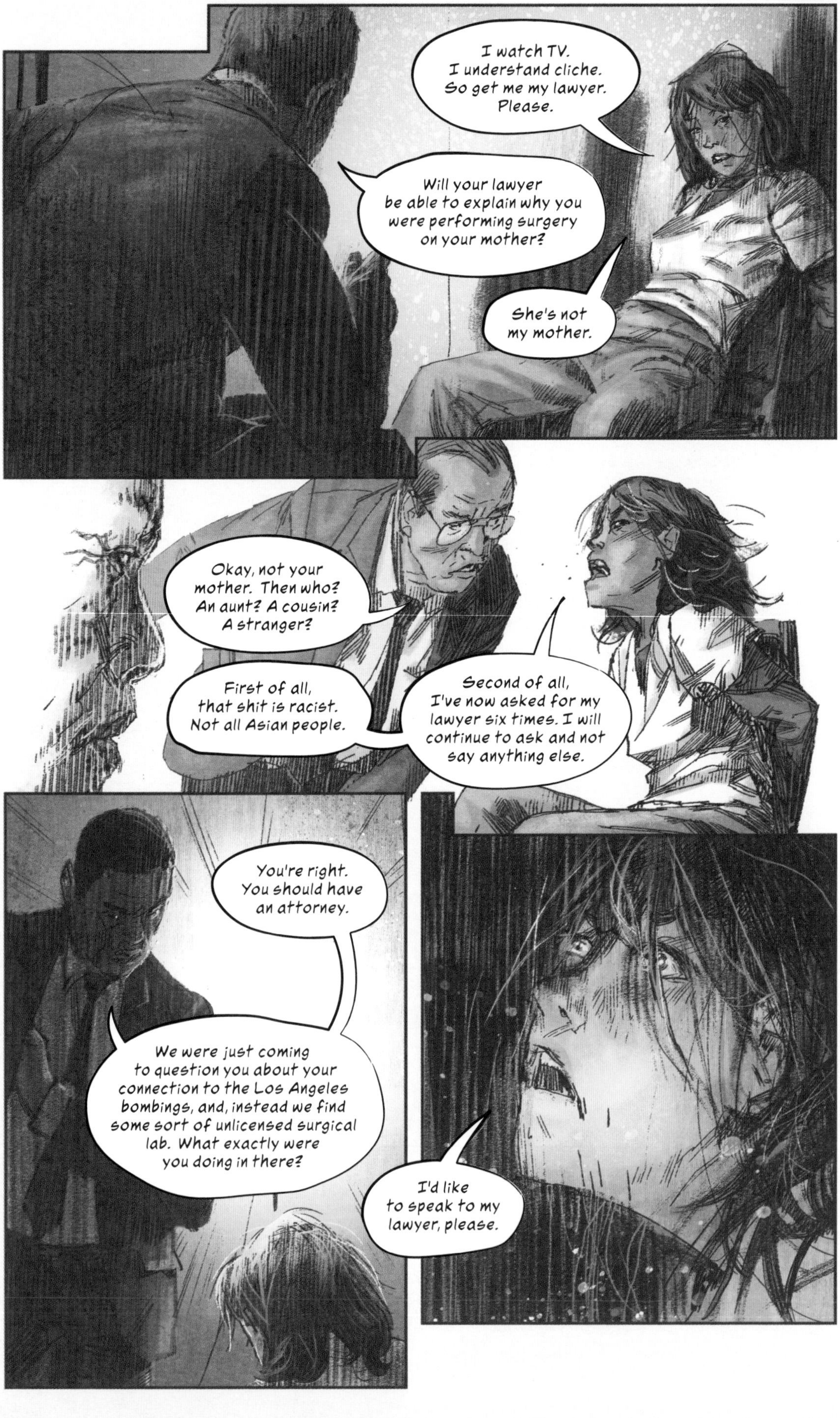
I watch TV. I understand cliche. So get me my lawyer. Please.
Will your lawyer be able to explain why you were performing surgery on your mother?
She's not my mother.
Okay, not your mother. Then who? An aunt? A cousin? A stranger?
First of all, that shit is racist. Not all Asian people.
Second of all, I've now asked for my lawyer six times. I will continue to ask and not say anything else.
You're right. You should have an attorney.
We were just coming to question you about your connection to the Los Angeles bombings, and, instead we find some sort of unlicensed surgical lab. What exactly were you doing in there?
I'd like to speak to my lawyer, please.

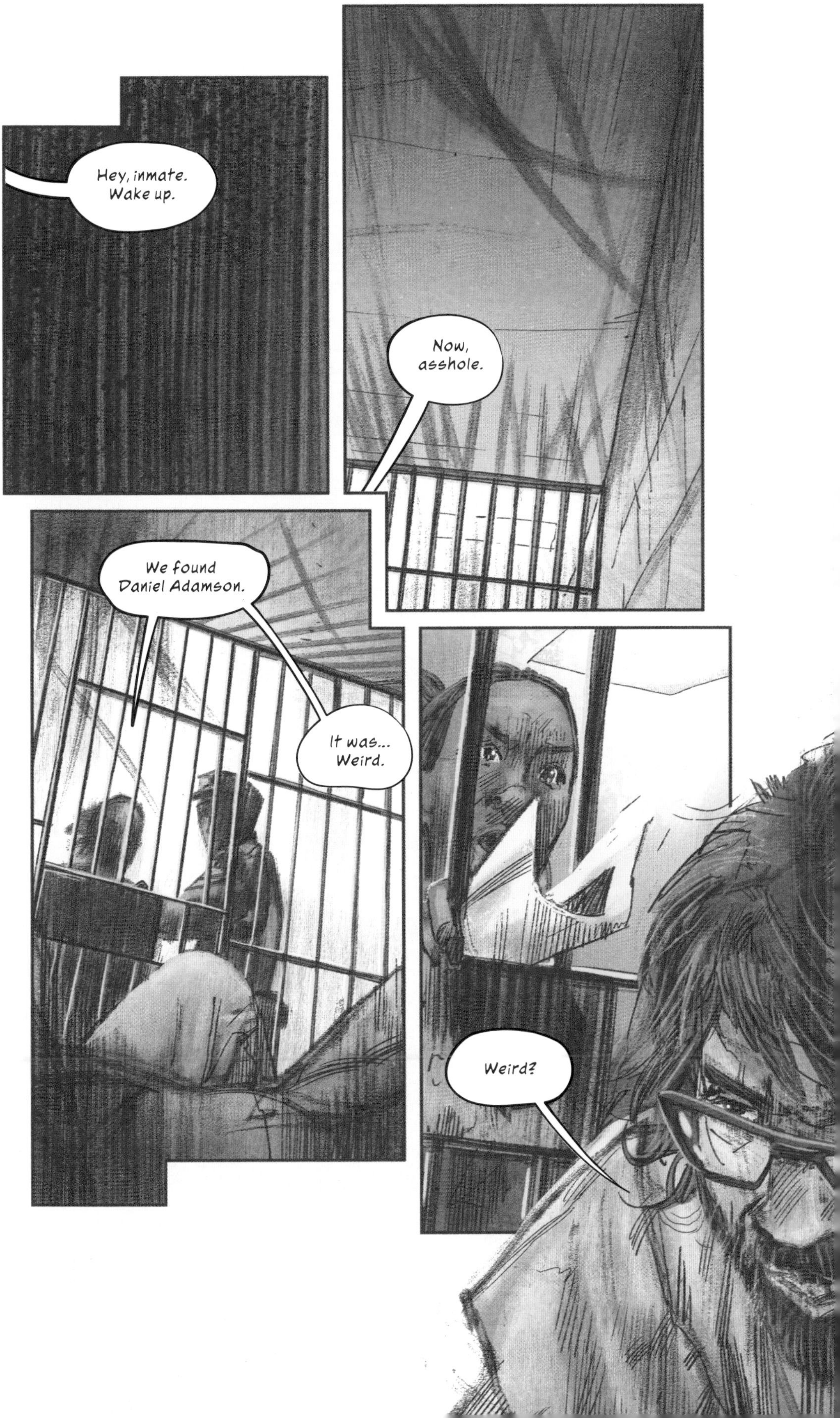
Hey, inmate.
Wake up.
Now,
asshole.
We found
Daniel Adamson.
It was...
Weird.
Weird?

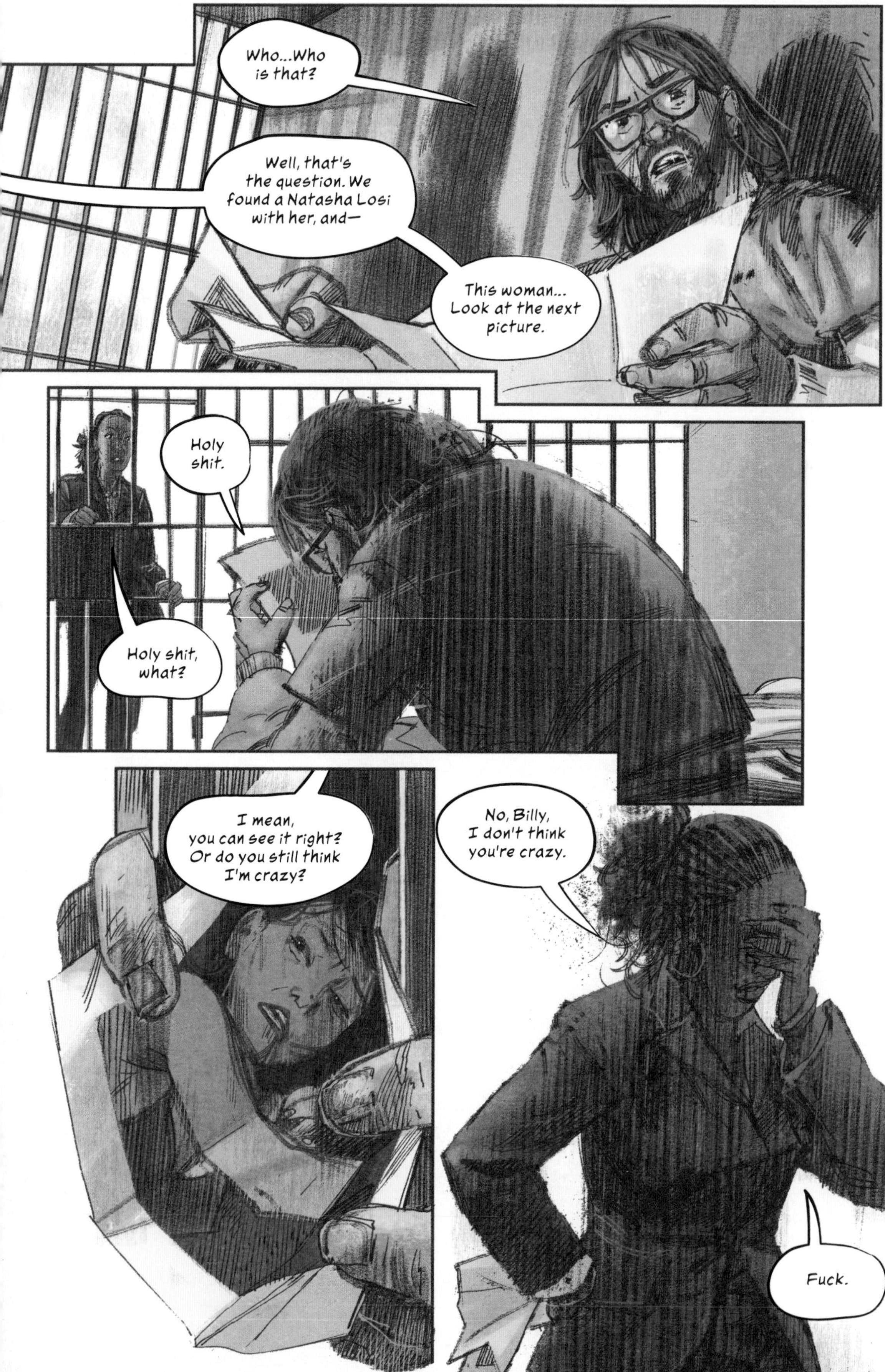
Who...Who is that?
Well, that's the question. We found a Natasha Losi with her, and—
This woman... Look at the next picture.
Holy shit.
Holy shit, what?
I mean, you can see it right? Or do you still think I'm crazy?
No, Billy, I don't think you're crazy.
Fuck.

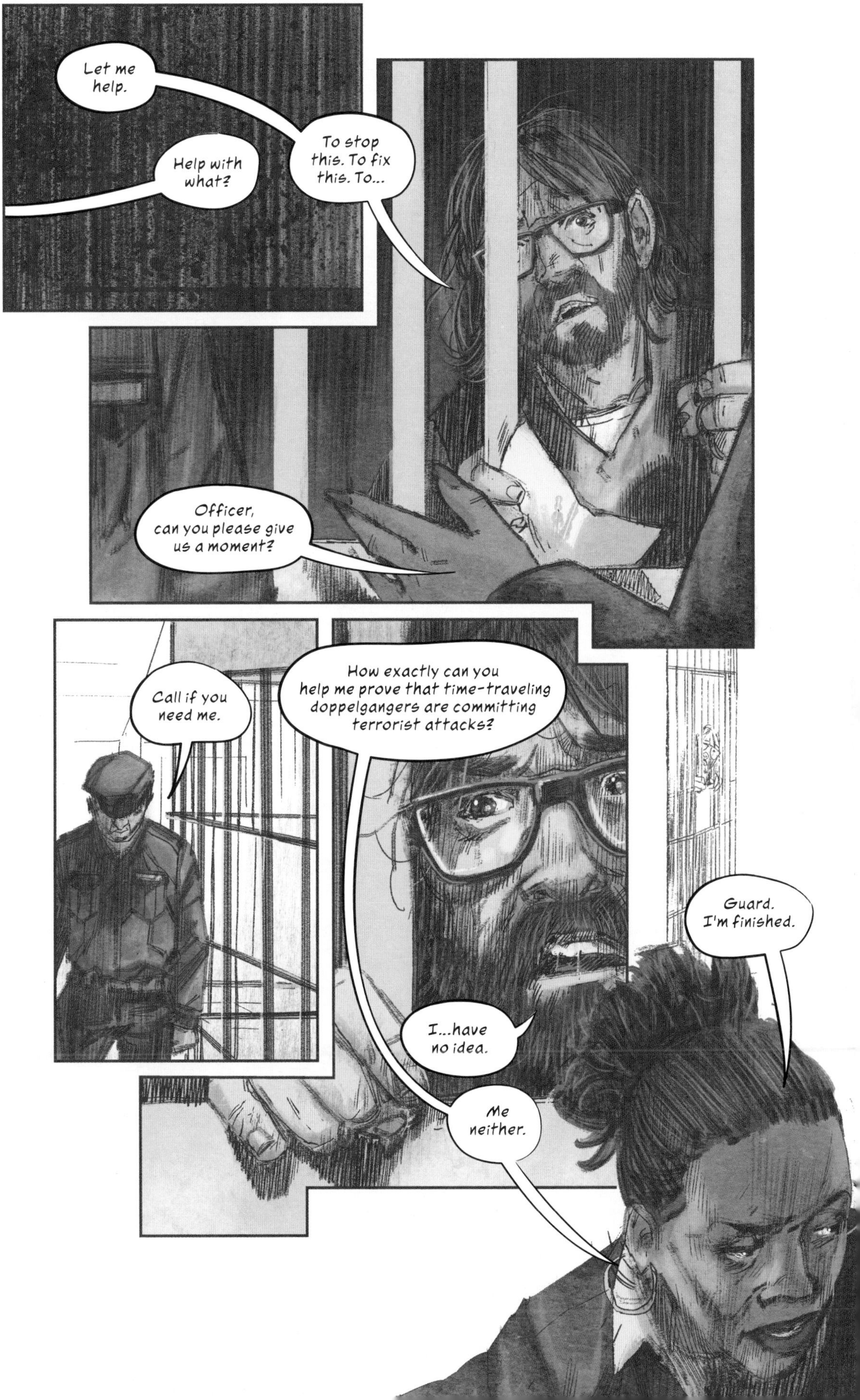
Let me help.
Help with what?
To stop this. To fix this. To...
Officer, can you please give us a moment?
Call if you need me.
How exactly can you help me prove that time-traveling doppelgangers are committing terrorist attacks?
I...have no idea.
Me neither.
Guard. I'm finished.

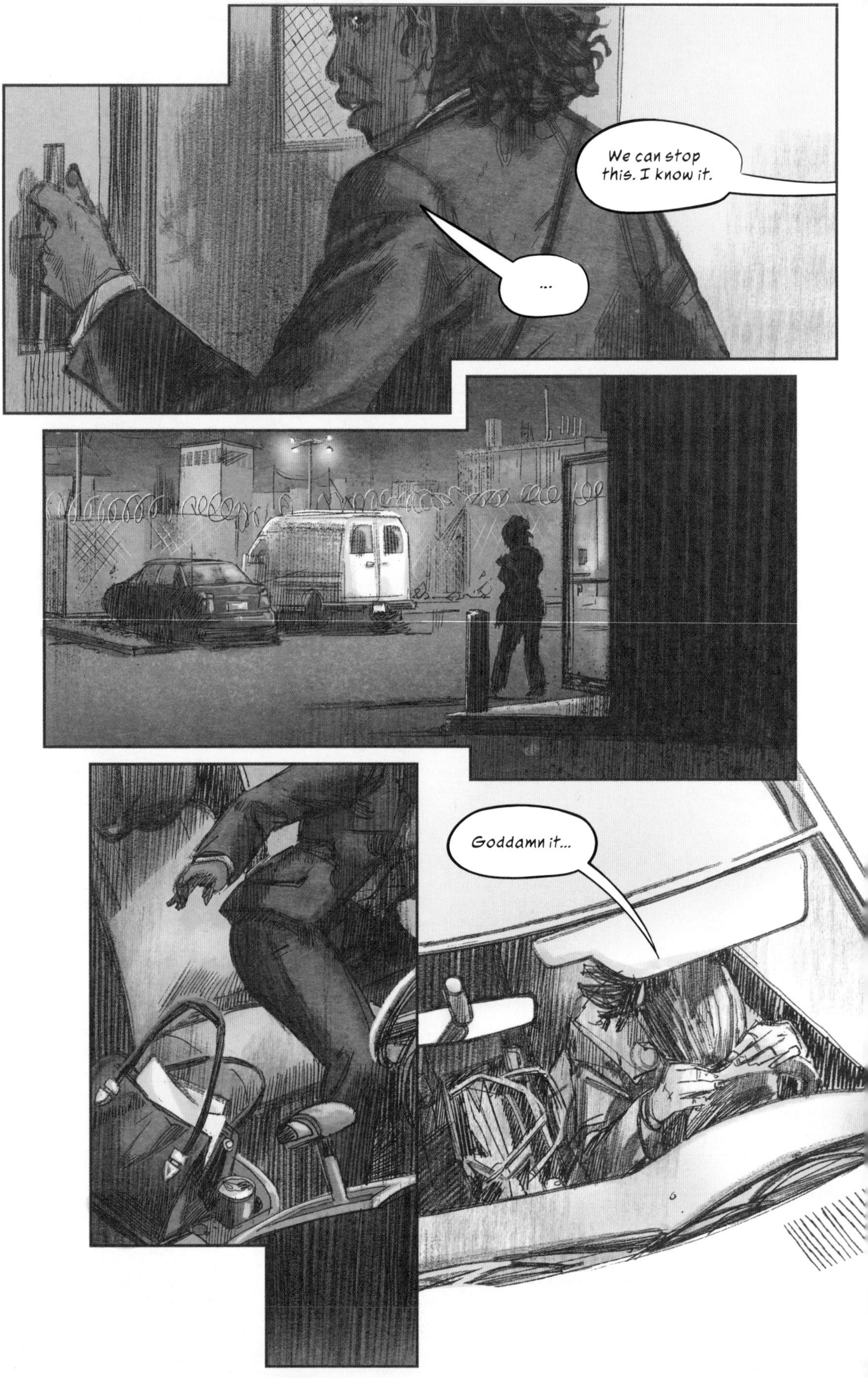
We can stop this. I know it.
...
Goddamn it...

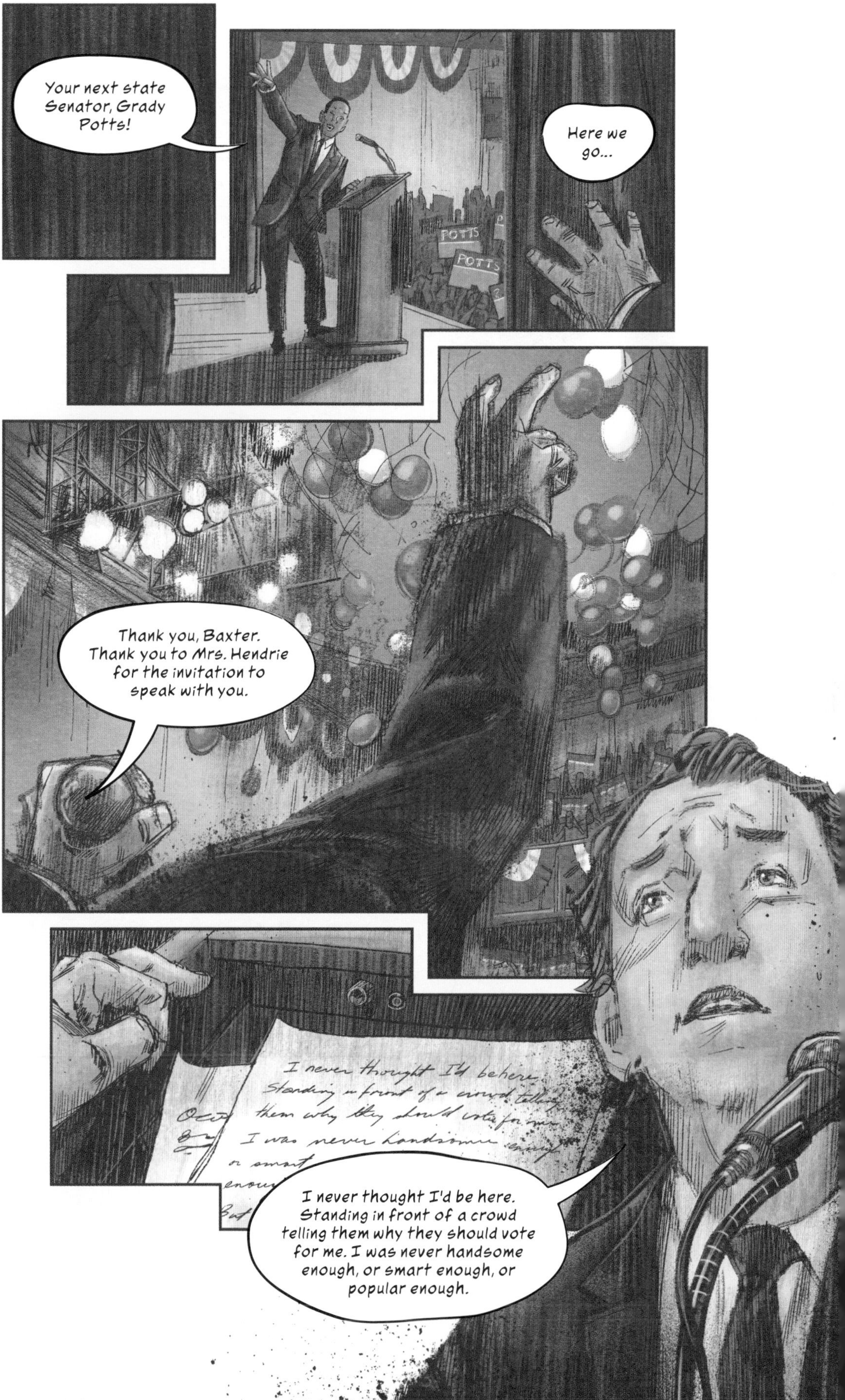
Your next state Senator, Grady Potts!
POTTS
POTTS
Here we go...
Thank you, Baxter. Thank you to Mrs. Hendrie for the invitation to speak with you.
I never thought I'd be here. Standing in front of a crowd telling them why they should vote for me. I was never handsome enough, or smart enough, or popular enough.

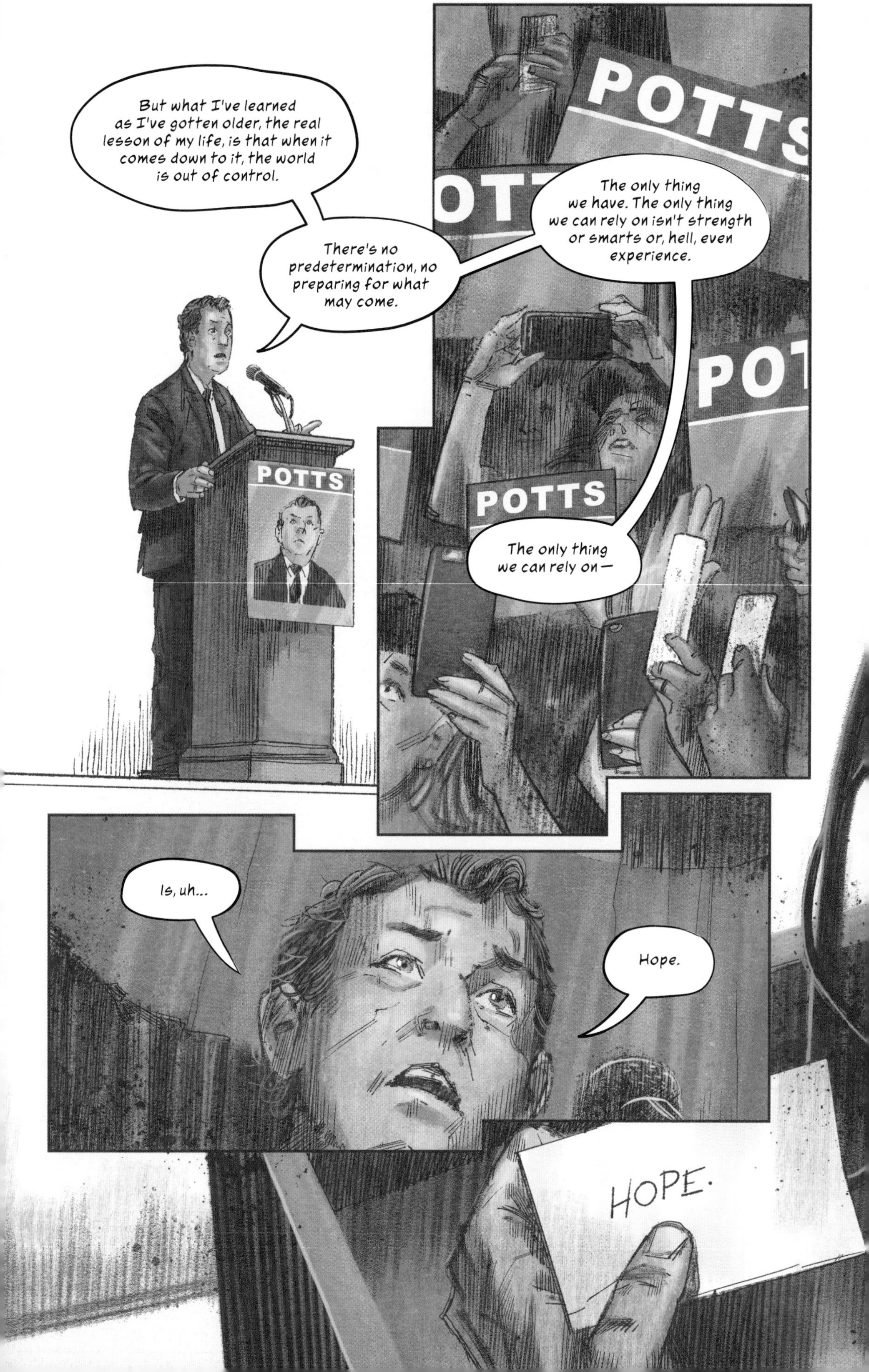
But what I've learned as I've gotten older, the real lesson of my life, is that when it comes down to it, the world is out of control.
There's no predetermination, no preparing for what may come.
POTTS
The only thing we have. The only thing we can rely on isn't strength or smarts or, hell, even experience.
POTTS
POT
POTTS
POTTS
The only thing we can rely on—
Is, uh...
Hope.
HOPE.

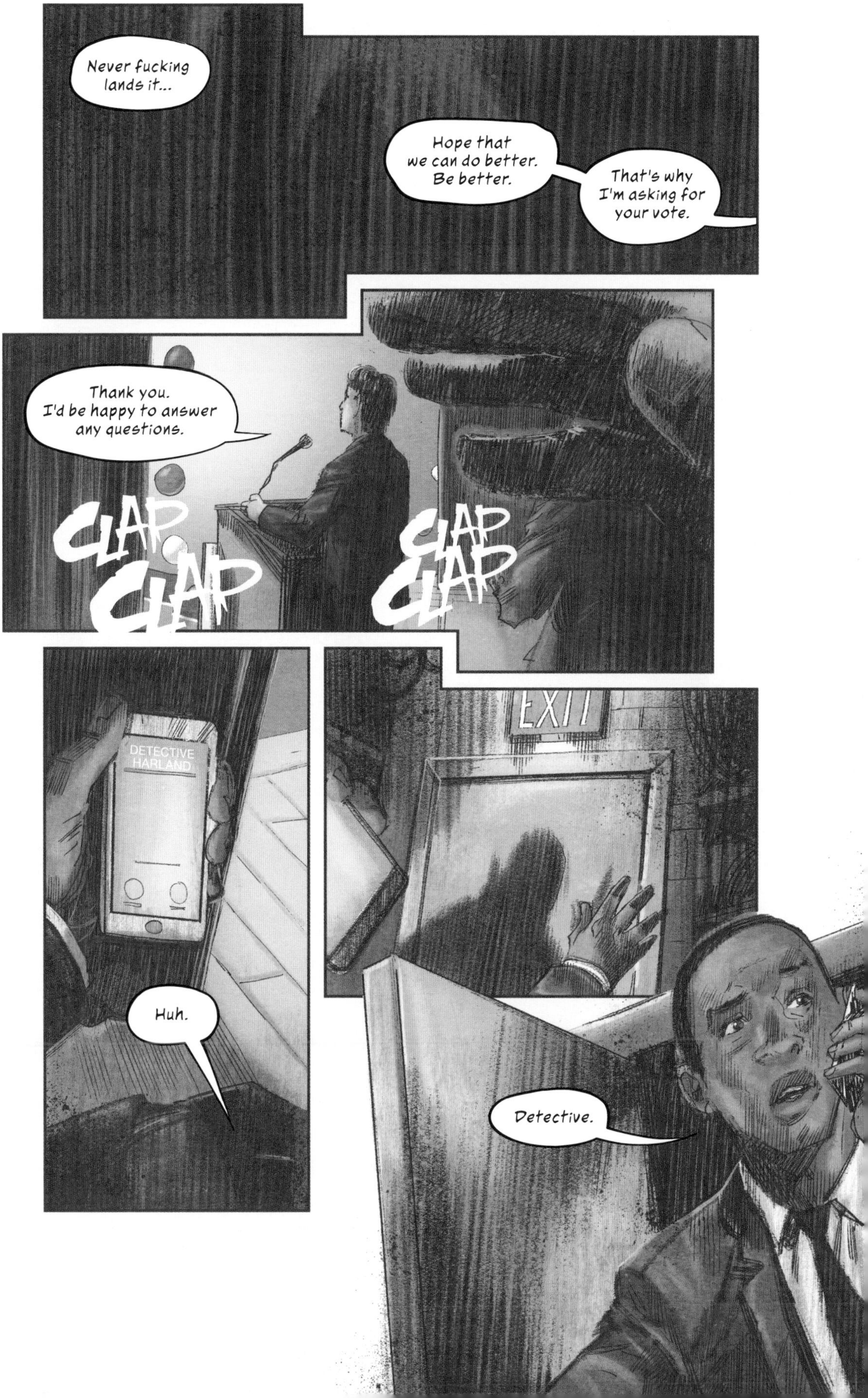

Never fucking lands it...
Hope that we can do better. Be better.
That's why I'm asking for your vote.
Thank you. I'd be happy to answer any questions.
CLAP CLAP
CLAP CLAP
DETECTIVE HARLAND
Huh.
EXIT
Detective.

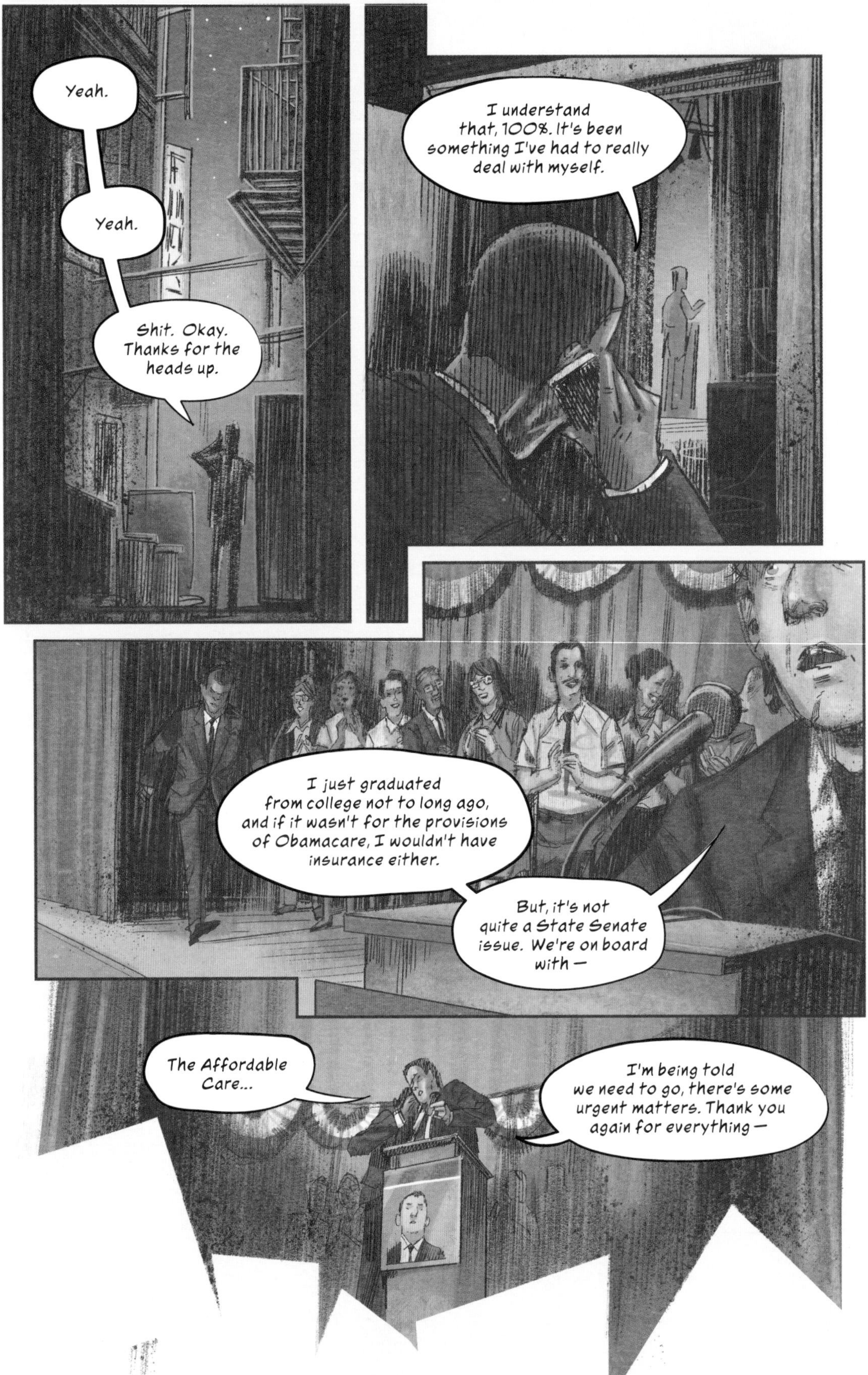
Yeah.
Yeah.
Shit. Okay. Thanks for the heads up.
I understand that, 100%. It's been something I've had to really deal with myself.
I just graduated from college not to long ago, and if it wasn't for the provisions of Obamacare, I wouldn't have insurance either.
But, it's not quite a State Senate issue. We're on board with —
The Affordable Care...
I'm being told we need to go, there's some urgent matters. Thank you again for everything —

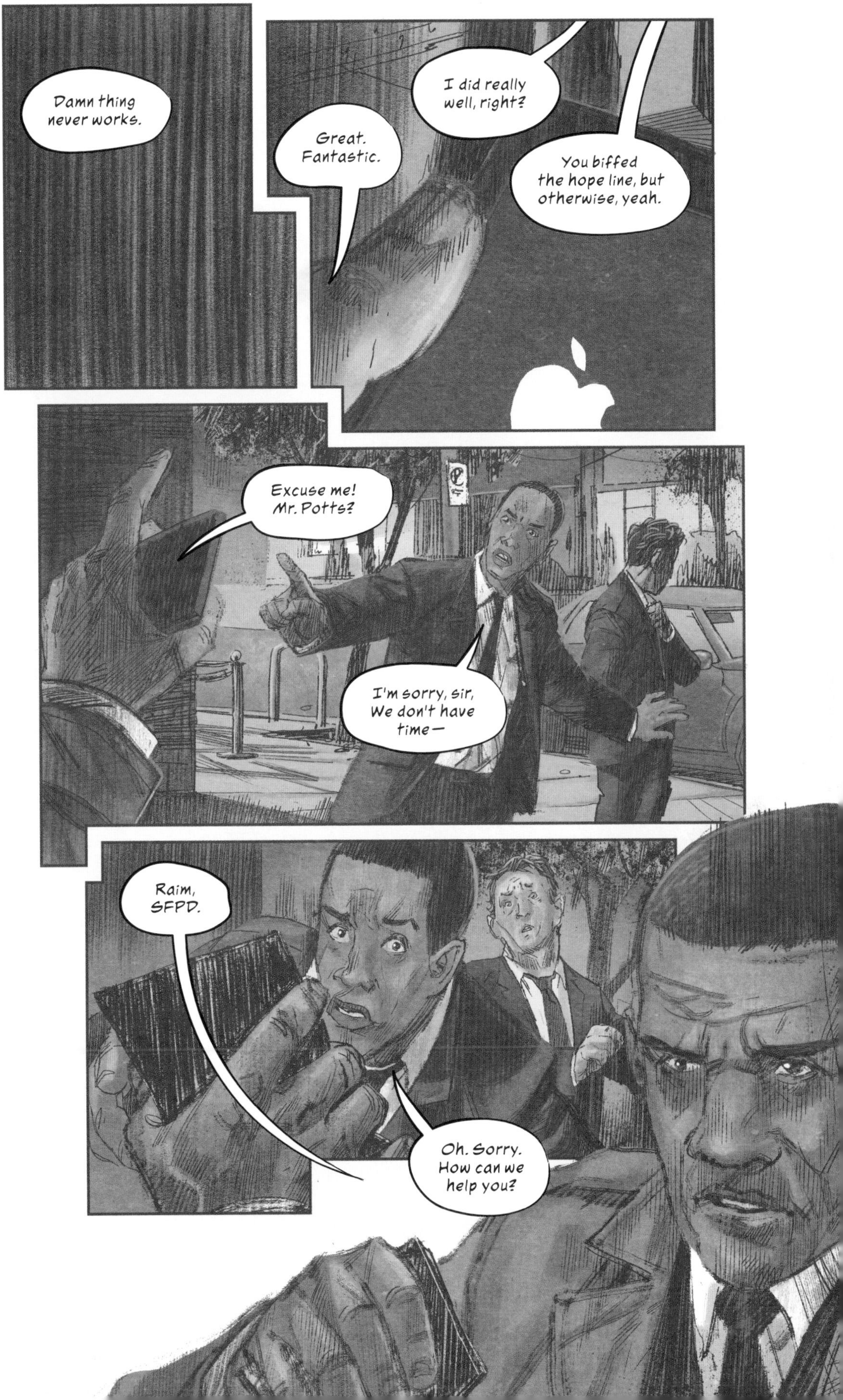
Damn thing never works.
I did really well, right?
Great. Fantastic.
You biffed the hope line, but otherwise, yeah.
Excuse me! Mr. Potts?
I'm sorry, sir, We don't have time—
Raim, SFPD.
Oh. Sorry. How can we help you?

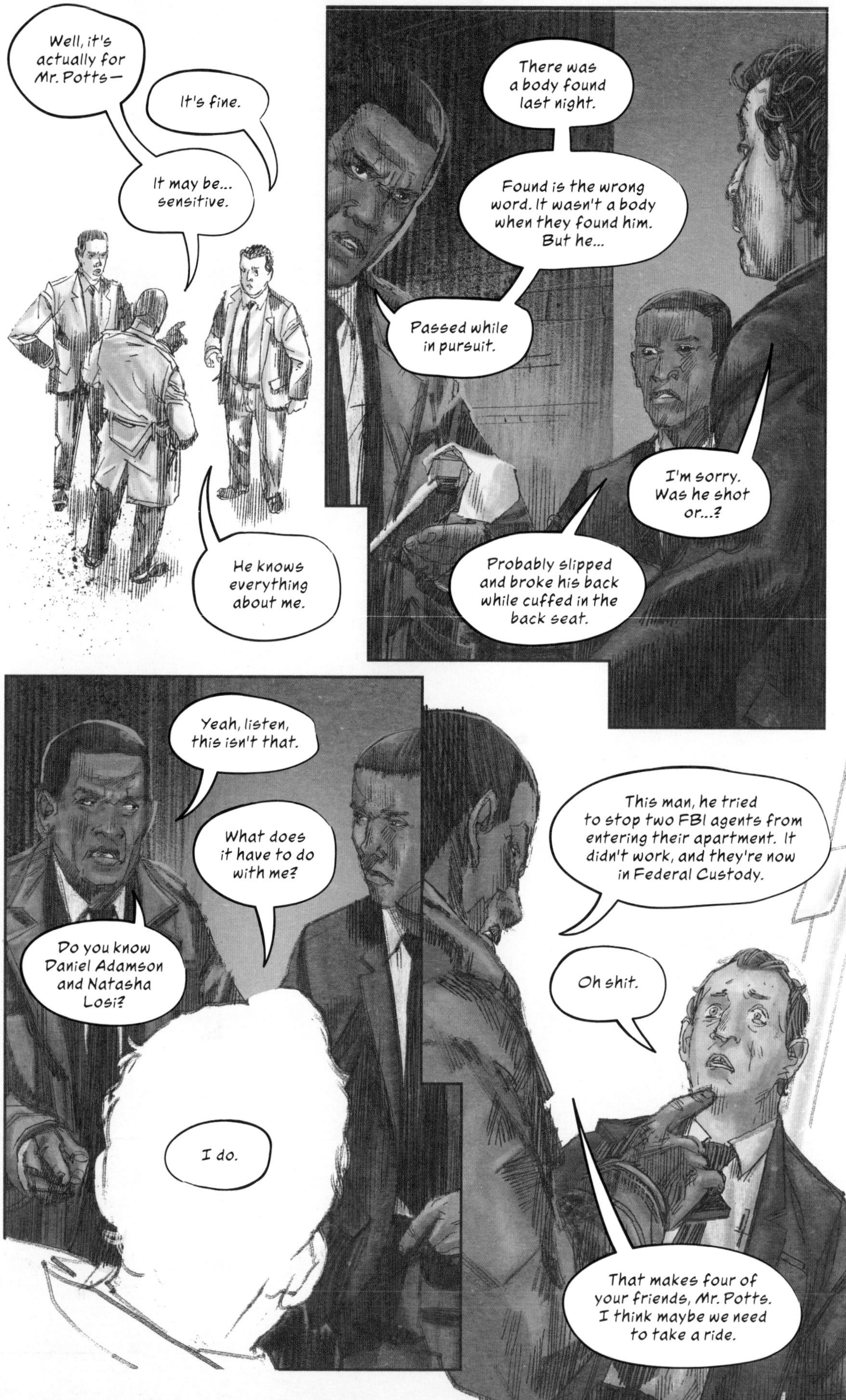
Well, it's actually for Mr. Potts—
It's fine.
It may be... sensitive.
He knows everything about me.
There was a body found last night.
Found is the wrong word. It wasn't a body when they found him. But he...
Passed while in pursuit.
I'm sorry. Was he shot or...?
Probably slipped and broke his back while cuffed in the back seat.
Yeah, listen, this isn't that.
What does it have to do with me?
Do you know Daniel Adamson and Natasha Losi?
I do.
This man, he tried to stop two FBI agents from entering their apartment. It didn't work, and they're now in Federal Custody.
Oh shit.
That makes four of your friends, Mr. Potts. I think maybe we need to take a ride.

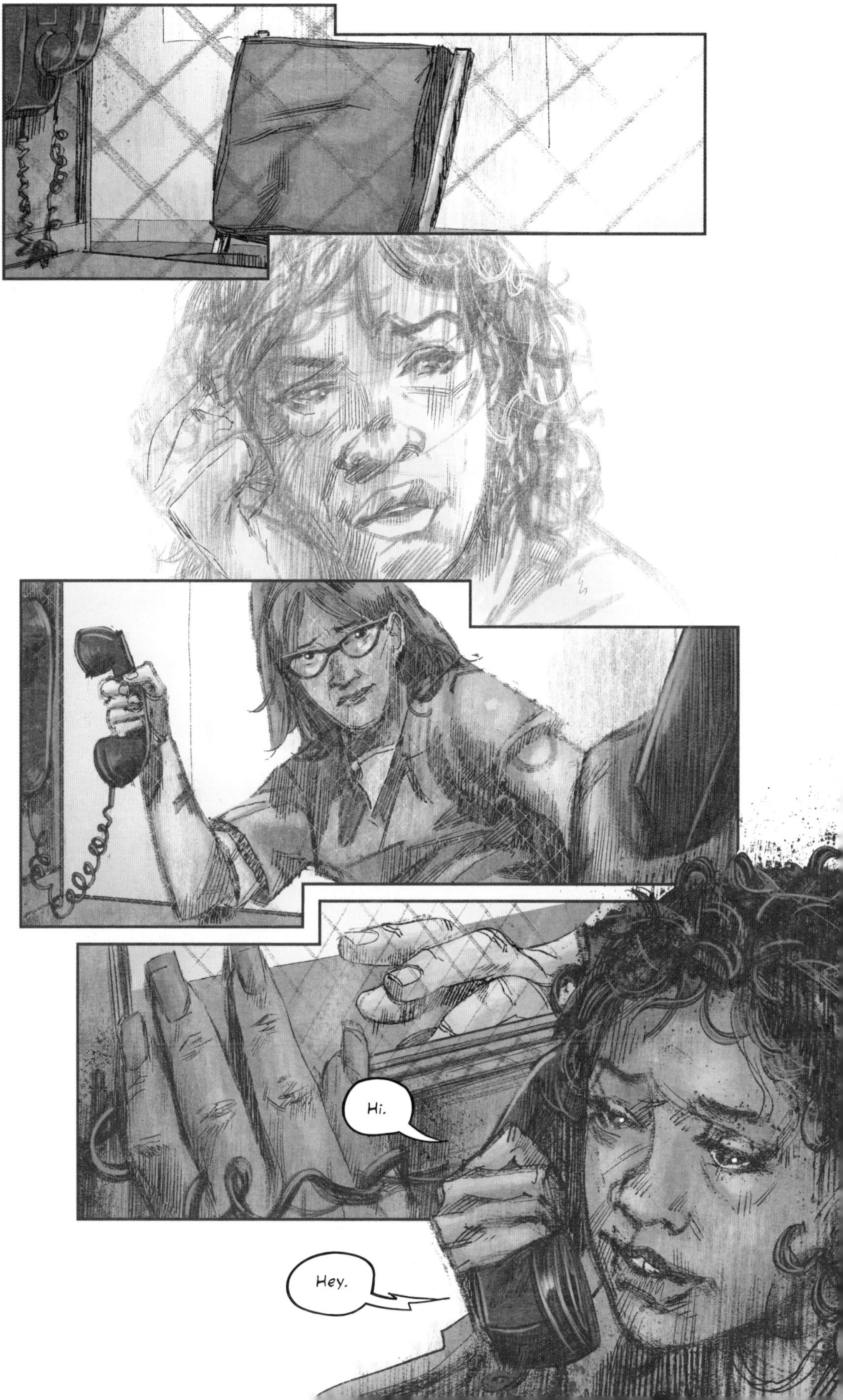
Hi.
Hey.

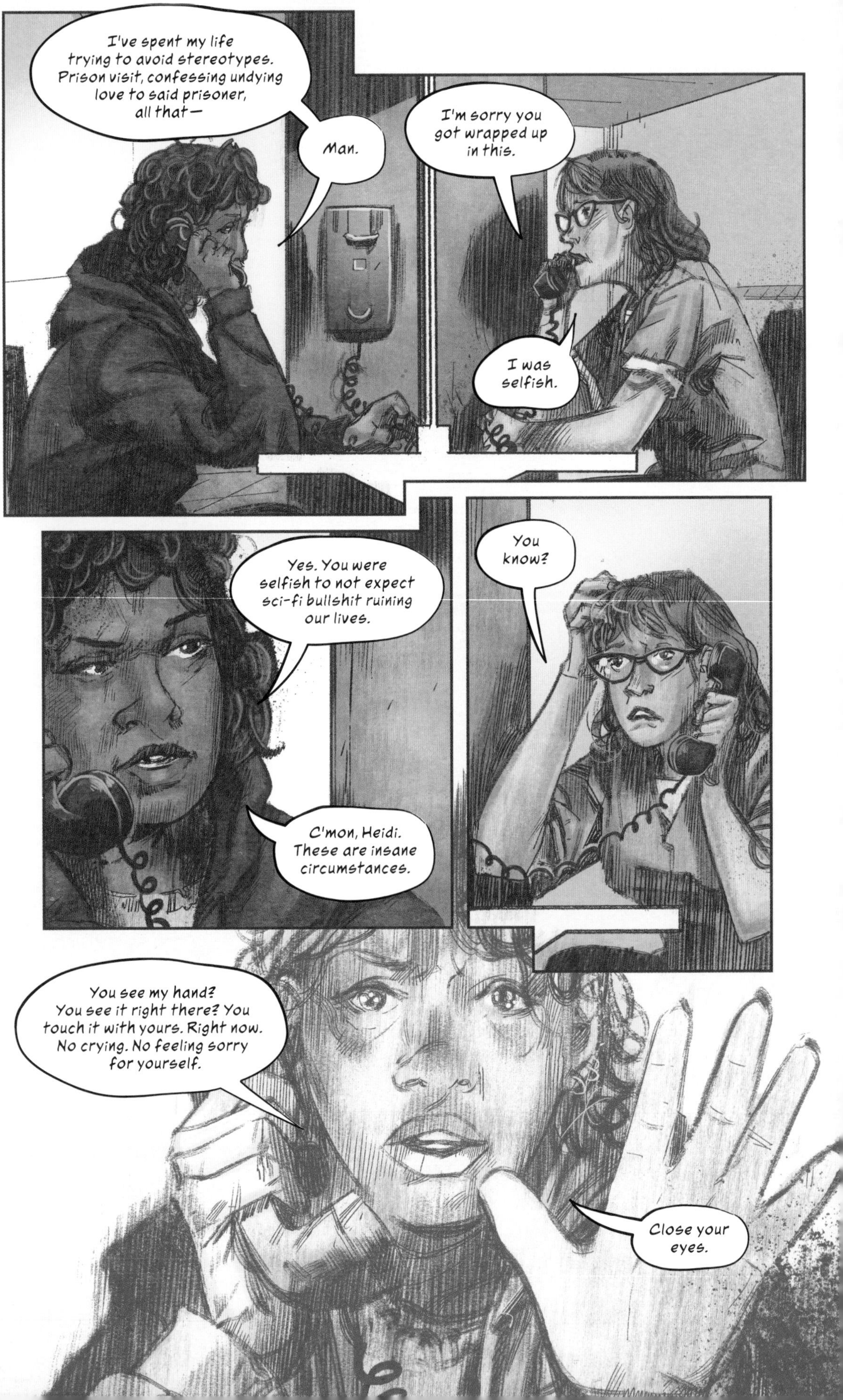
I've spent my life trying to avoid stereotypes. Prison visit, confessing undying love to said prisoner, all that—
Man.
I'm sorry you got wrapped up in this.
I was selfish.
Yes. You were selfish to not expect sci-fi bullshit ruining our lives.
C'mon, Heidi. These are insane circumstances.
You know?
You see my hand? You see it right there? You touch it with yours. Right now. No crying. No feeling sorry for yourself.
Close your eyes.

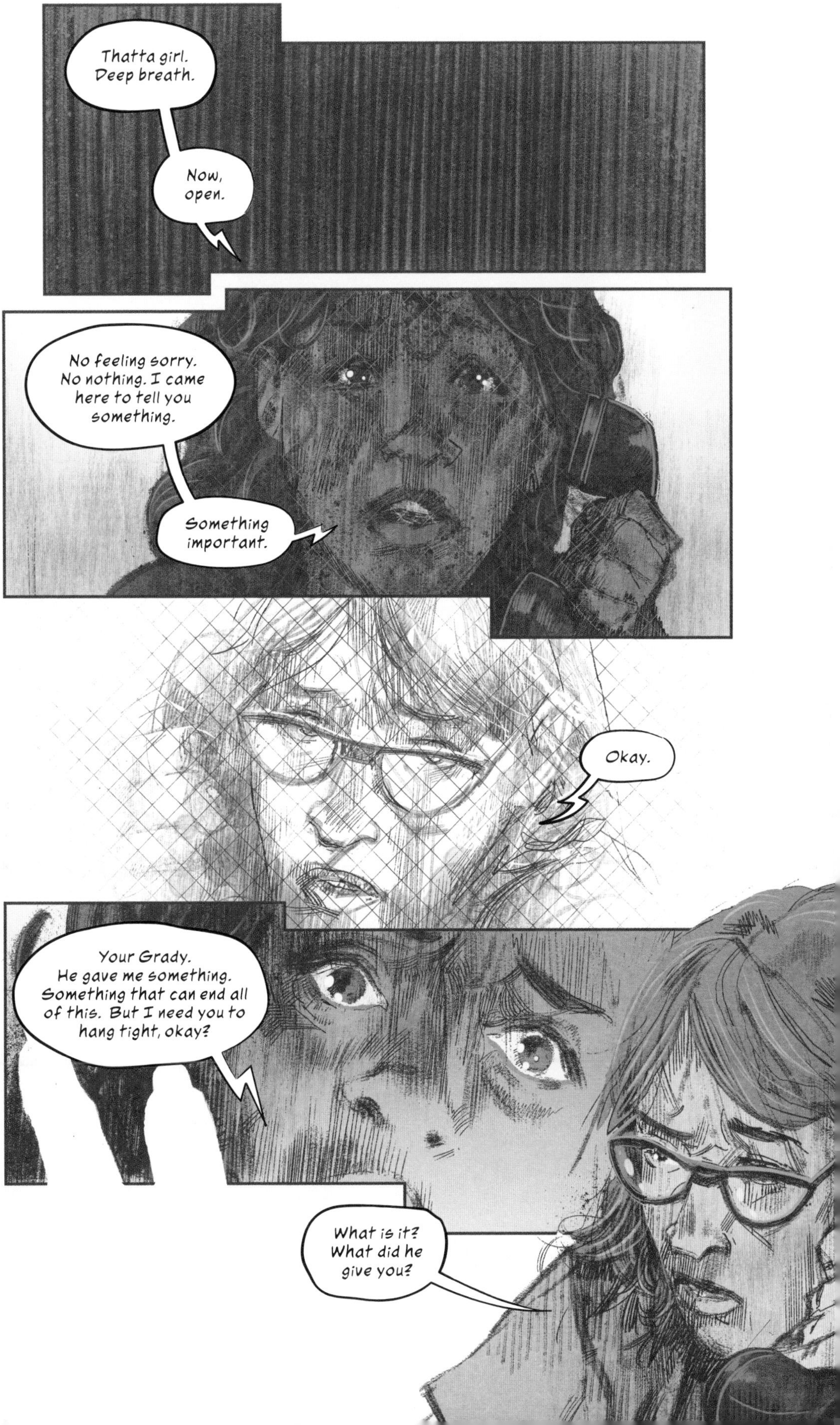
Thatta girl. Deep breath.
Now, open.
No feeling sorry. No nothing. I came here to tell you something.
Something important.
Okay.
Your Grady. He gave me something. Something that can end all of this. But I need you to hang tight, okay?
What is it? What did he give you?

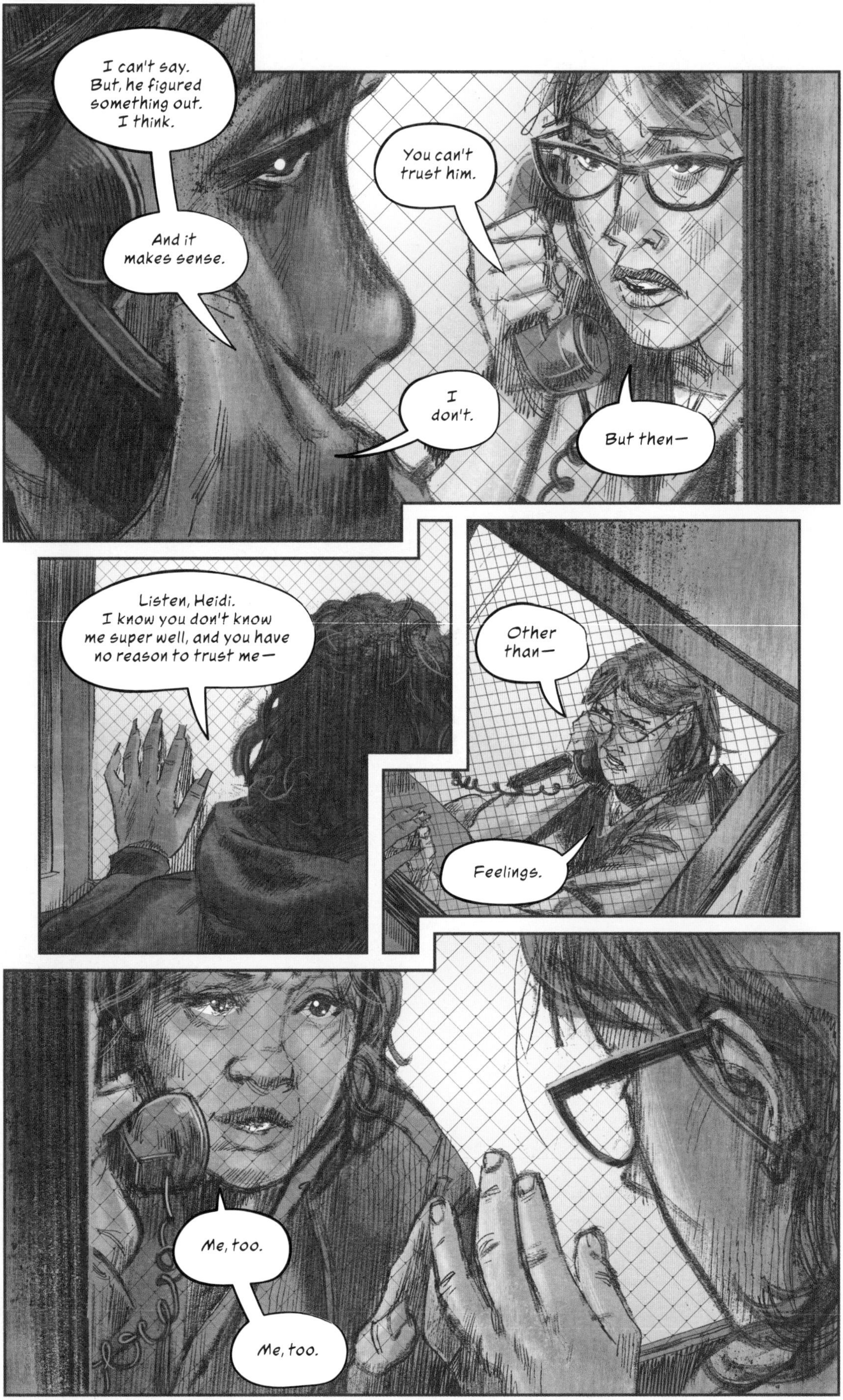

I can't say. But, he figured something out. I think.
And it makes sense.
You can't trust him.
I don't.
But then—
Listen, Heidi. I know you don't know me super well, and you have no reason to trust me—
Other than—
Feelings.
Me, too.
Me, too.

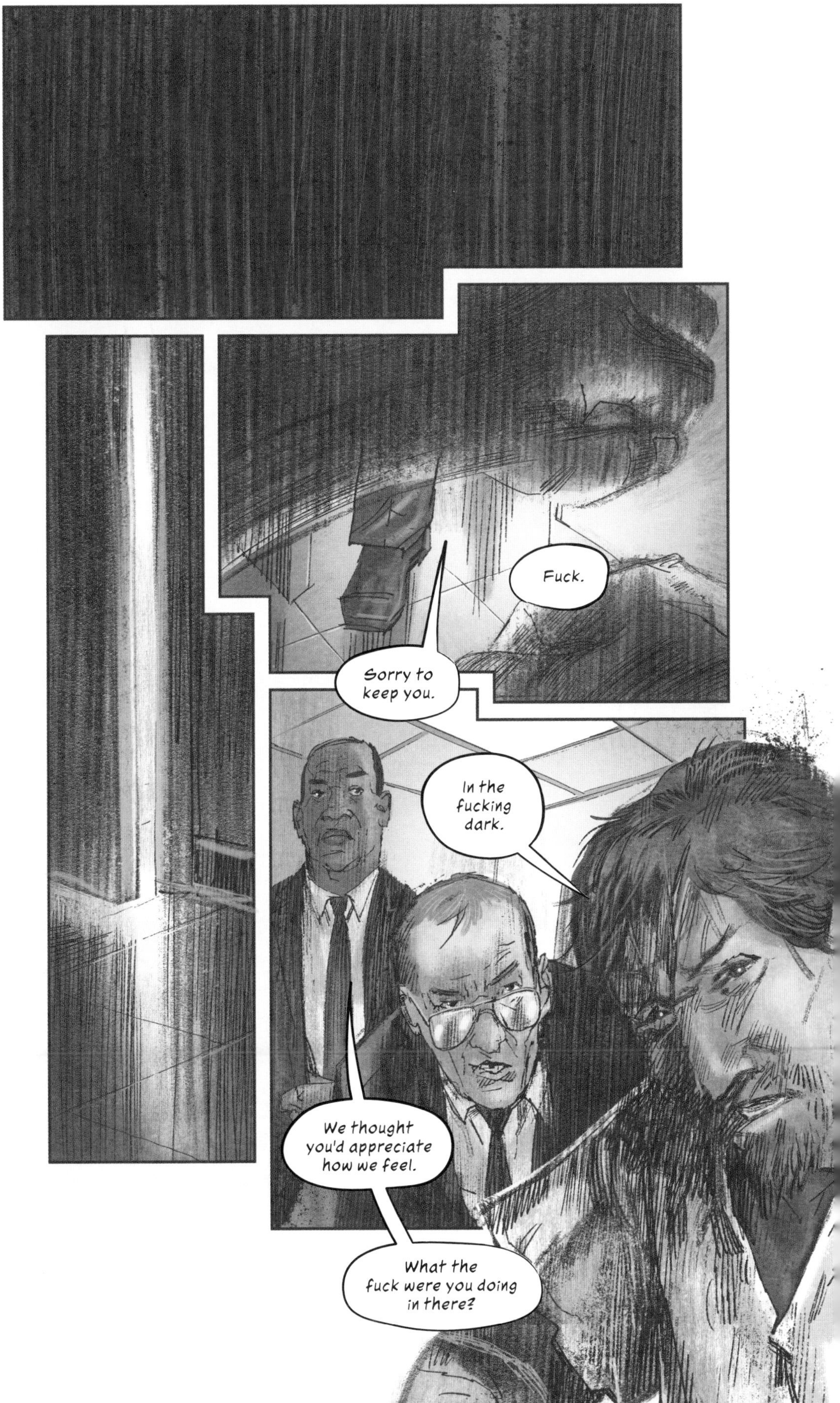
Fuck.
Sorry to keep you.
In the fucking dark.
We thought you'd appreciate how we feel.
What the fuck were you doing in there?

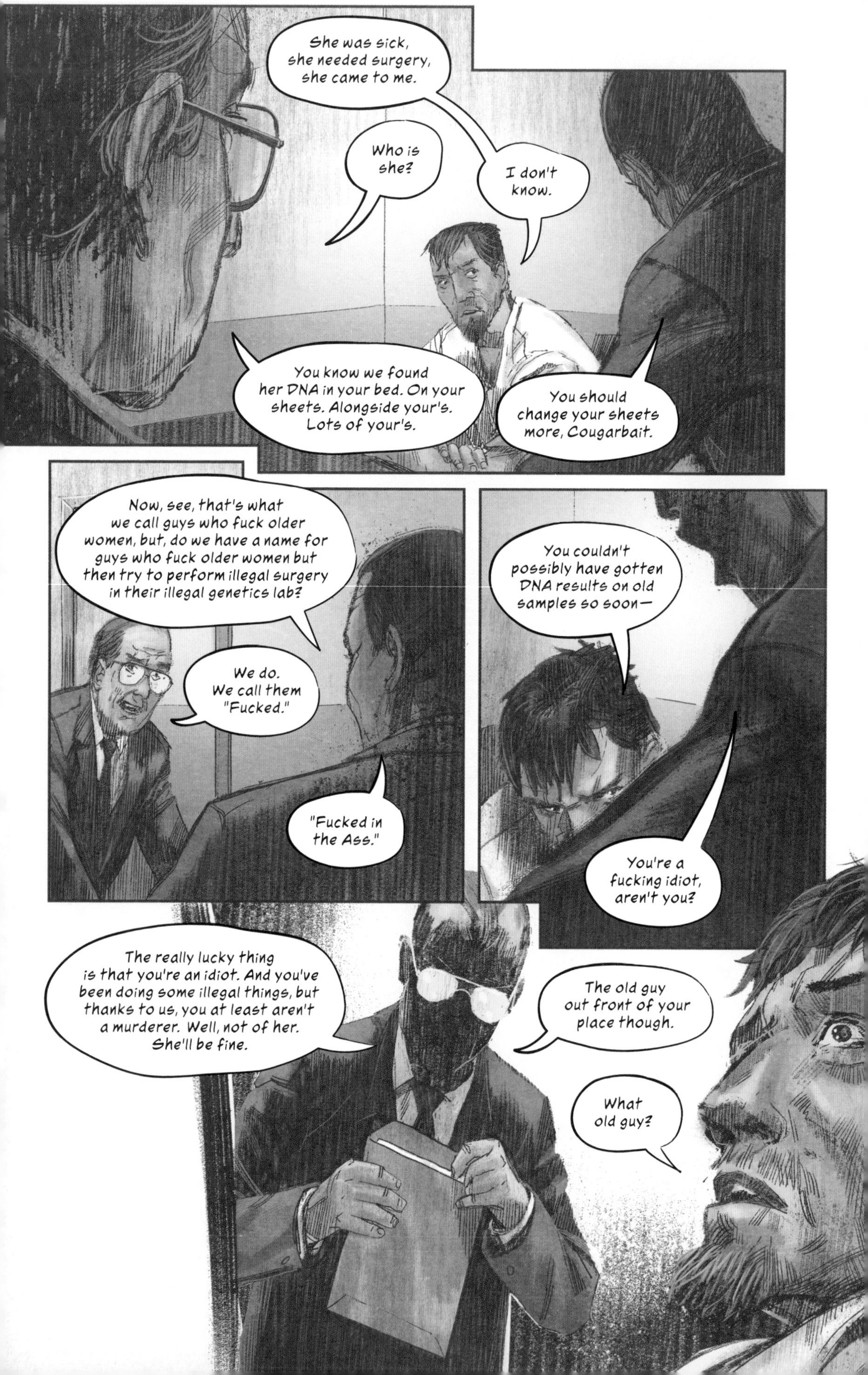
She was sick, she needed surgery, she came to me.
Who is she?
I don't know.
You know we found her DNA in your bed. On your sheets. Alongside your's. Lots of your's.
You should change your sheets more, Cougarbait.
Now, see, that's what we call guys who fuck older women, but, do we have a name for guys who fuck older women but then try to perform illegal surgery in their illegal genetics lab?
We do. We call them "Fucked."
"Fucked in the Ass."
You couldn't possibly have gotten DNA results on old samples so soon—
You're a fucking idiot, aren't you?
The really lucky thing is that you're an idiot. And you've been doing some illegal things, but thanks to us, you at least aren't a murderer. Well, not of her. She'll be fine.
The old guy out front of your place though.
What old guy?

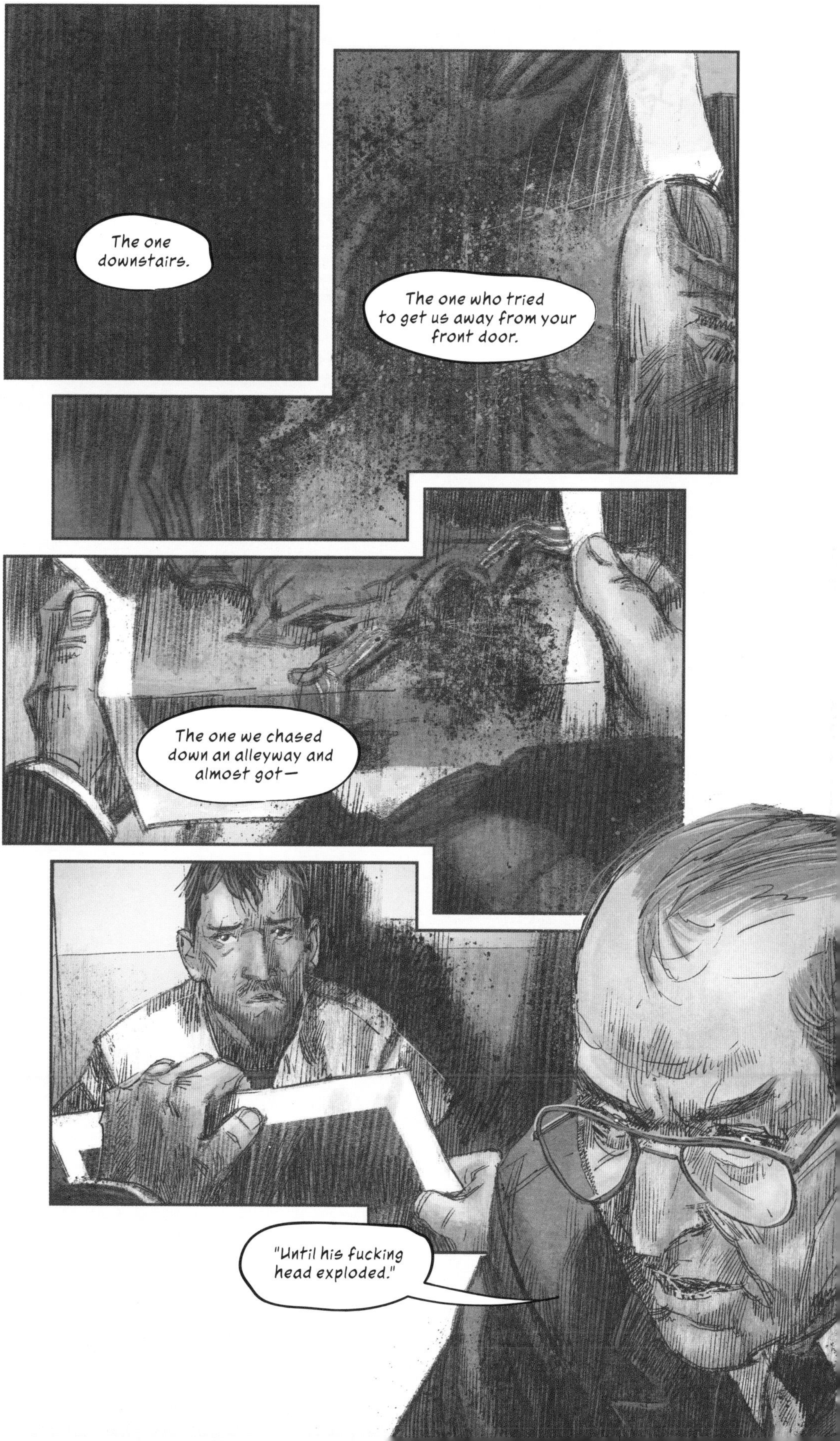
The one downstairs.
The one who tried to get us away from your front door.
The one we chased down an alleyway and almost got—
"Until his fucking head exploded."

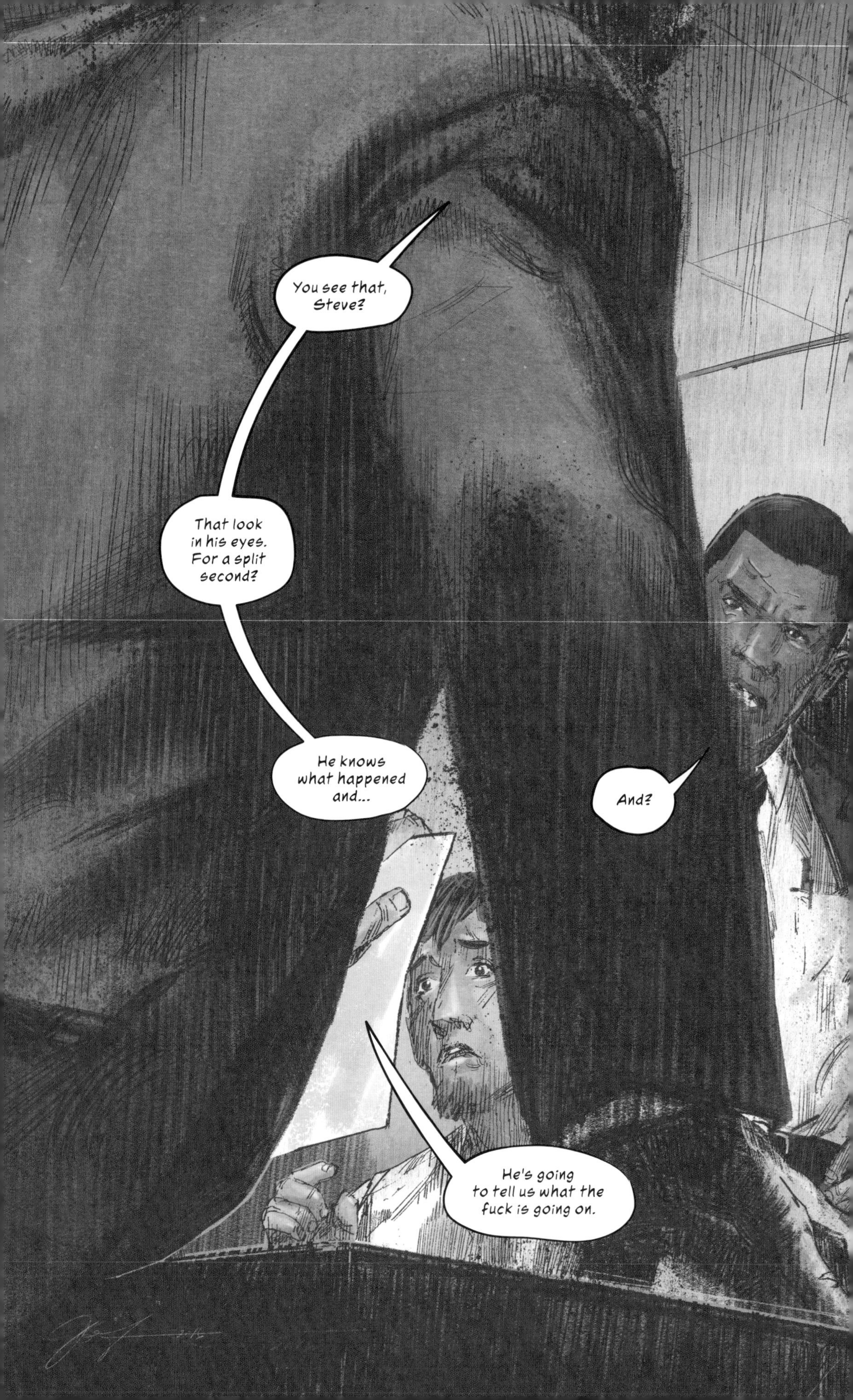
You see that, Steve?
That look in his eyes. For a split second?
He knows what happened and...
And?
He's going to tell us what the fuck is going on.

CHAPTER
18

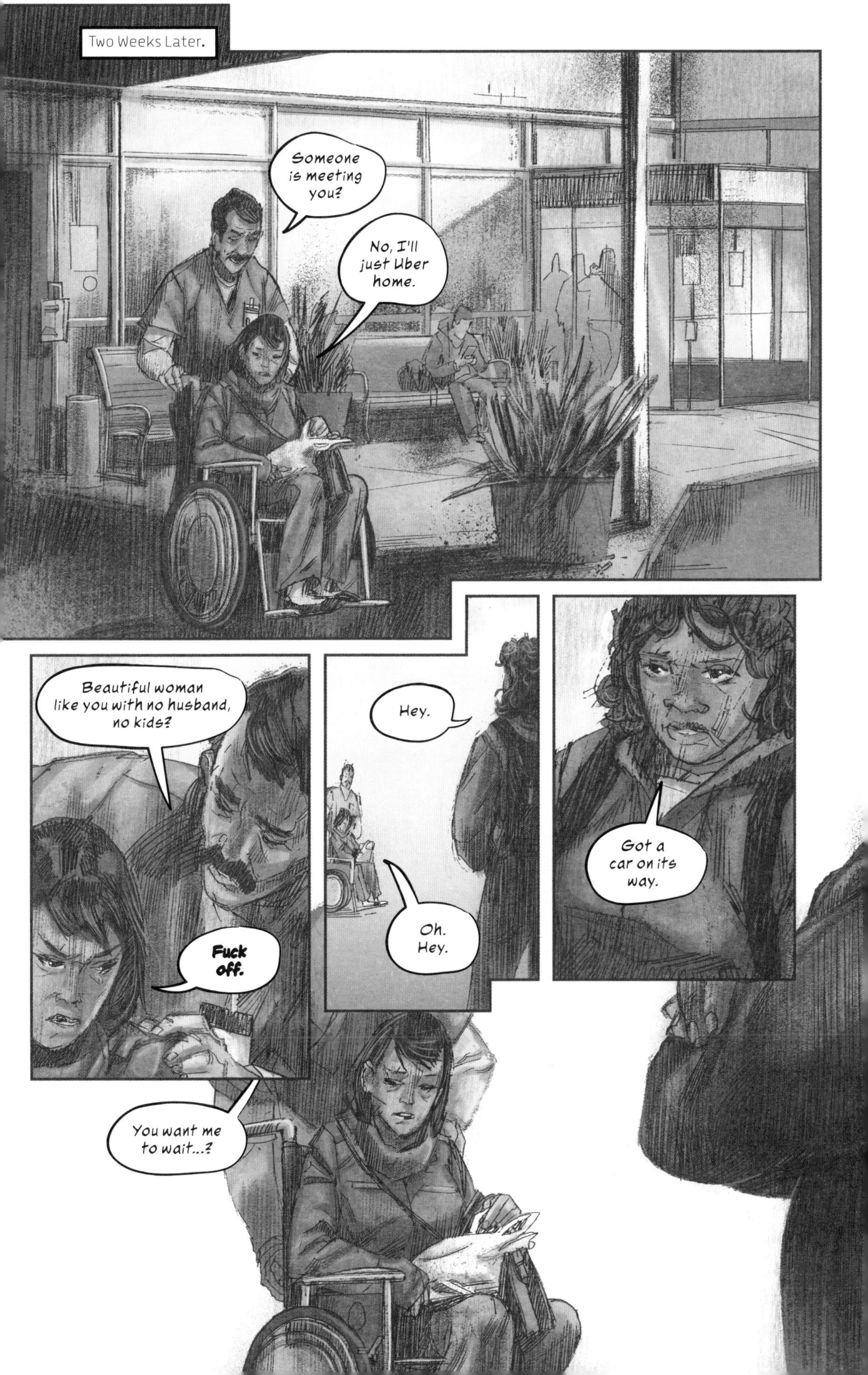
Two Weeks Later.
Someone is meeting you?
No, I'll just Uber home.
Beautiful woman like you with no husband, no kids?
Fuck off.
Hey.
Oh. Hey.
Got a car on its way.
You want me to wait...?

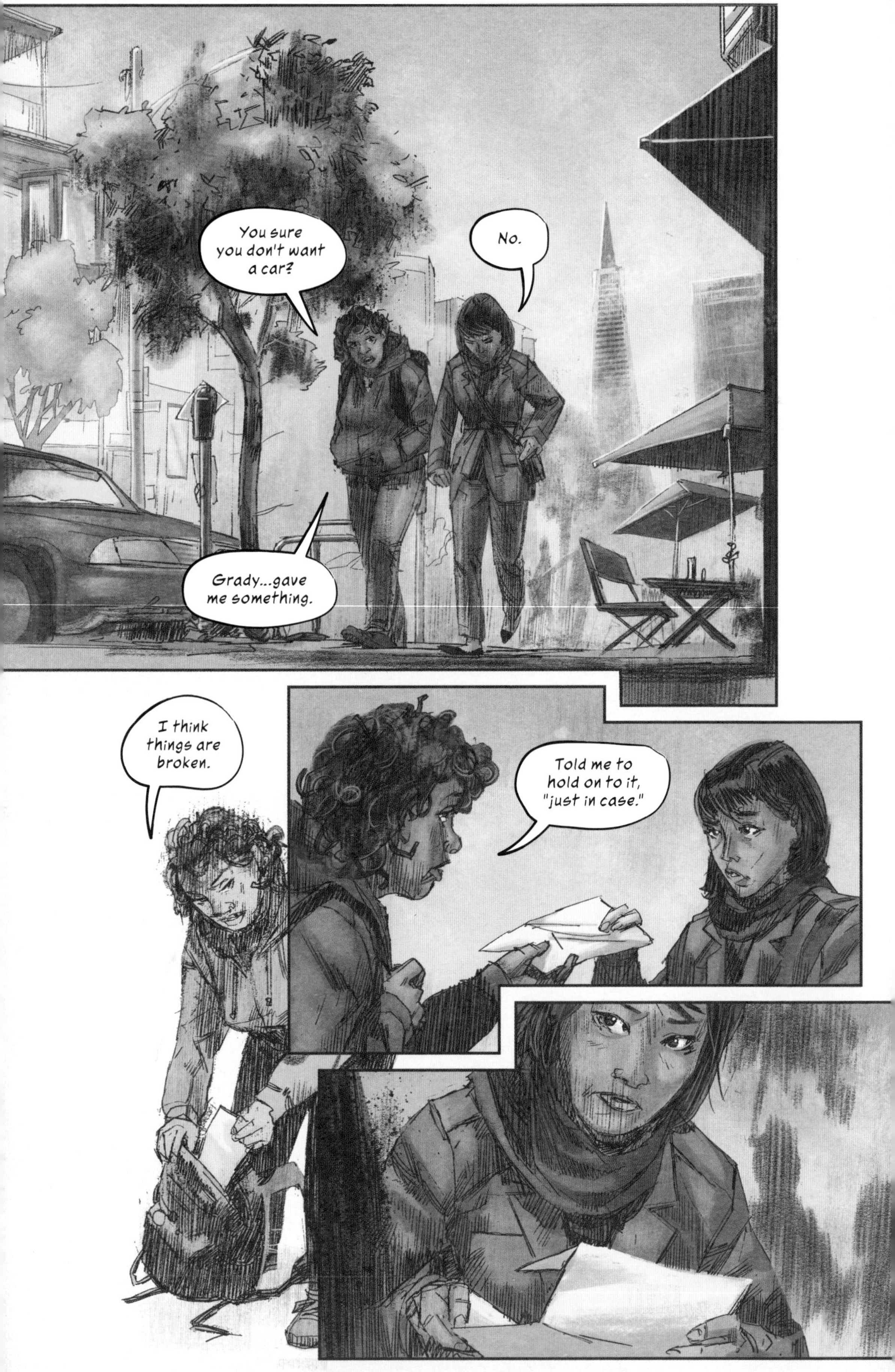
You sure you don't want a car?
No.
Grady...gave me something.
I think things are broken.
Told me to hold on to it, "just in case."

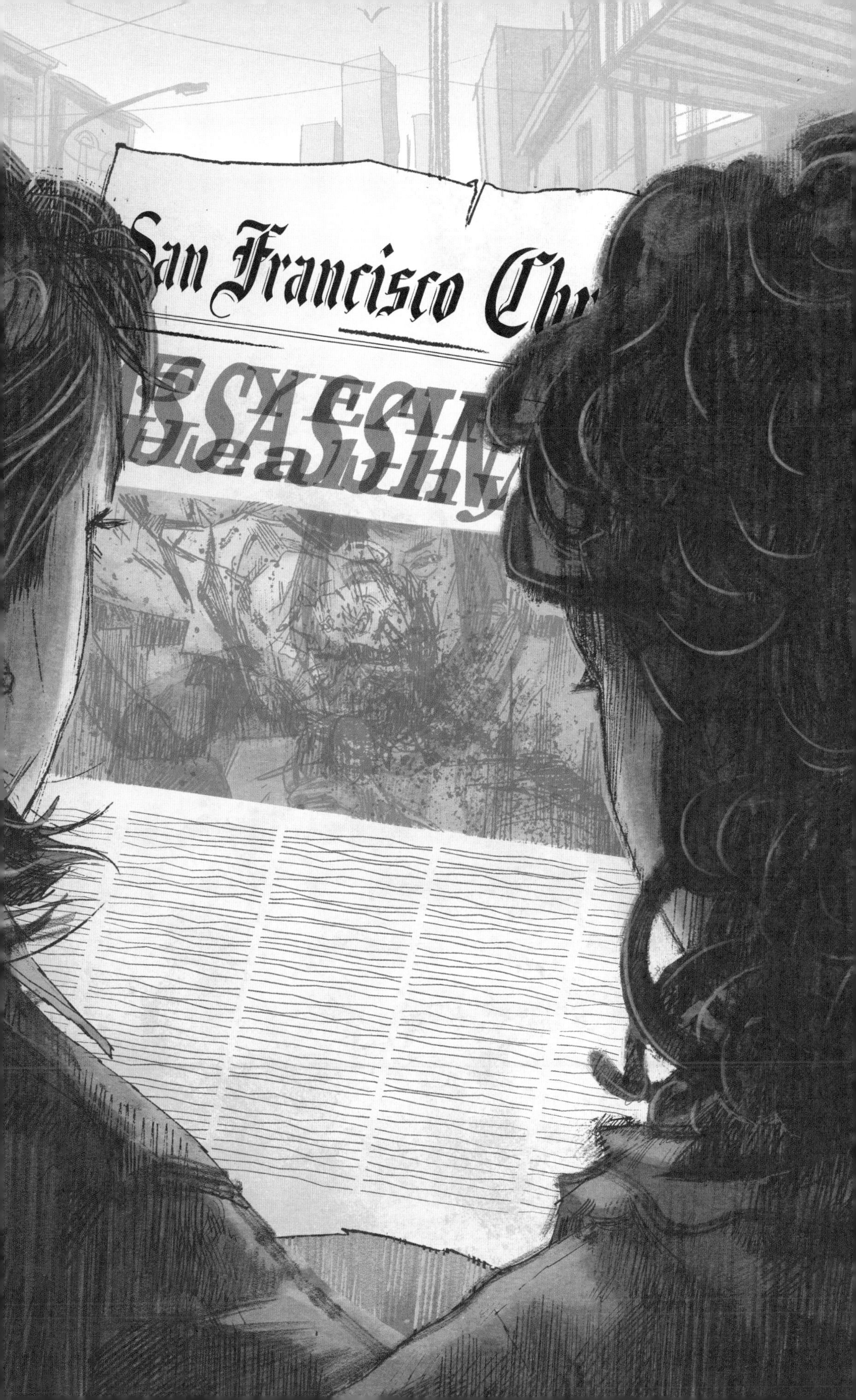
San Francisco Ch

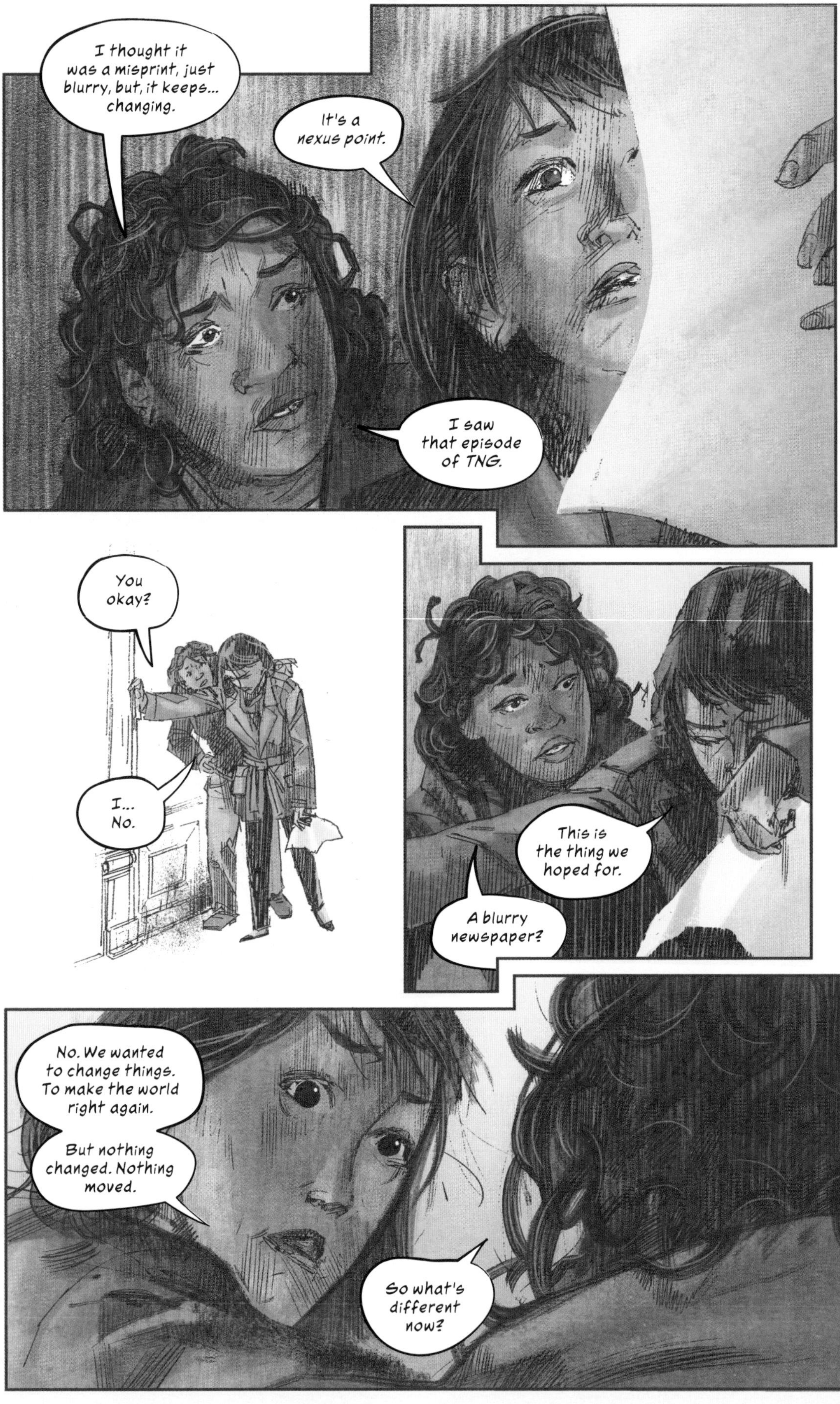
I thought it was a misprint, just blurry, but, it keeps... changing.
It's a nexus point.
I saw that episode of TNG.
You okay?
I... No.
This is the thing we hoped for.
A blurry newspaper?
No. We wanted to change things. To make the world right again.
But nothing changed. Nothing moved.
So what's different now?

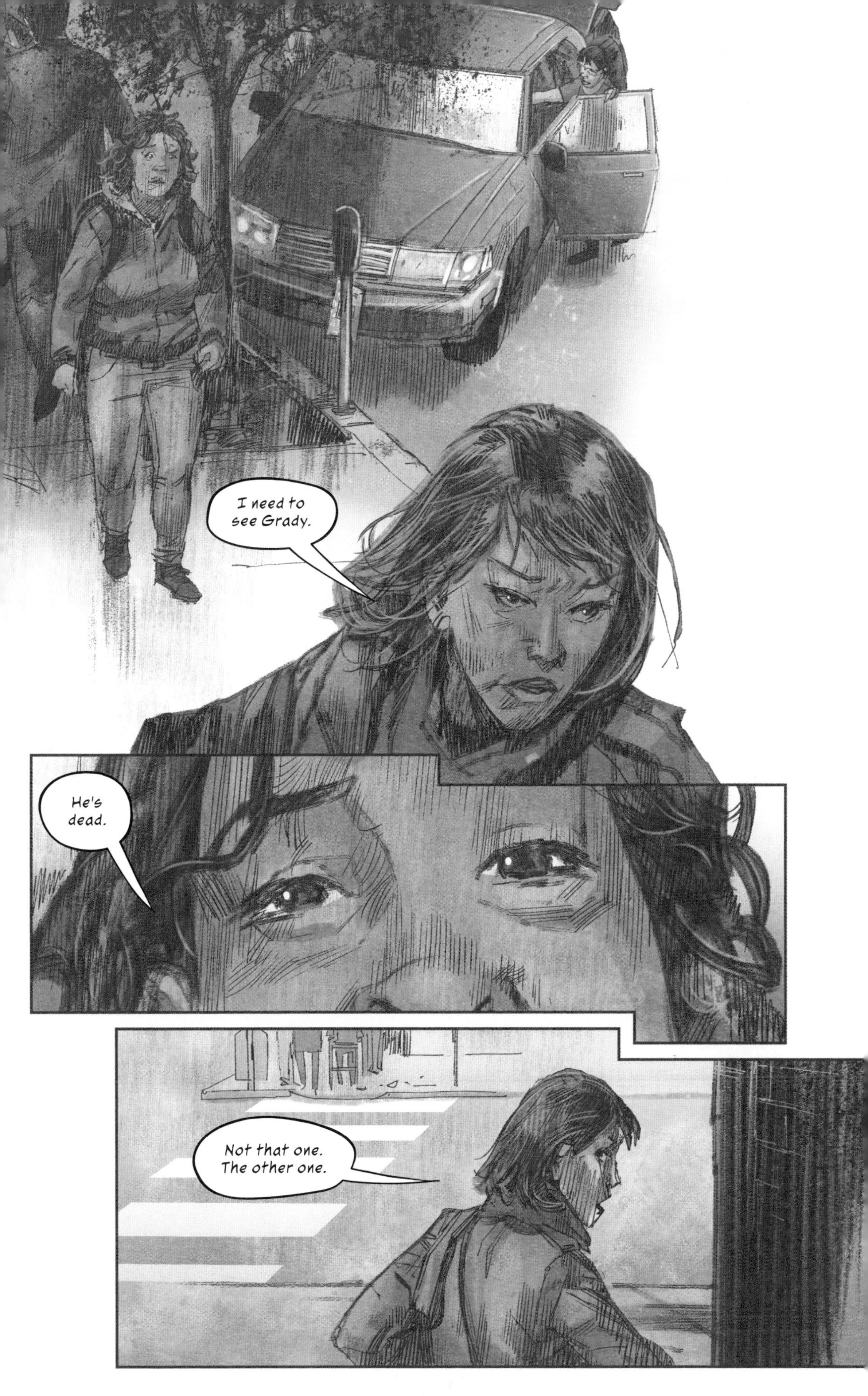
I need to see Grady.
He's dead.
Not that one. The other one.

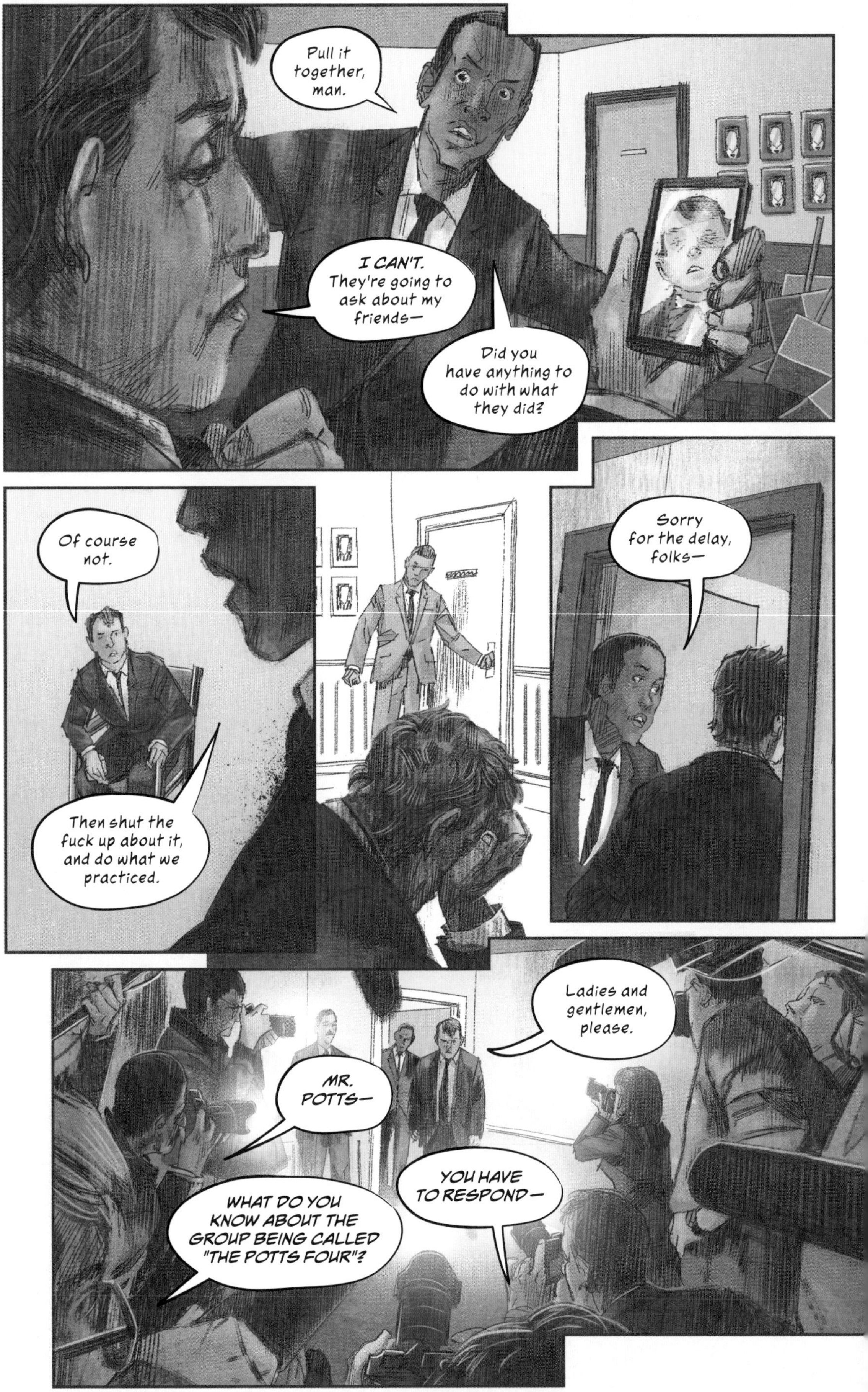
Pull it together, man.
I CAN'T. They're going to ask about my friends—
Did you have anything to do with what they did?
Of course not.
Then shut the fuck up about it, and do what we practiced.
Sorry for the delay, folks—
Ladies and gentlemen, please.
MR. POTTS—
WHAT DO YOU KNOW ABOUT THE GROUP BEING CALLED "THE POTTS FOUR"?
YOU HAVE TO RESPOND—

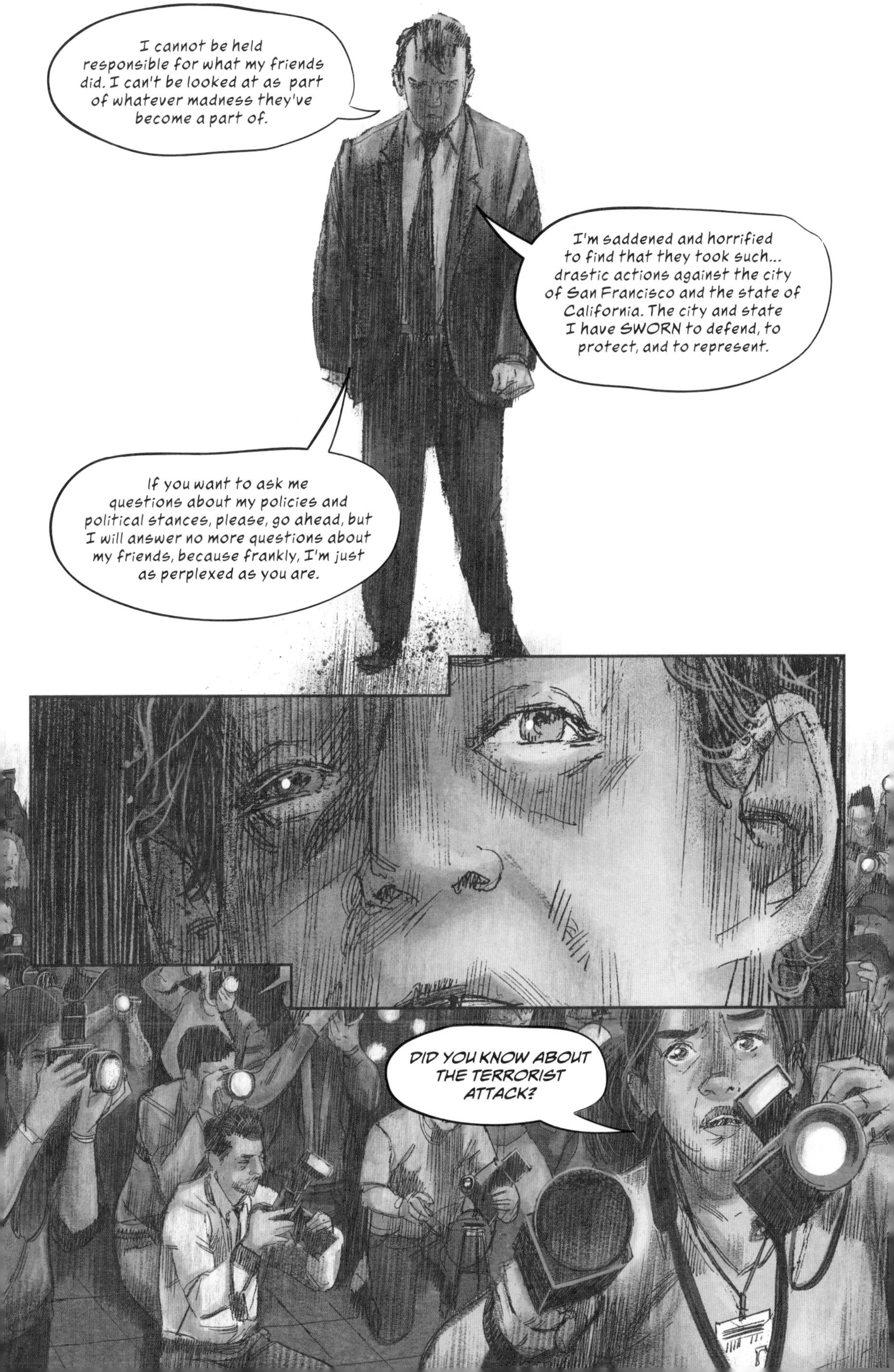
I cannot be held responsible for what my friends did. I can't be looked at as part of whatever madness they've become a part of.
I'm saddened and horrified to find that they took such... drastic actions against the city of San Francisco and the state of California. The city and state I have SWORN to defend, to protect, and to represent.
If you want to ask me questions about my policies and political stances, please, go ahead, but I will answer no more questions about my friends, because frankly, I'm just as perplexed as you are.
DID YOU KNOW ABOUT THE TERRORIST ATTACK?

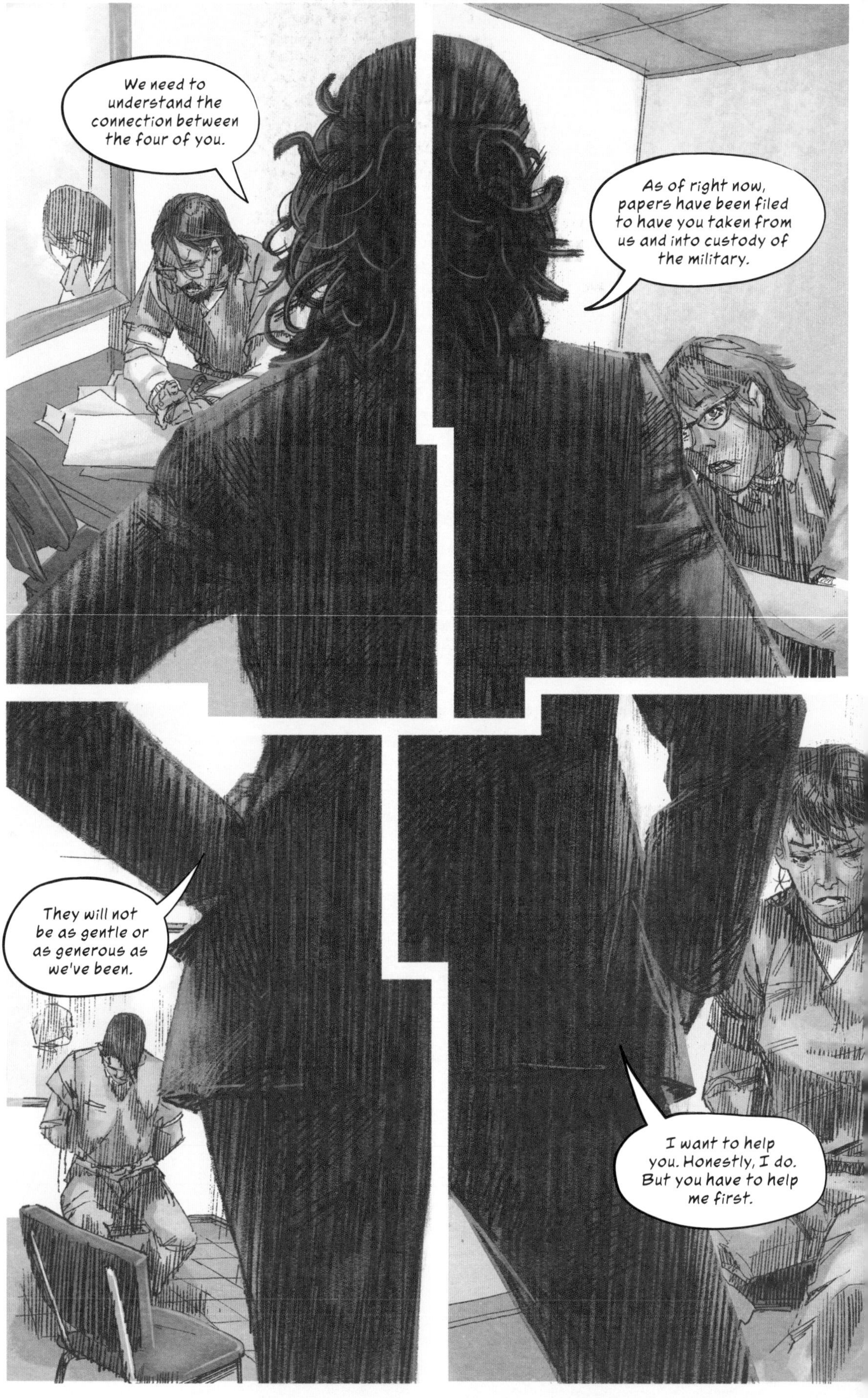
We need to understand the connection between the four of you.
As of right now, papers have been filed to have you taken from us and into custody of the military.
They will not be as gentle or as generous as we've been.
I want to help you. Honestly, I do. But you have to help me first.

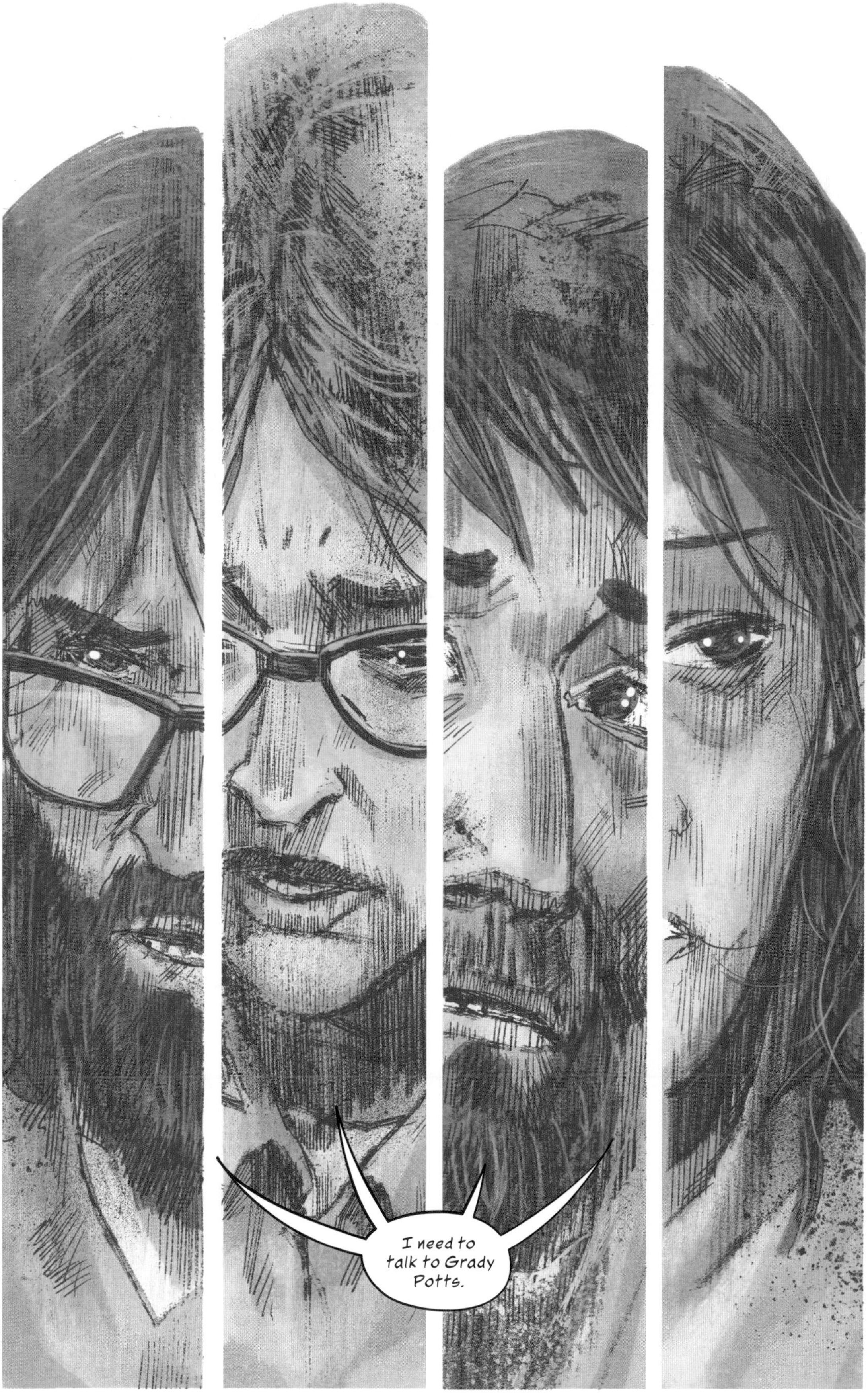
I need to talk to Grady Potts.

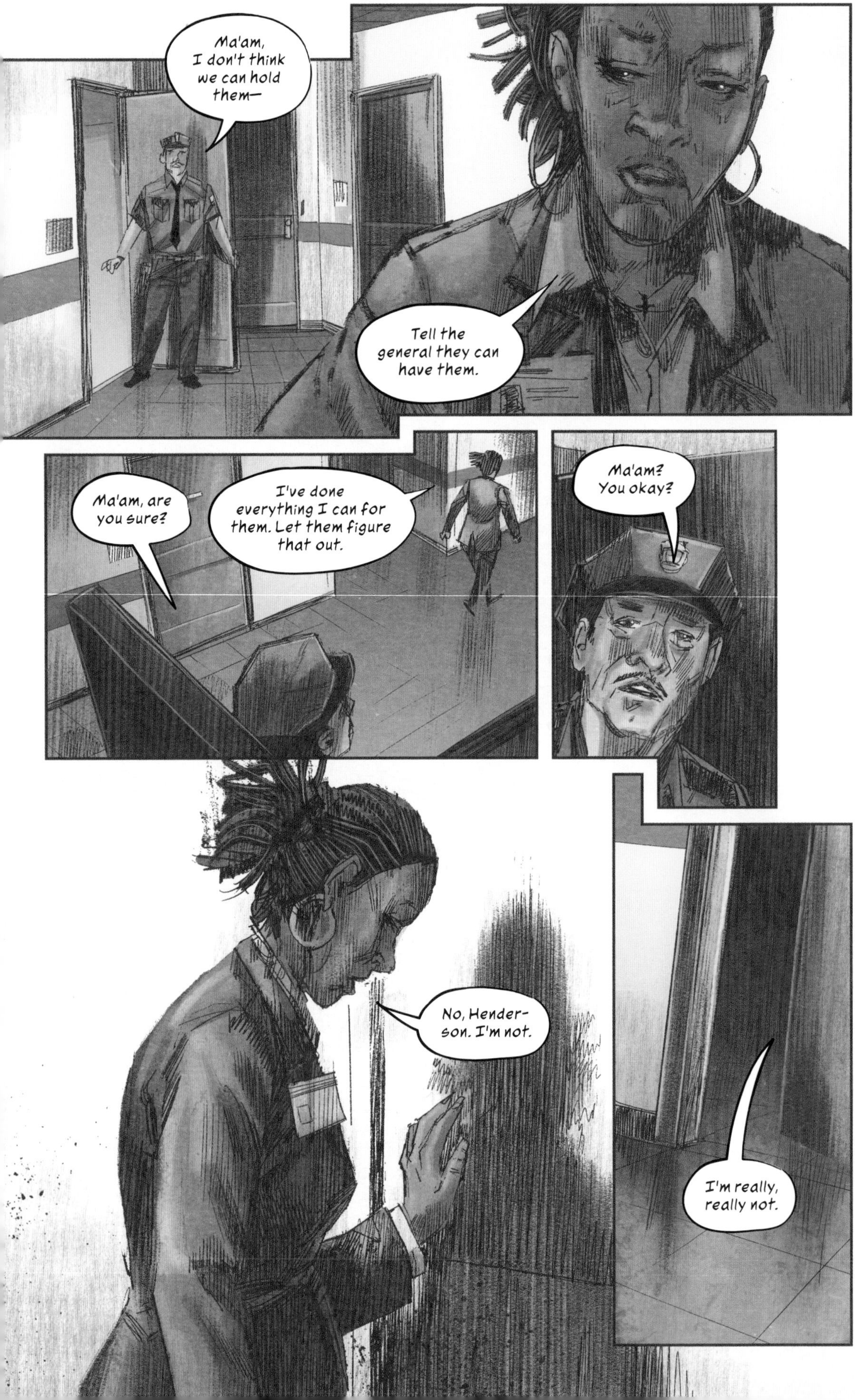
Ma'am, I don't think we can hold them—
Tell the general they can have them.
Ma'am, are you sure?
I've done everything I can for them. Let them figure that out.
Ma'am? You okay?
No, Henderson. I'm not.
I'm really, really not.

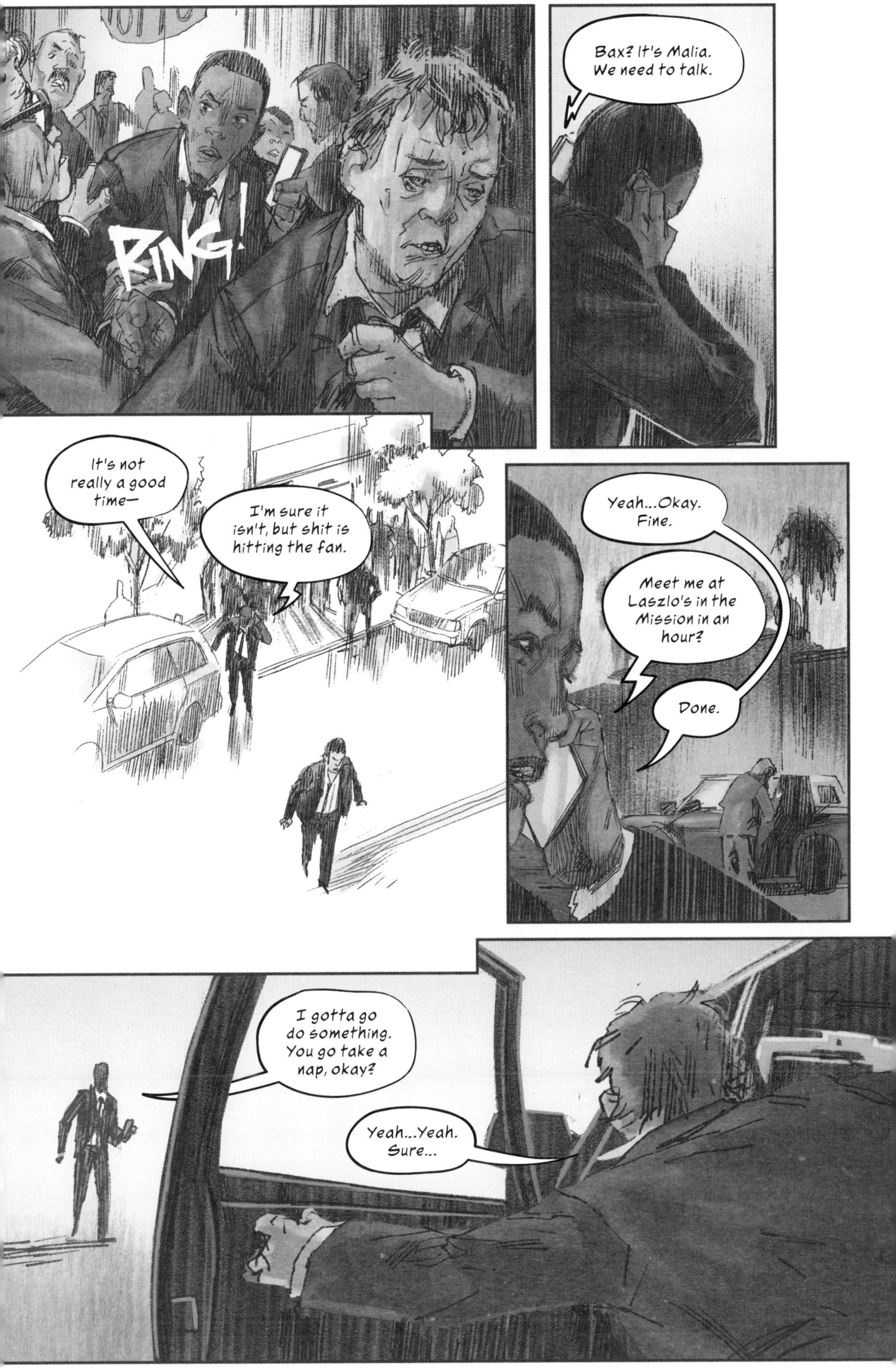
RING!
Bax? It's Malia. We need to talk.
It's not really a good time—
I'm sure it isn't, but shit is hitting the fan.
Yeah...Okay. Fine.
Meet me at Laszlo's in the Mission in an hour?
Done.
I gotta go do something. You go take a nap, okay?
Yeah...Yeah. Sure...

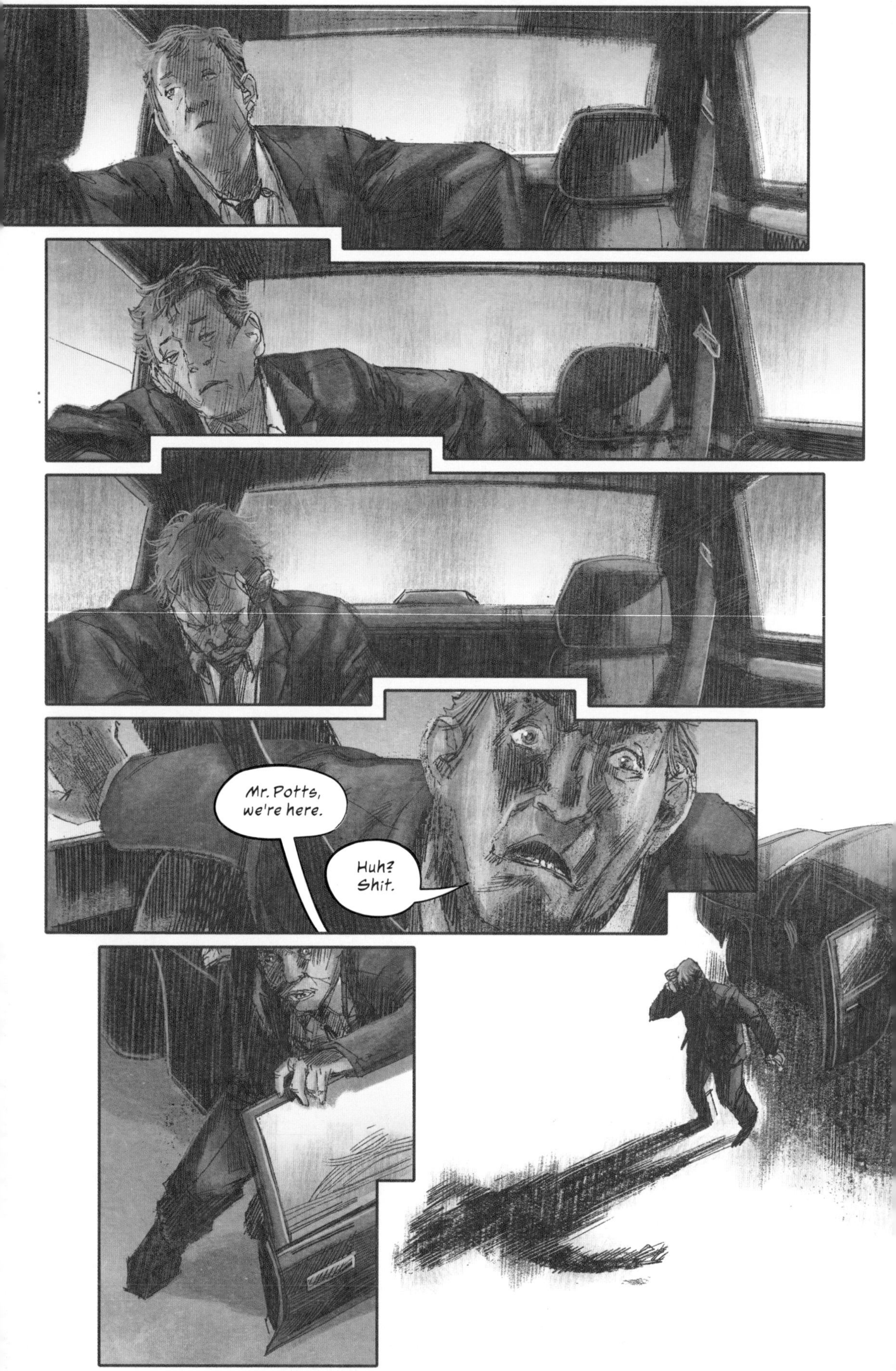
Mr. Potts,
we're here.
Huh?
Shit.

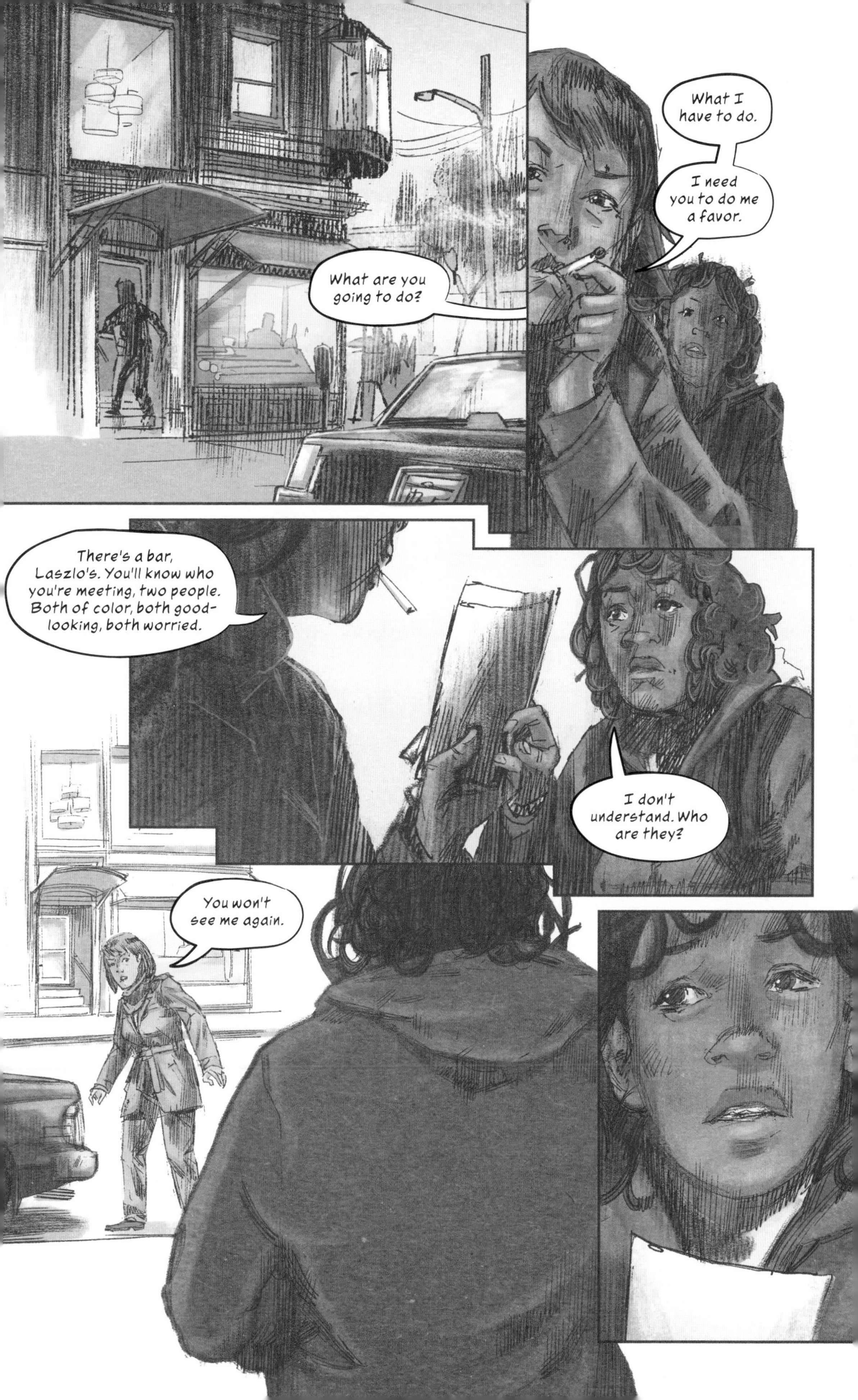
What are you going to do?
What I have to do.
I need you to do me a favor.
There's a bar, Laszlo's. You'll know who you're meeting, two people. Both of color, both good-looking, both worried.
I don't understand. Who are they?
You won't see me again.

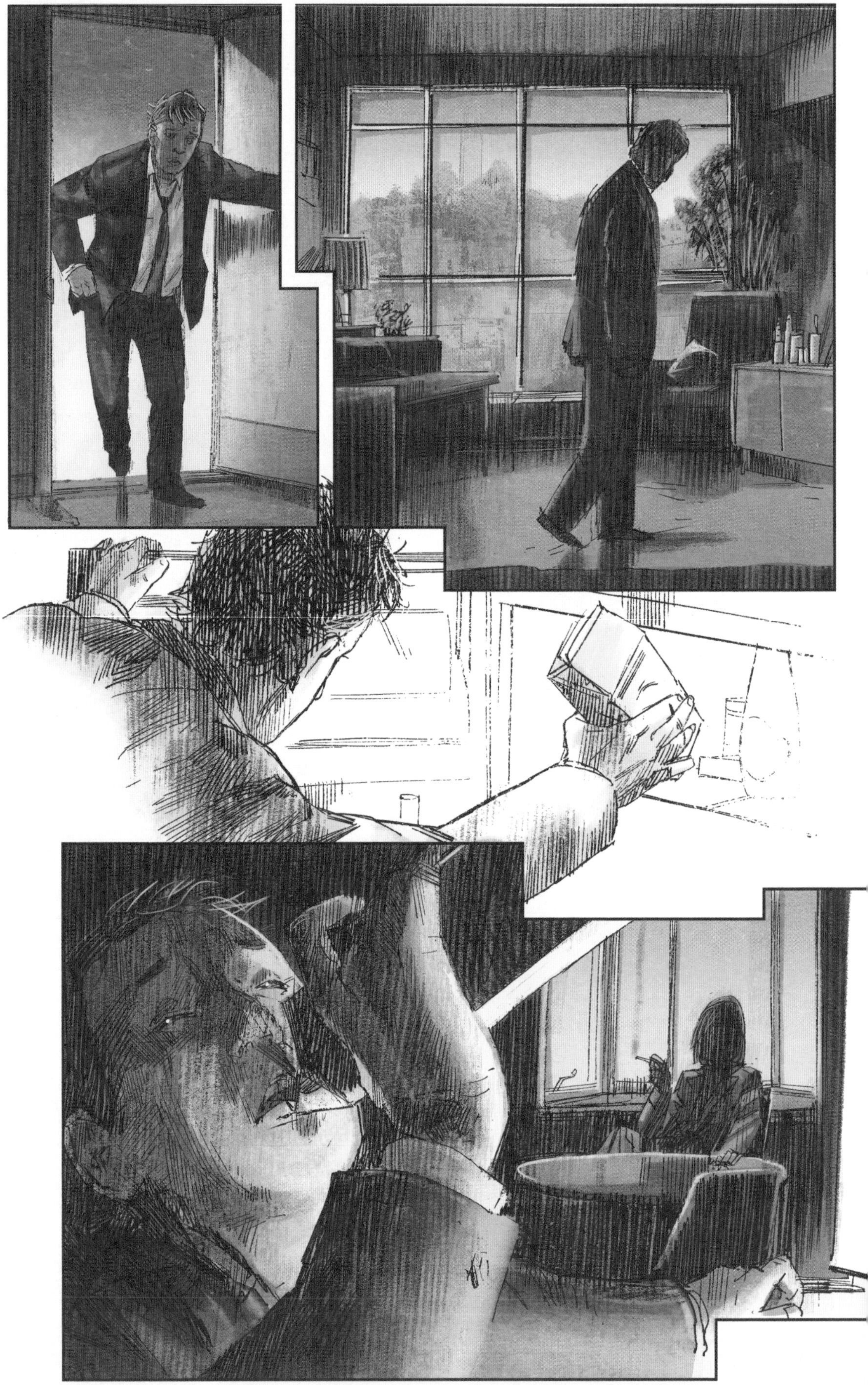

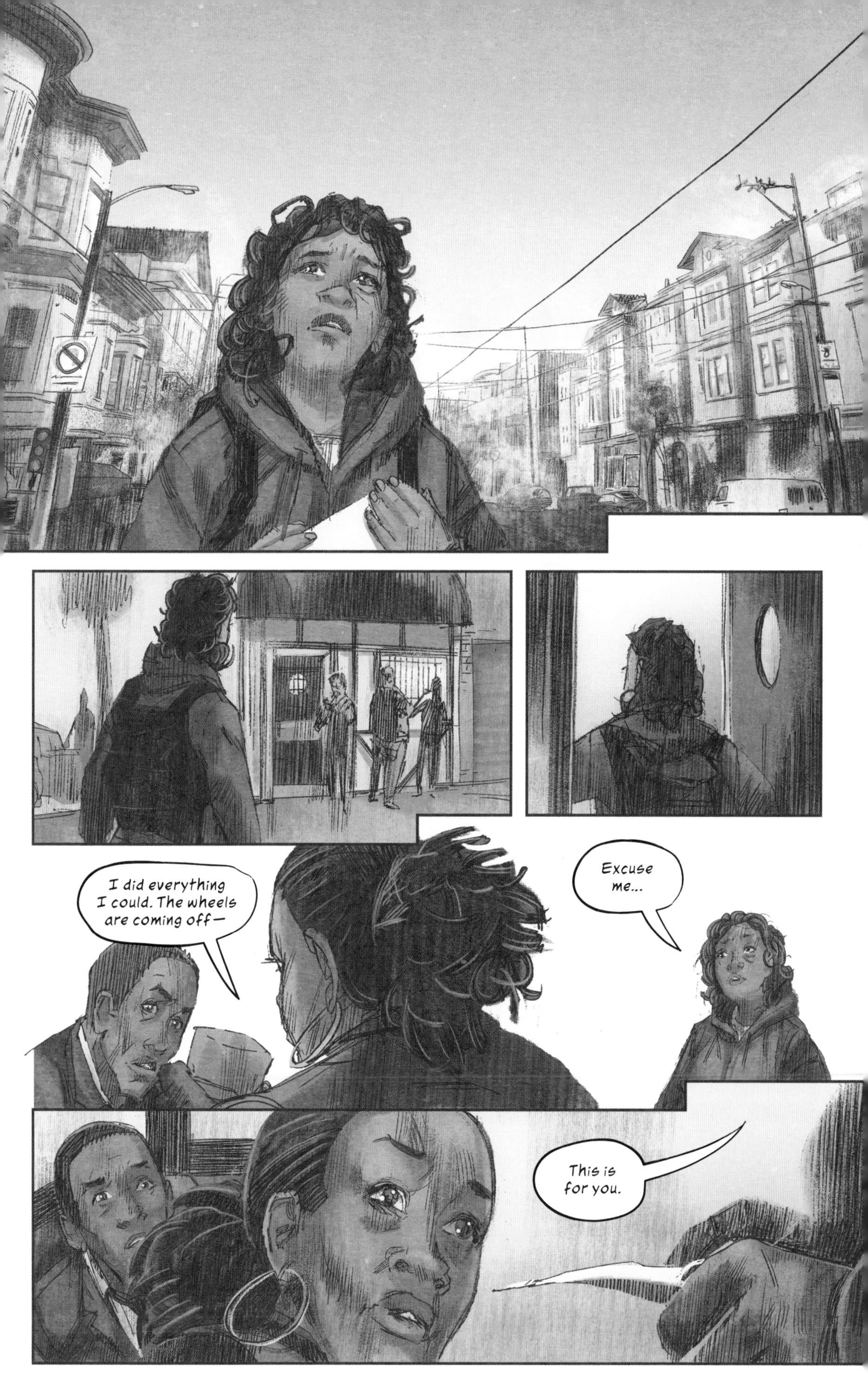
I did everything I could. The wheels are coming off—
Excuse me...
This is for you.

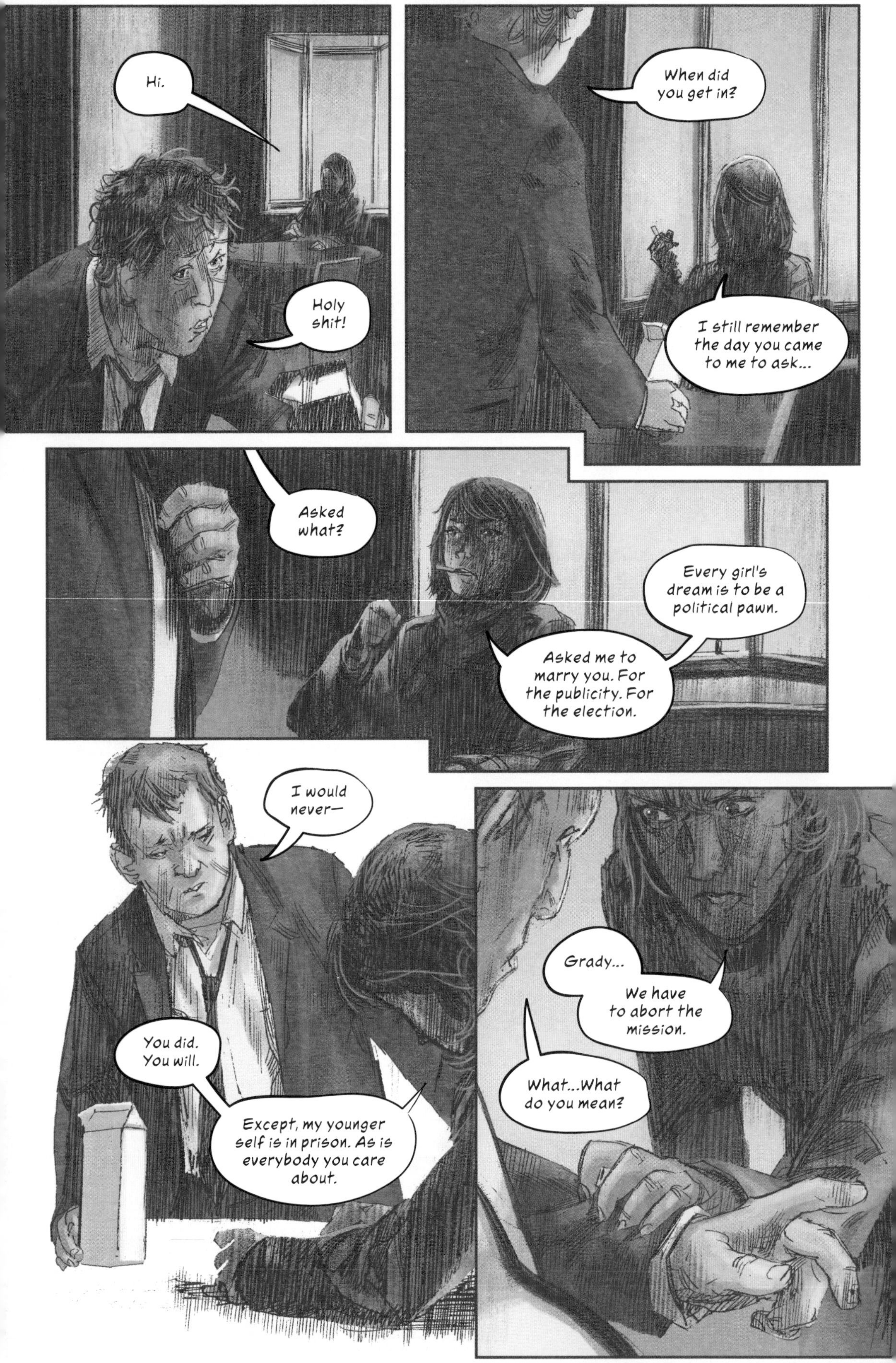
Hi.
Holy shit!
When did you get in?
I still remember the day you came to me to ask...
Asked what?
Asked me to marry you. For the publicity. For the election.
Every girl's dream is to be a political pawn.
I would never—
You did. You will.
Except, my younger self is in prison. As is everybody you care about.
Grady...
We have to abort the mission.
What...What do you mean?

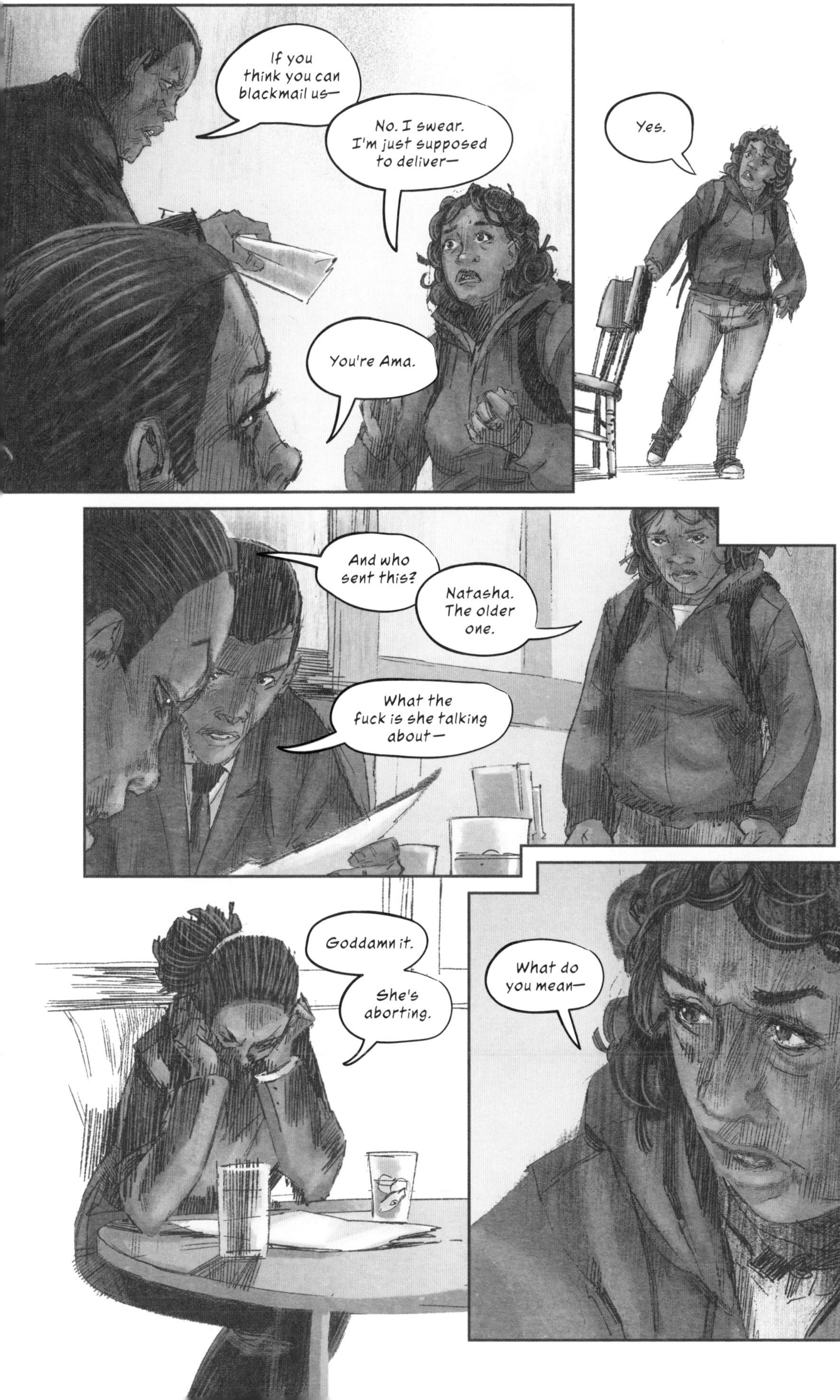
If you think you can blackmail us—
No. I swear. I'm just supposed to deliver—
You're Ama.
Yes.
And who sent this?
Natasha. The older one.
What the fuck is she talking about—
Goddamn it.
She's aborting.
What do you mean—

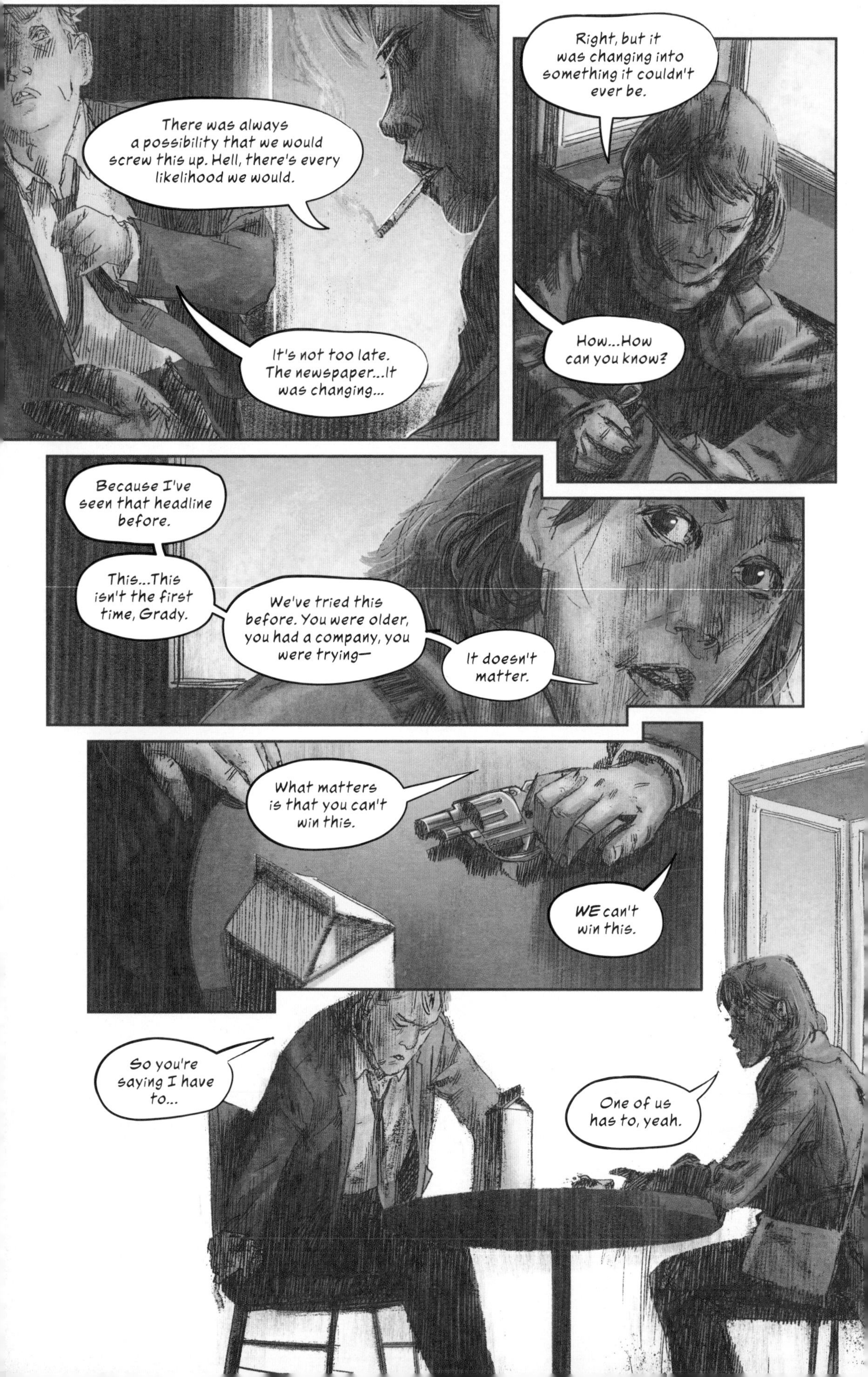
There was always a possibility that we would screw this up. Hell, there's every likelihood we would.
It's not too late. The newspaper...It was changing...
Right, but it was changing into something it couldn't ever be.
How...How can you know?
Because I've seen that headline before.
This...This isn't the first time, Grady.
We've tried this before. You were older, you had a company, you were trying—
It doesn't matter.
What matters is that you can't win this.
WE can't win this.
So you're saying I have to...
One of us has to, yeah.

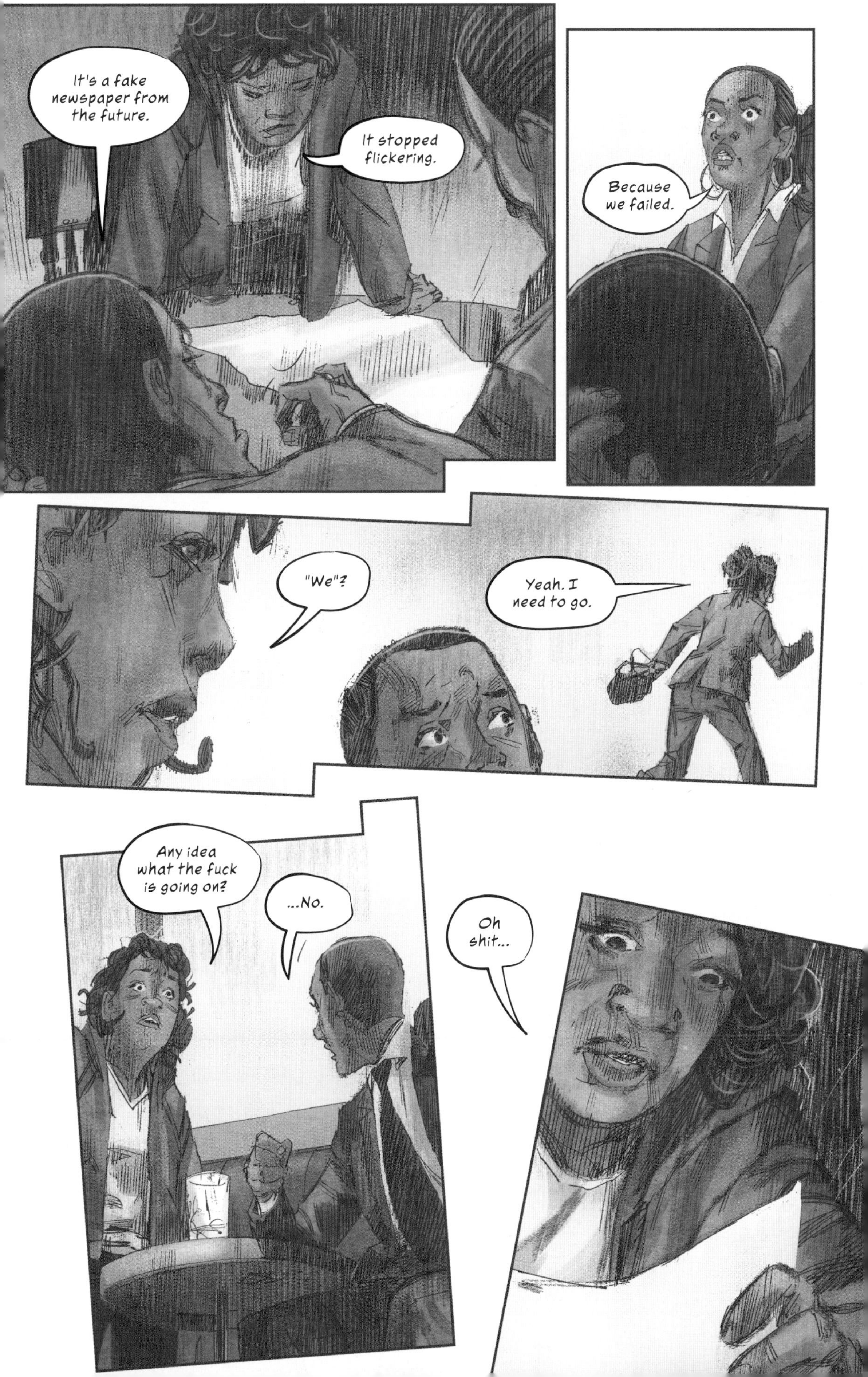
It's a fake newspaper from the future.
It stopped flickering.
Because we failed.
"We"?
Yeah. I need to go.
Any idea what the fuck is going on?
...No.
Oh shit...

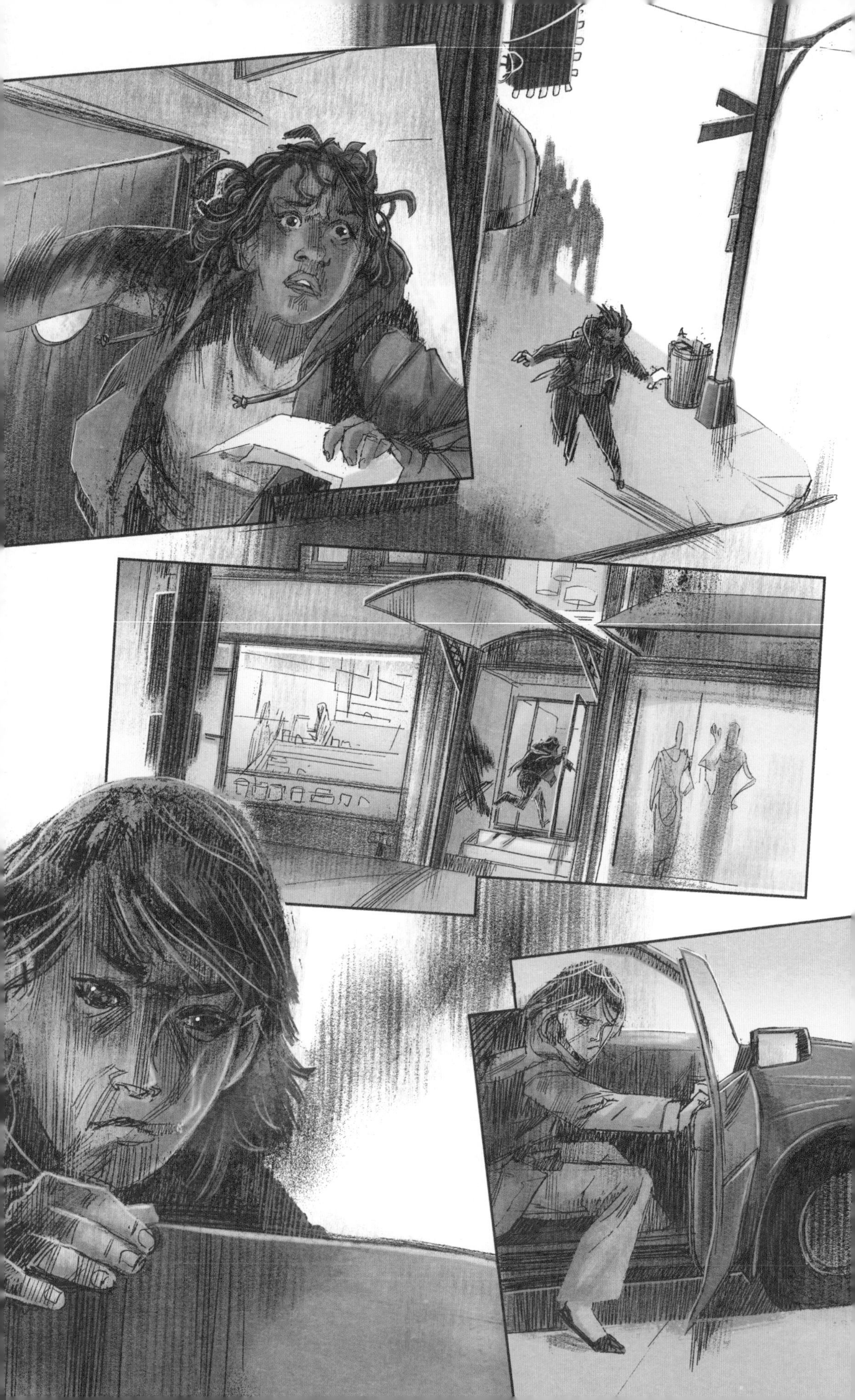

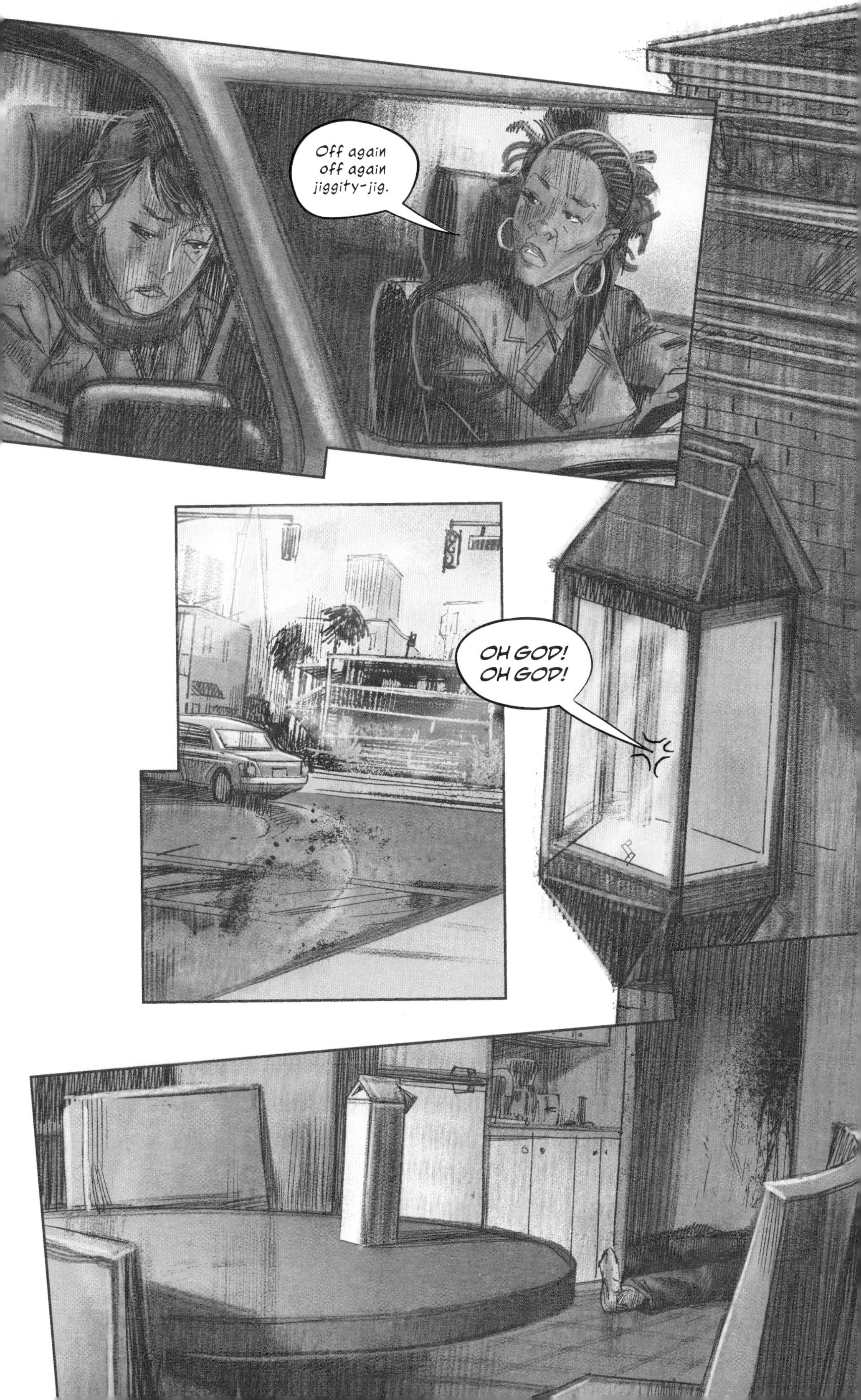
Off again off again jiggity-jig.
OH GOD! OH GOD!

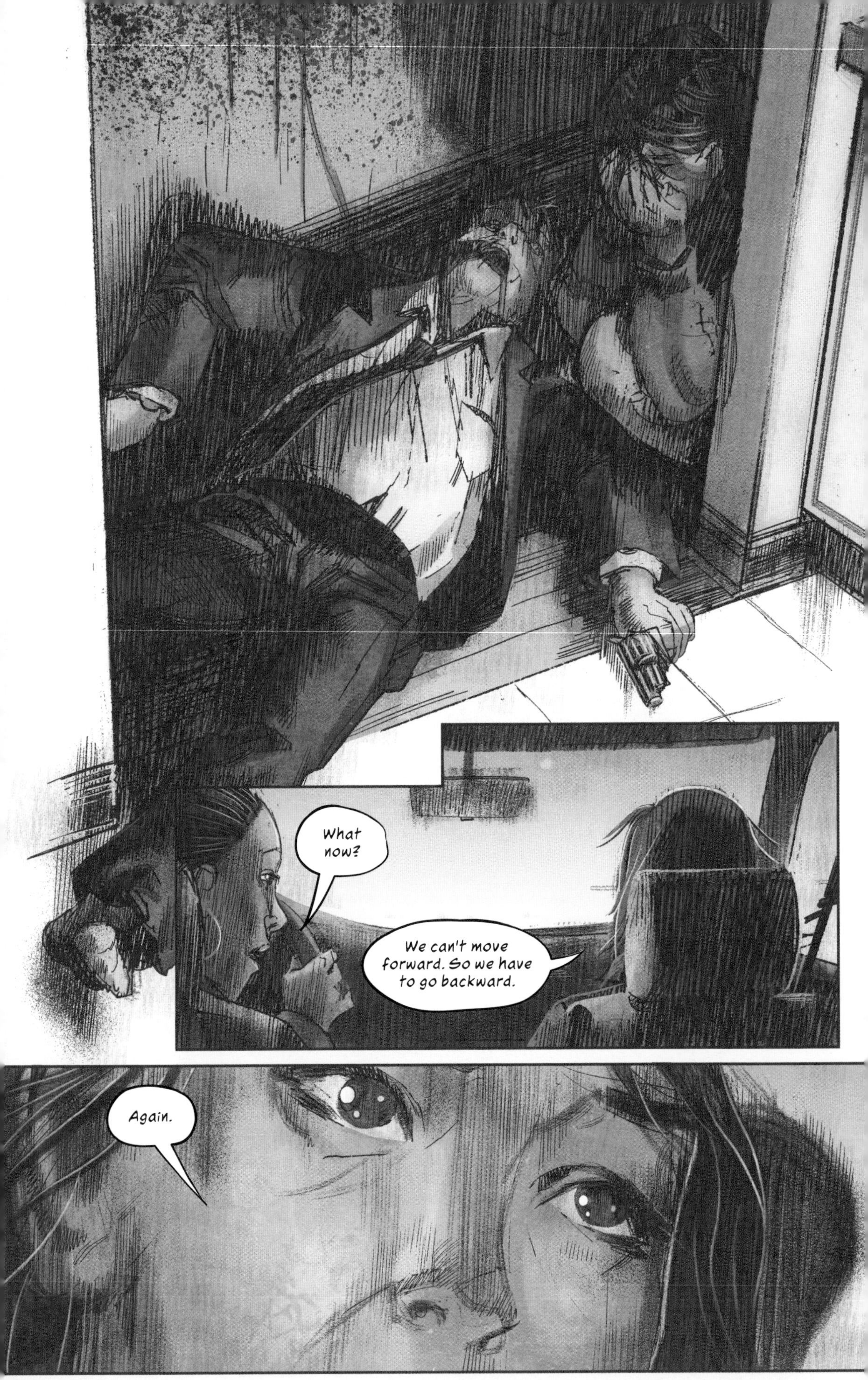
What now?
We can't move forward. So we have to go backward.
Again.

CHAPTER
19

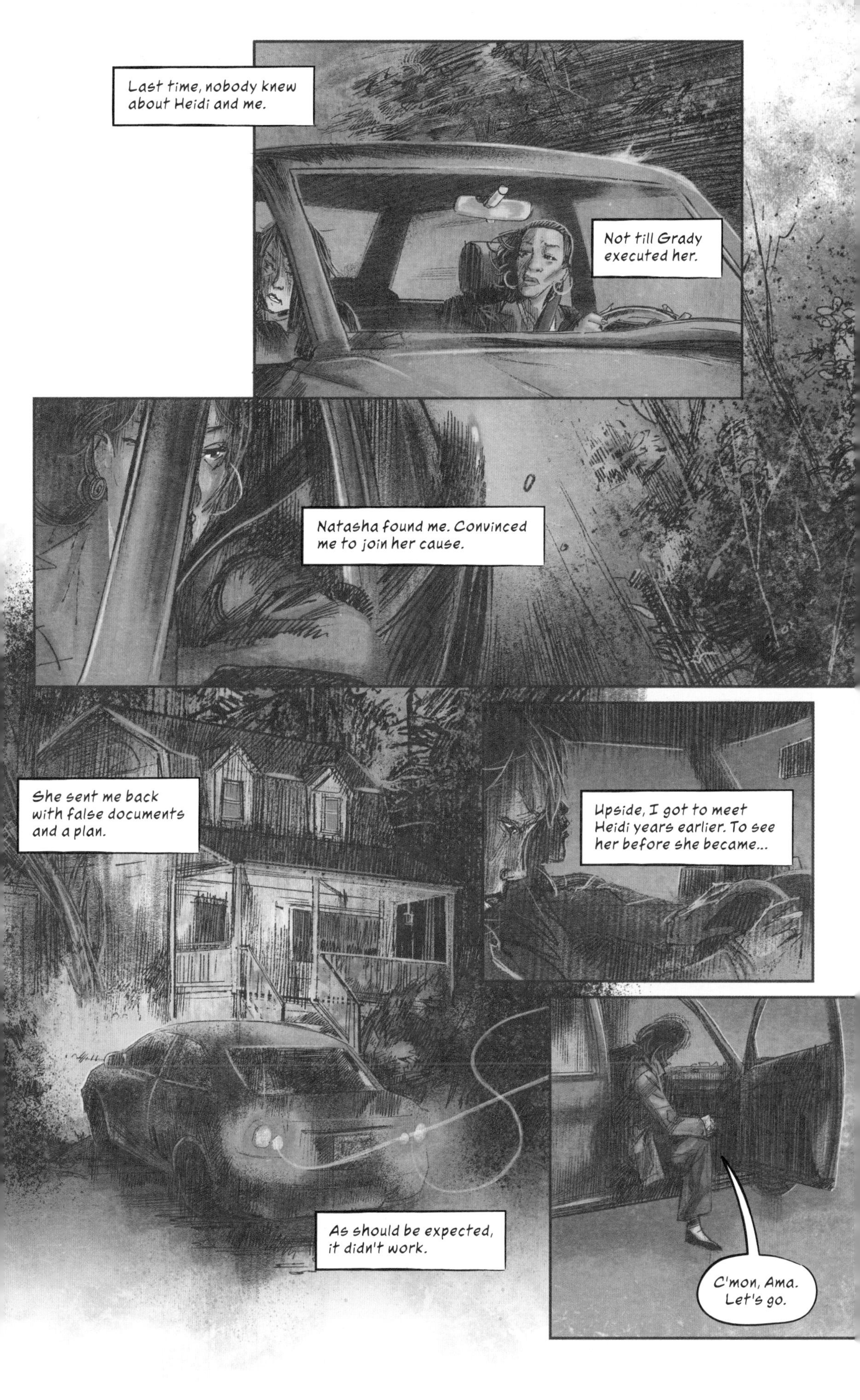
Last time, nobody knew about Heidi and me.
Not till Grady executed her.
Natasha found me. Convinced me to join her cause.
She sent me back with false documents and a plan.
Upside, I got to meet Heidi years earlier. To see her before she became...
As should be expected, it didn't work.
C'mon, Ama. Let's go.

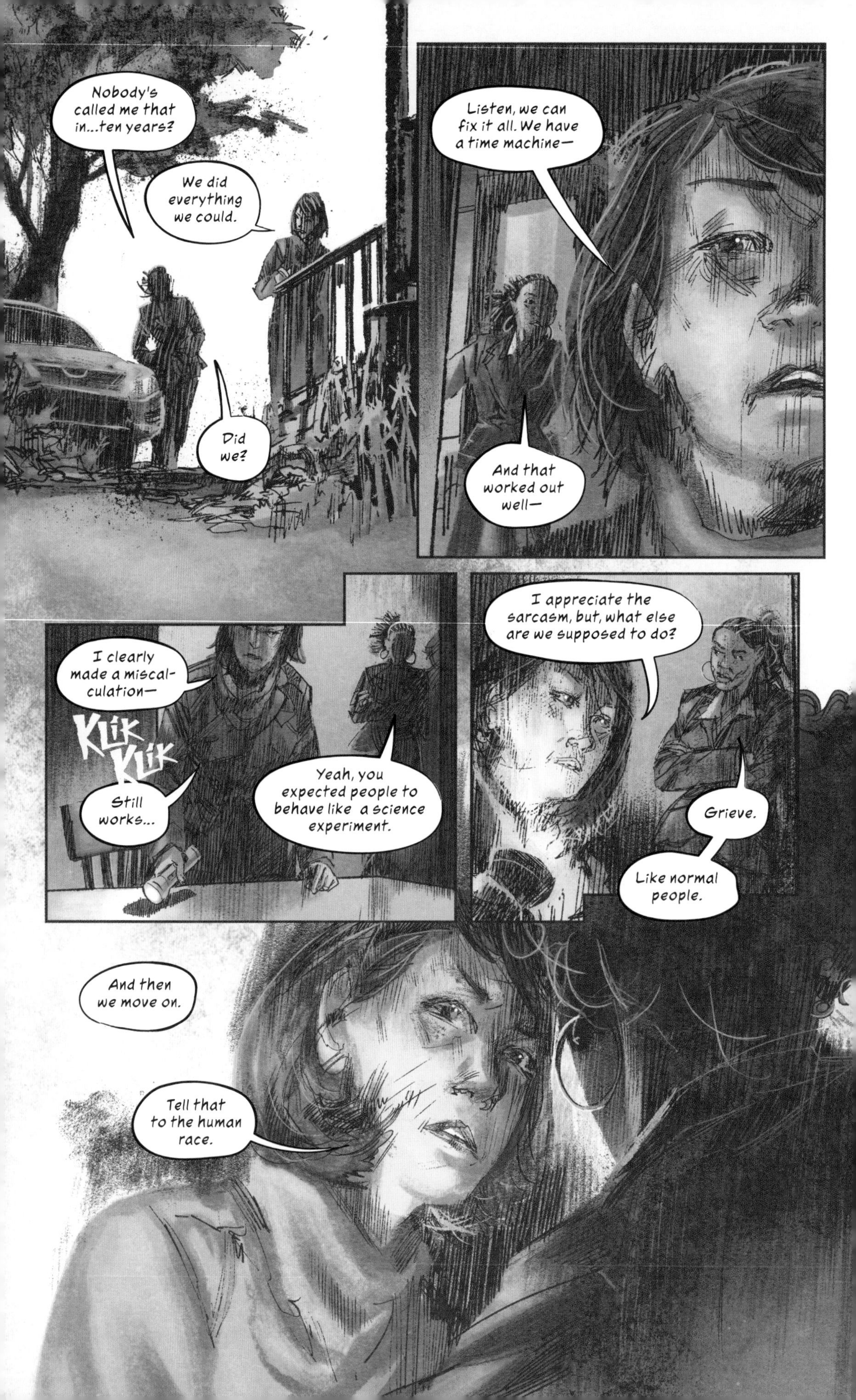
Nobody's called me that in...ten years?
We did everything we could.
Did we?
Listen, we can fix it all. We have a time machine—
And that worked out well—
I clearly made a miscal-culation—
KLIK KLIK
Still works...
Yeah, you expected people to behave like a science experiment.
I appreciate the sarcasm, but, what else are we supposed to do?
Grieve.
Like normal people.
And then we move on.
Tell that to the human race.

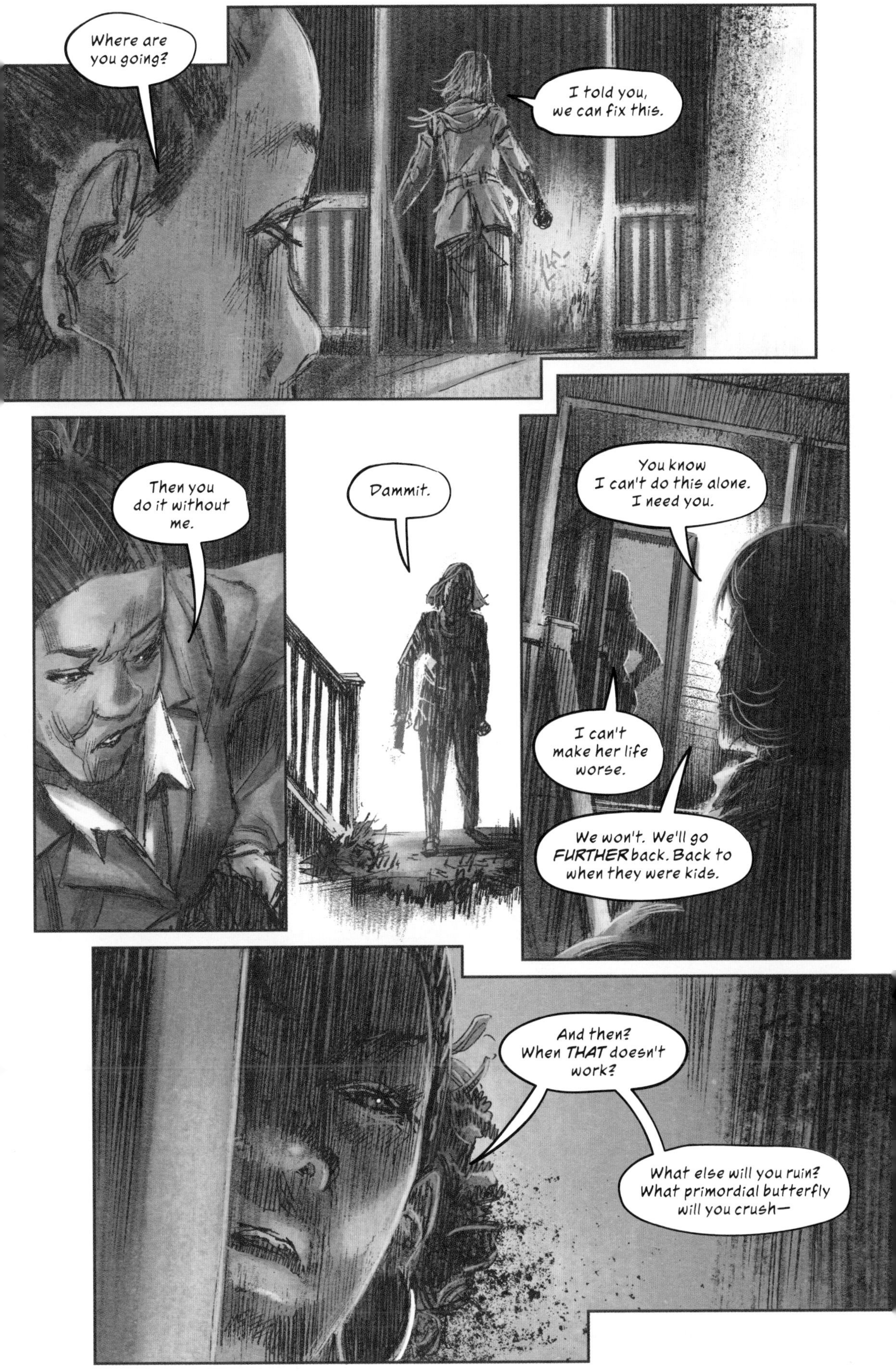
Where are you going?
I told you, we can fix this.
Then you do it without me.
Dammit.
You know I can't do this alone. I need you.
I can't make her life worse.
We won't. We'll go FURTHER back. Back to when they were kids.
And then? When THAT doesn't work?
What else will you ruin? What primordial butterfly will you crush—

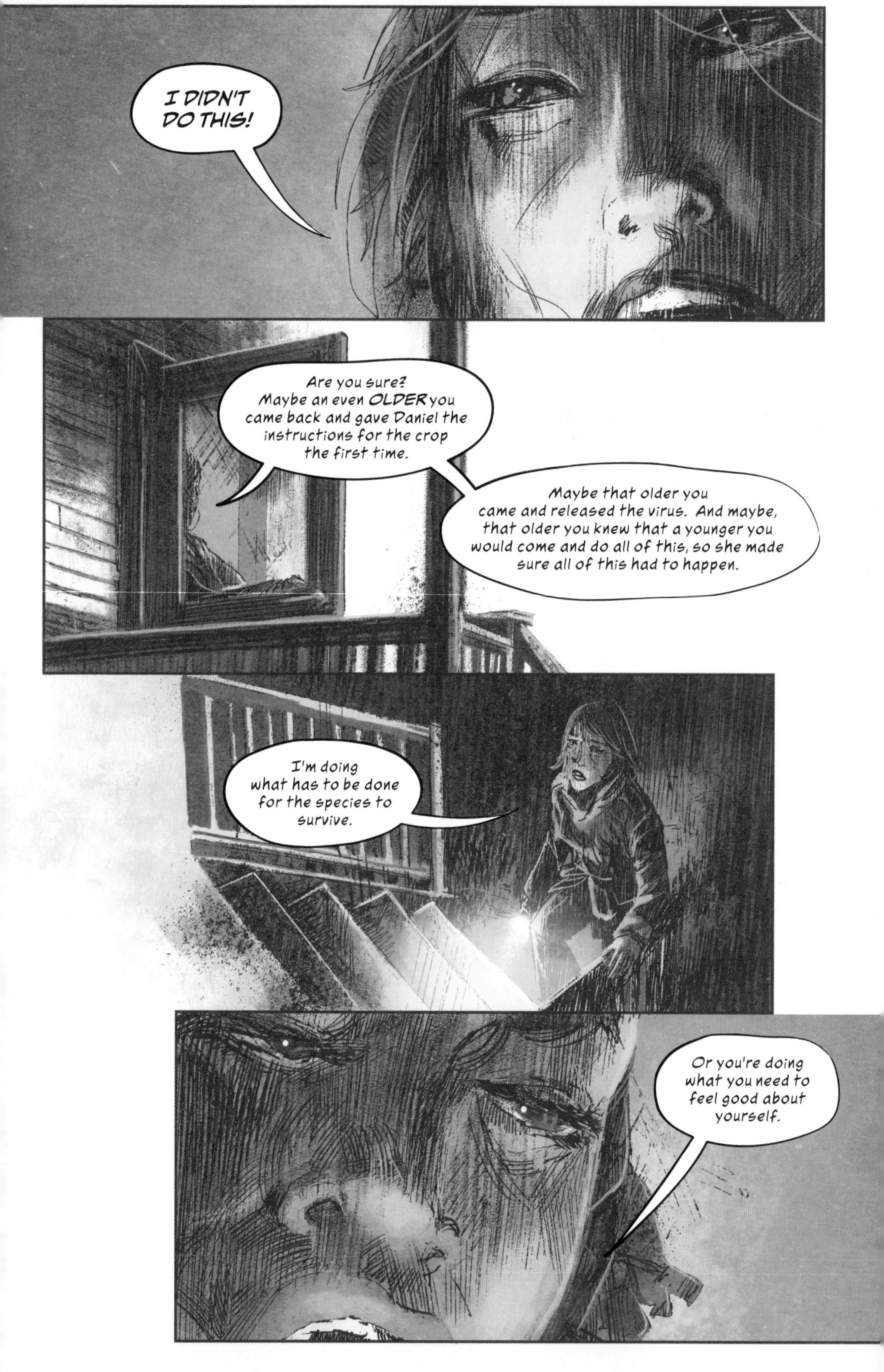
I DIDN'T DO THIS!
Are you sure? Maybe an even OLDER you came back and gave Daniel the instructions for the crop the first time.
Maybe that older you came and released the virus. And maybe, that older you knew that a younger you would come and do all of this, so she made sure all of this had to happen.
I'm doing what has to be done for the species to survive.
Or you're doing what you need to feel good about yourself.

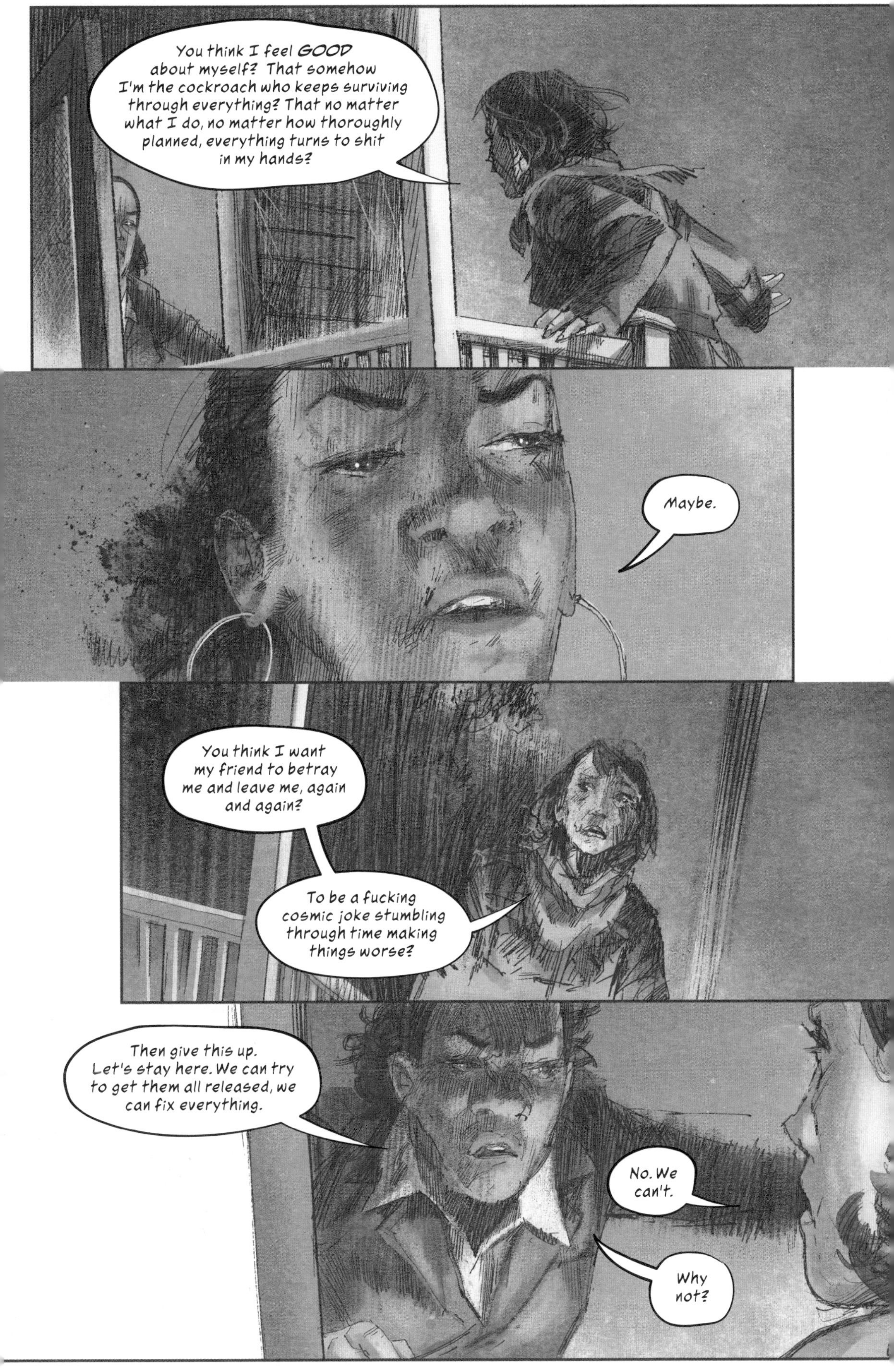
You think I feel GOOD about myself? That somehow I'm the cockroach who keeps surviving through everything? That no matter what I do, no matter how thoroughly planned, everything turns to shit in my hands?
Maybe.
You think I want my friend to betray me and leave me, again and again?
To be a fucking cosmic joke stumbling through time making things worse?
Then give this up. Let's stay here. We can try to get them all released, we can fix everything.
No. We can't.
Why not?

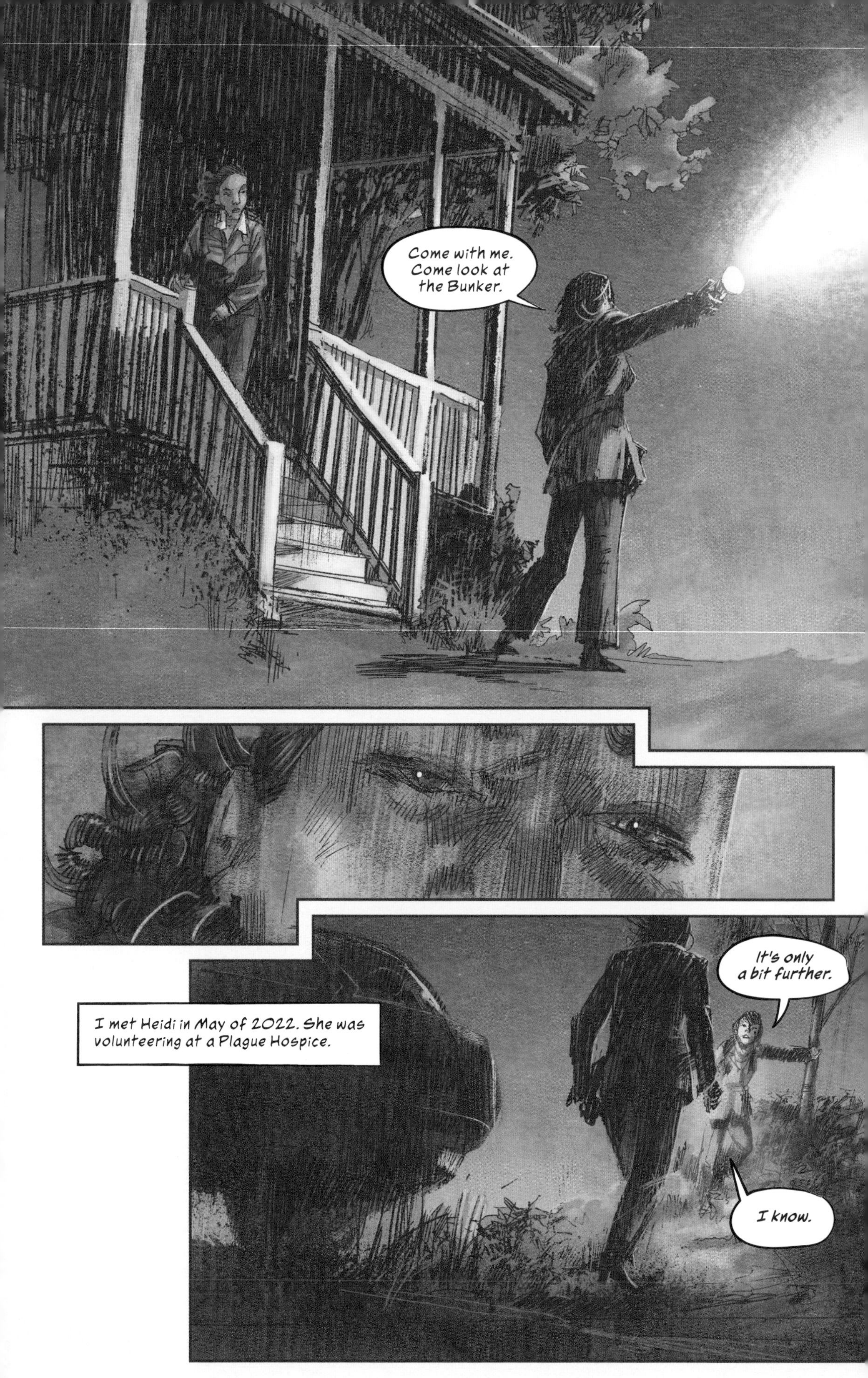
Come with me. Come look at the Bunker.
I met Heidi in May of 2022. She was volunteering at a Plague Hospice.
It's only a bit further.
I know.

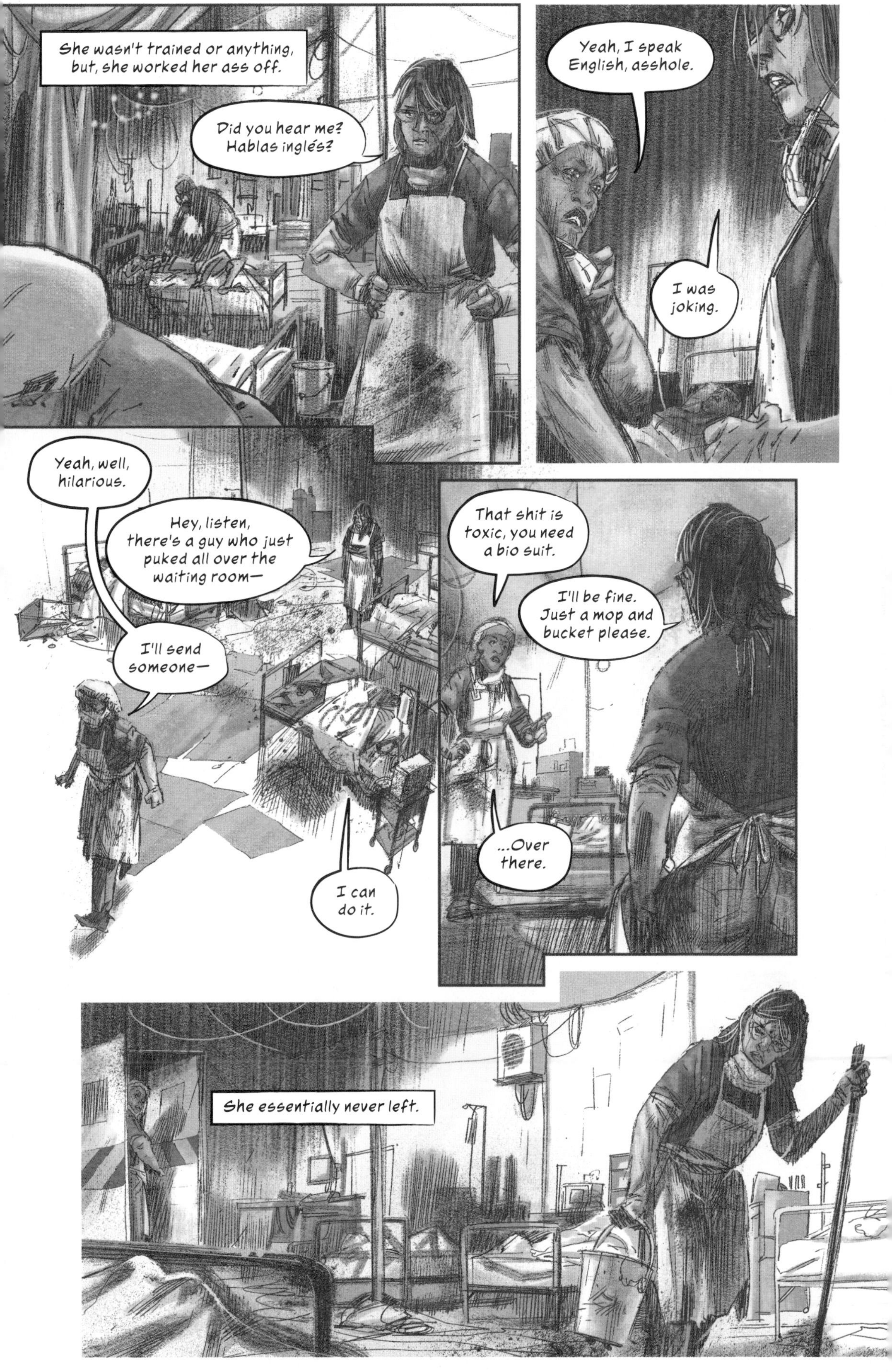
She wasn't trained or anything, but, she worked her ass off.
Did you hear me? Hablas inglés?
Yeah, I speak English, asshole.
I was joking.
Yeah, well, hilarious.
Hey, listen, there's a guy who just puked all over the waiting room—
I'll send someone—
I can do it.
That shit is toxic, you need a bio suit.
I'll be fine. Just a mop and bucket please.
...Over there.
She essentially never left.

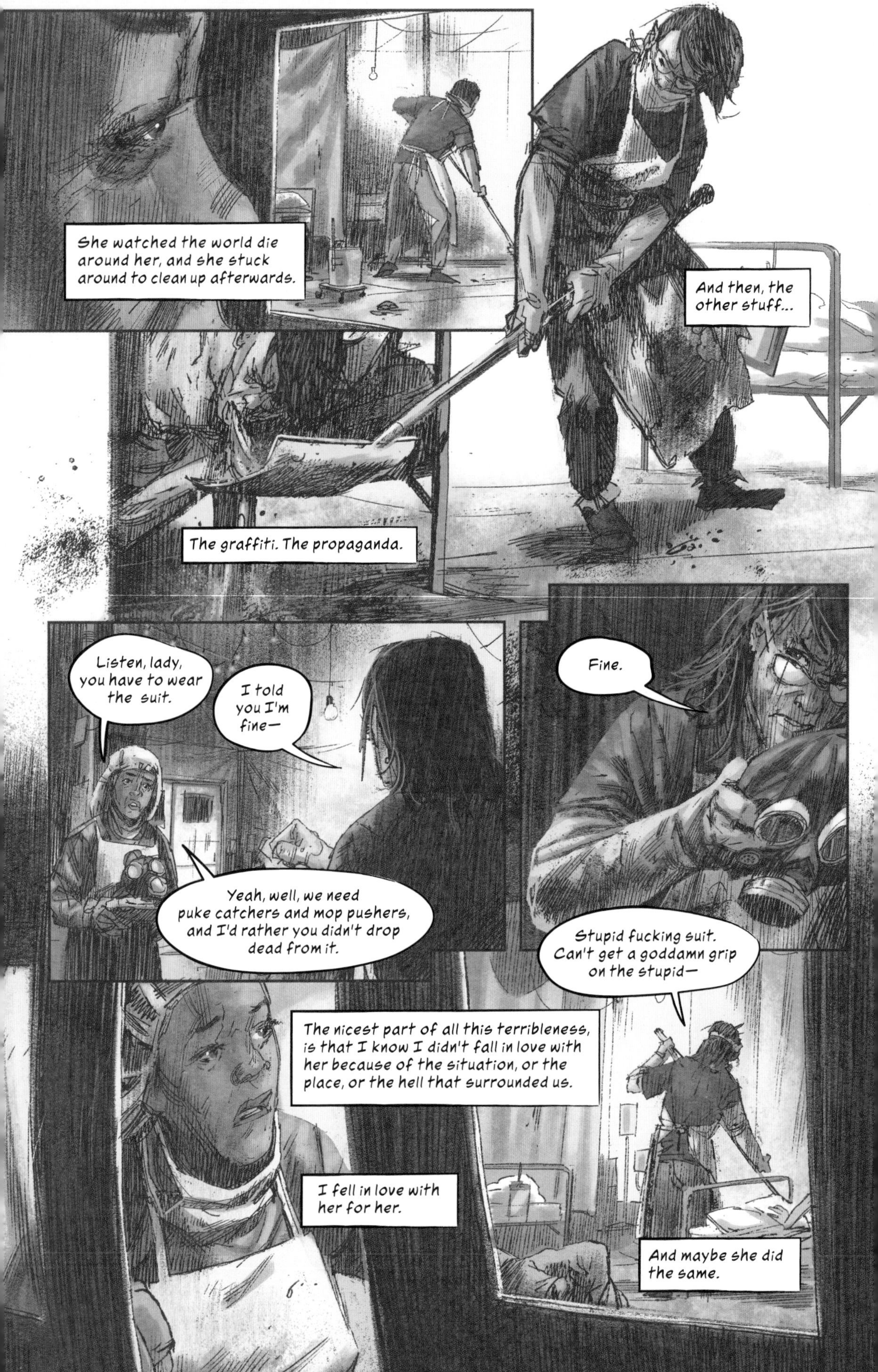

She watched the world die around her, and she stuck around to clean up afterwards.
And then, the other stuff...
The graffiti. The propaganda.
Listen, lady, you have to wear the suit.
I told you I'm fine—
Yeah, well, we need puke catchers and mop pushers, and I'd rather you didn't drop dead from it.
Fine.
Stupid fucking suit. Can't get a goddamn grip on the stupid—
The nicest part of all this terribleness, is that I know I didn't fall in love with her because of the situation, or the place, or the hell that surrounded us.
I fell in love with her for her.
And maybe she did the same.

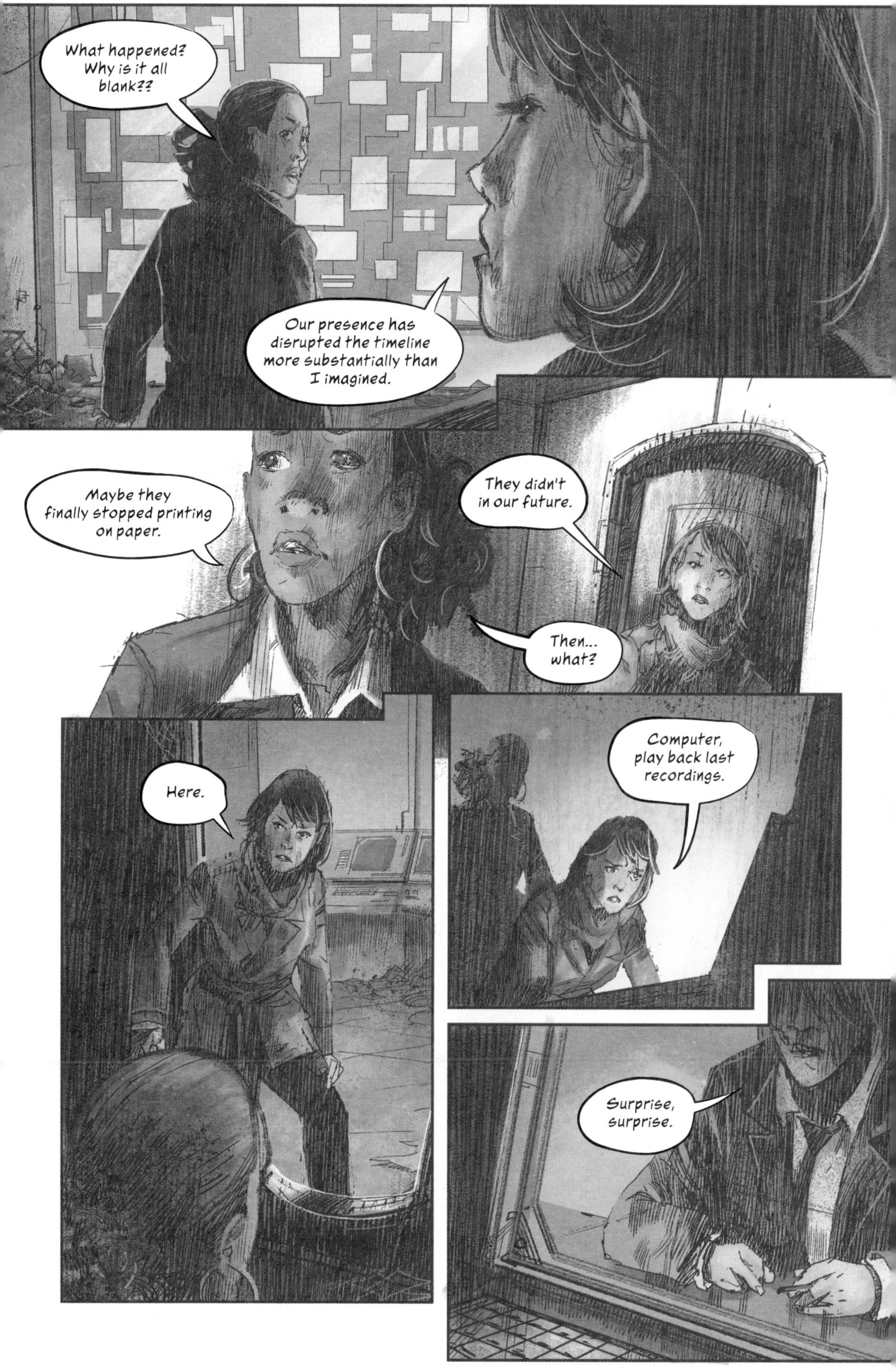
What happened? Why is it all blank??
Our presence has disrupted the timeline more substantially than I imagined.
Maybe they finally stopped printing on paper.
They didn't in our future.
Then... what?
Here.
Computer, play back last recordings.
Surprise, surprise.

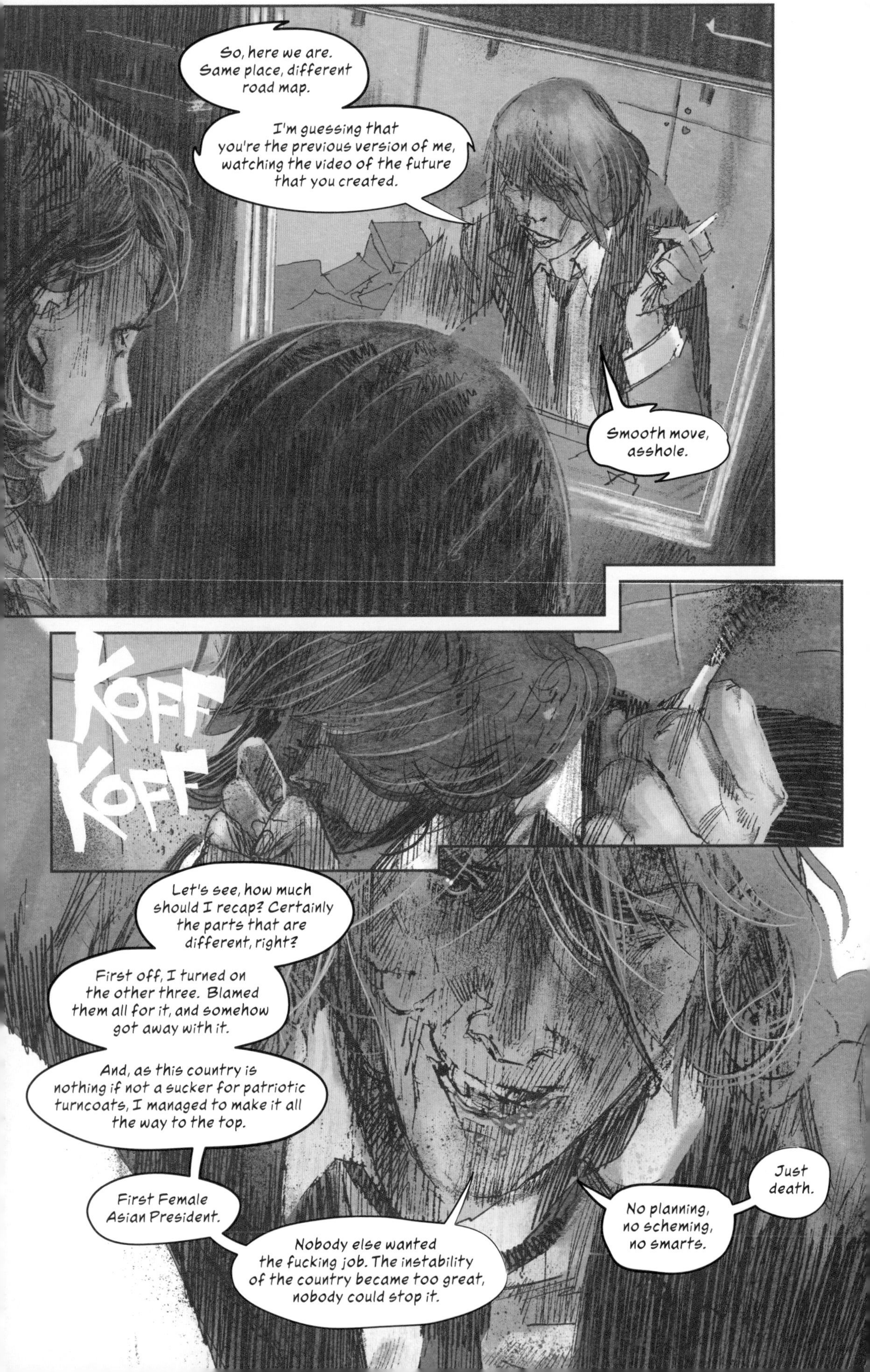

So, here we are. Same place, different road map.
I'm guessing that you're the previous version of me, watching the video of the future that you created.
Smooth move, asshole.
KOFF KOFF
Let's see, how much should I recap? Certainly the parts that are different, right?
First off, I turned on the other three. Blamed them all for it, and somehow got away with it.
And, as this country is nothing if not a sucker for patriotic turncoats, I managed to make it all the way to the top.
First Female Asian President.
Nobody else wanted the fucking job. The instability of the country became too great, nobody could stop it.
No planning, no scheming, no smarts.
Just death.

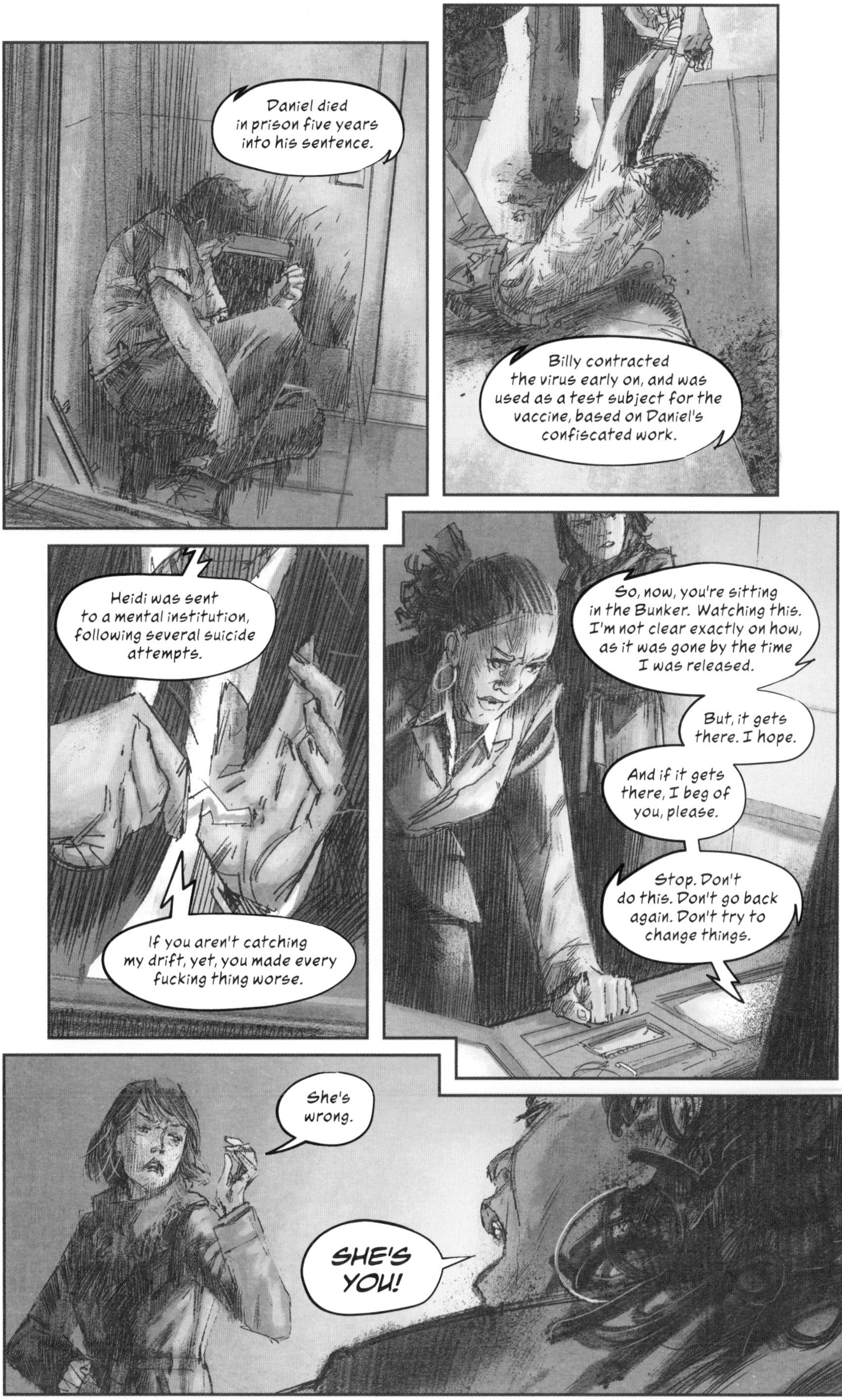
Daniel died in prison five years into his sentence.
Billy contracted the virus early on, and was used as a test subject for the vaccine, based on Daniel's confiscated work.
Heidi was sent to a mental institution, following several suicide attempts.
If you aren't catching my drift, yet, you made every fucking thing worse.
So, now, you're sitting in the Bunker. Watching this. I'm not clear exactly on how, as it was gone by the time I was released.
But, it gets there. I hope.
And if it gets there, I beg of you, please.
Stop. Don't do this. Don't go back again. Don't try to change things.
She's wrong.
SHE'S YOU!

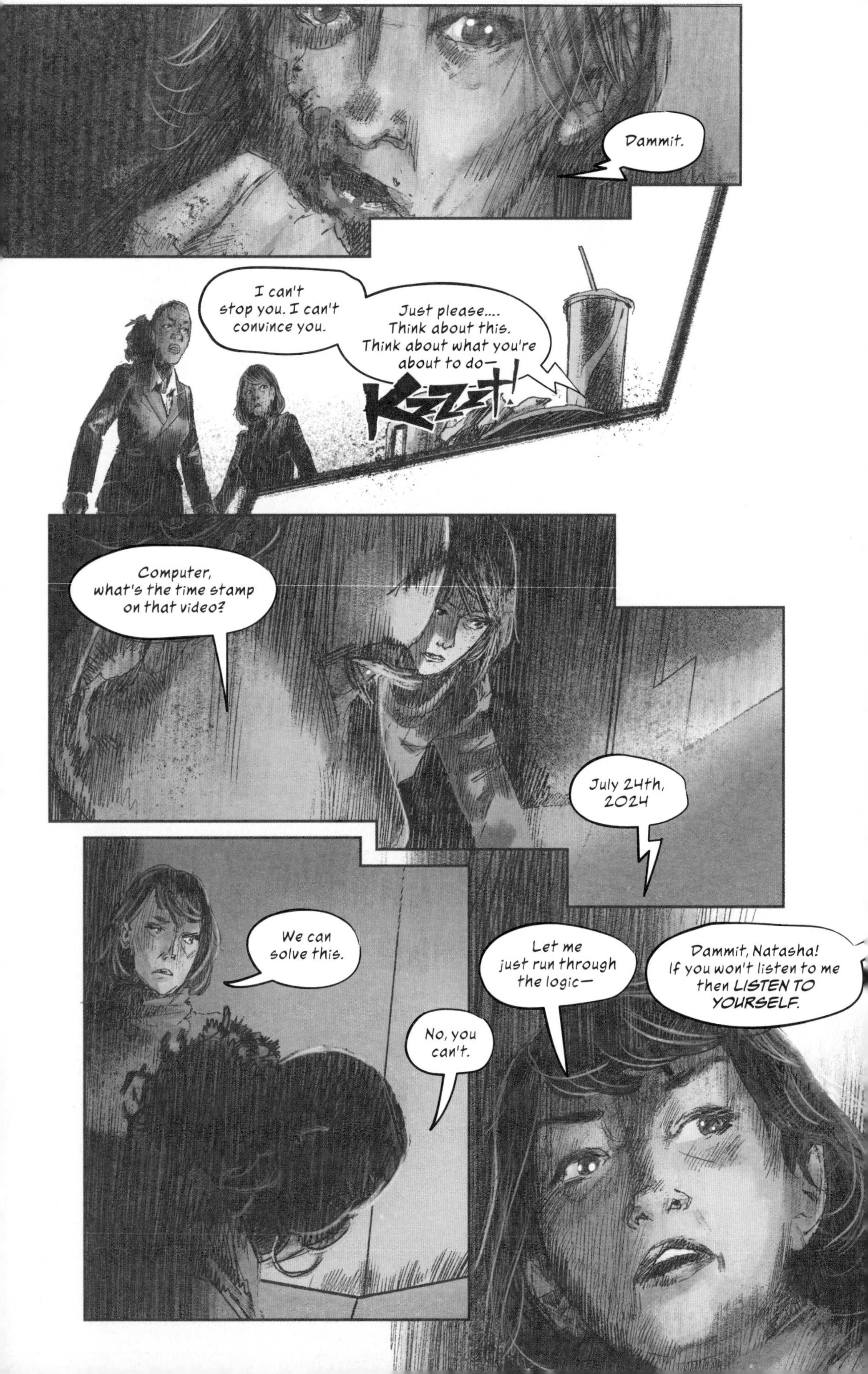
Dammit.
I can't stop you. I can't convince you.
Just please.... Think about this. Think about what you're about to do—
KZZZT!
Computer, what's the time stamp on that video?
July 24th, 2024
We can solve this.
No, you can't.
Let me just run through the logic—
Dammit, Natasha! If you won't listen to me then LISTEN TO YOURSELF.

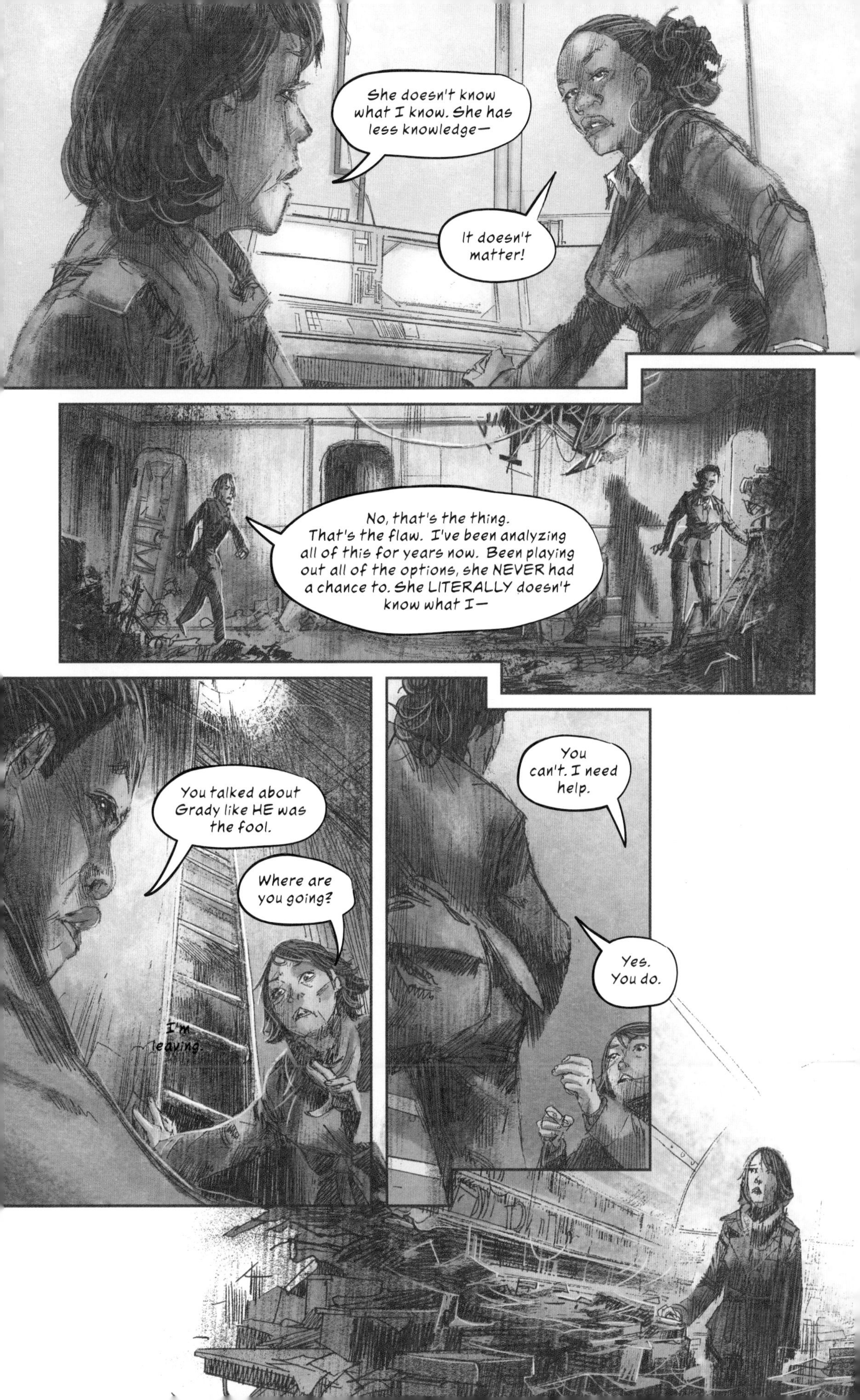
She doesn't know what I know. She has less knowledge—
It doesn't matter!
No, that's the thing. That's the flaw. I've been analyzing all of this for years now. Been playing out all of the options, she NEVER had a chance to. She LITERALLY doesn't know what I—
You talked about Grady like HE was the fool.
Where are you going?
I'm leaving.
You can't. I need help.
Yes. You do.

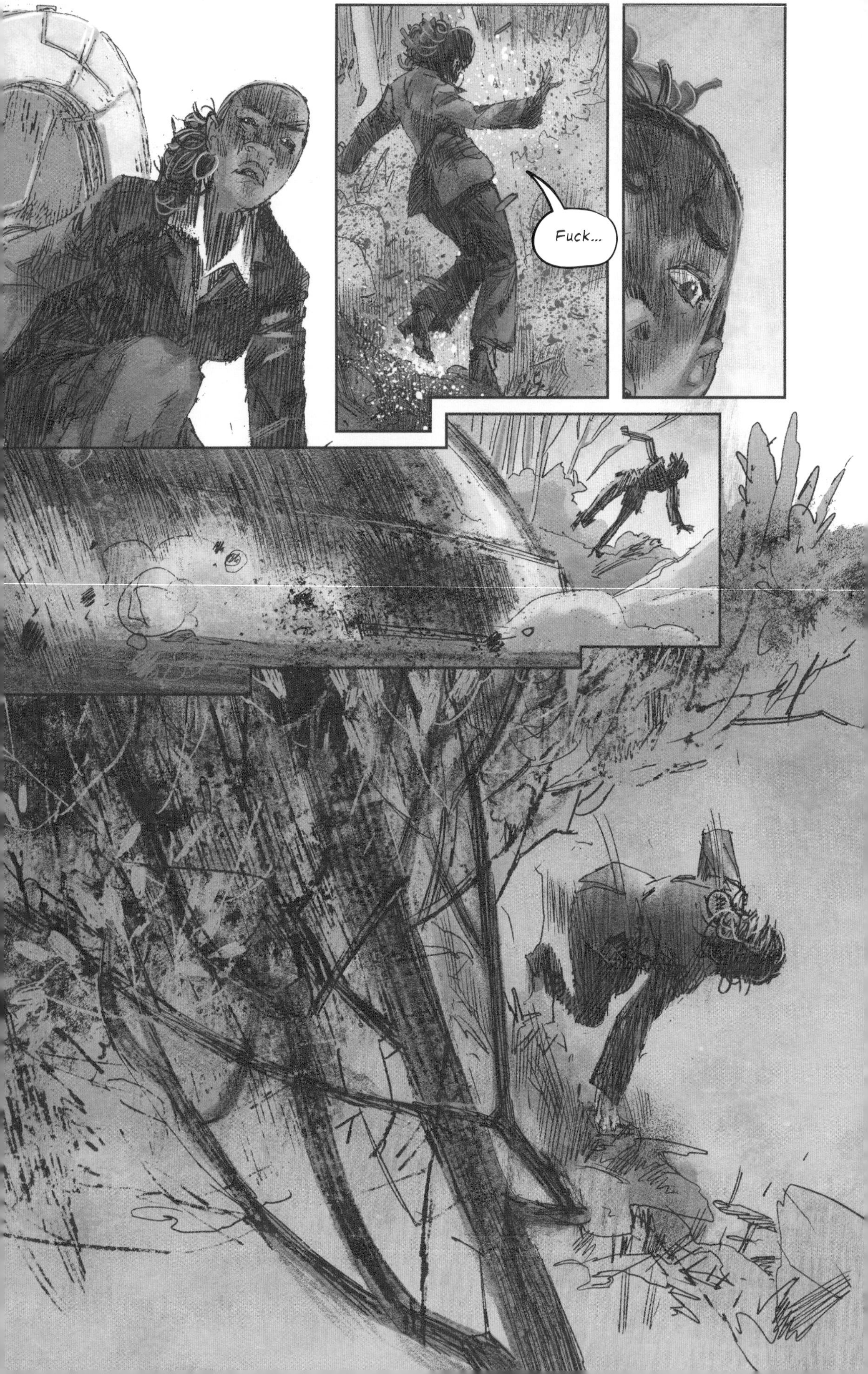
Fuck...

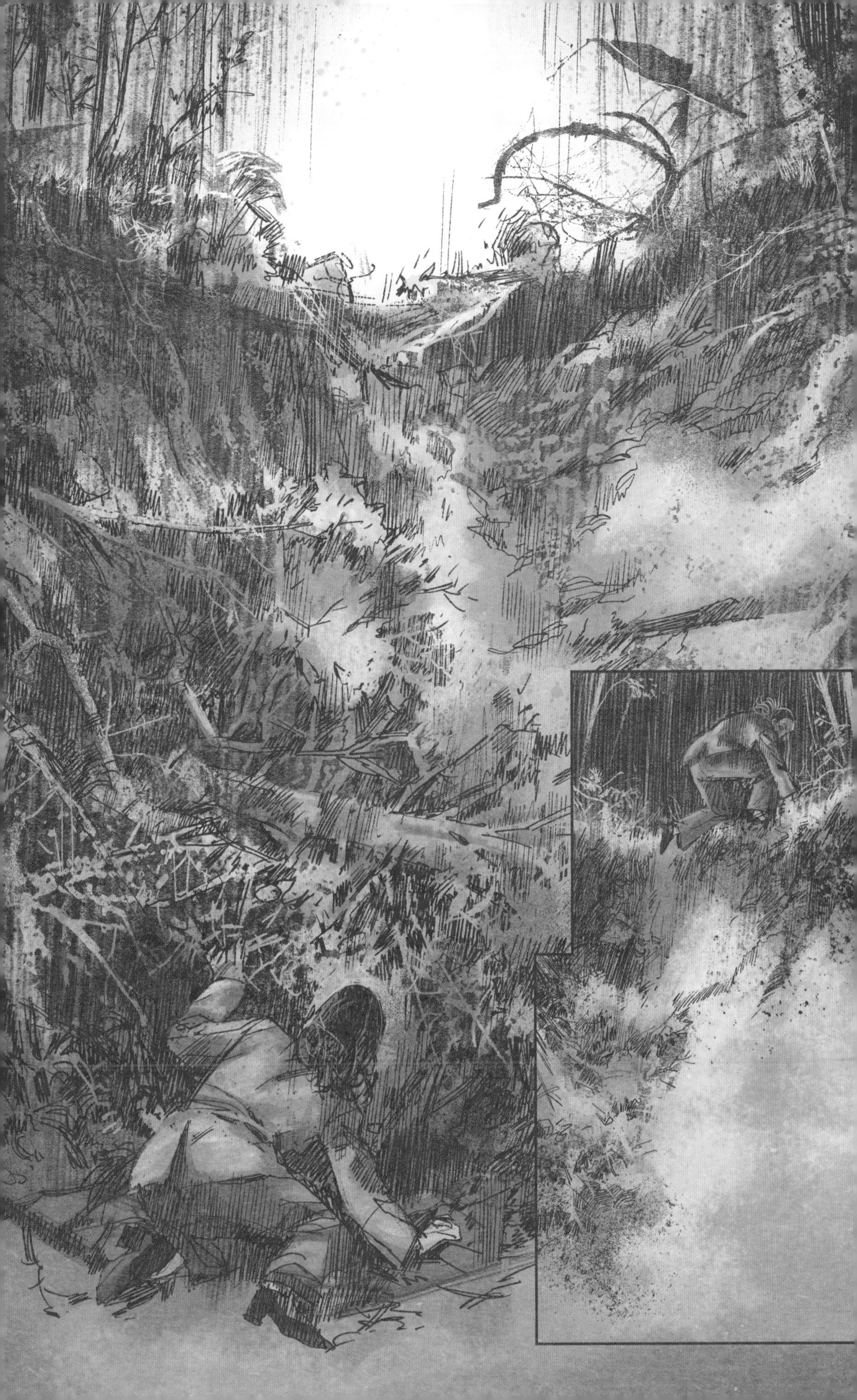

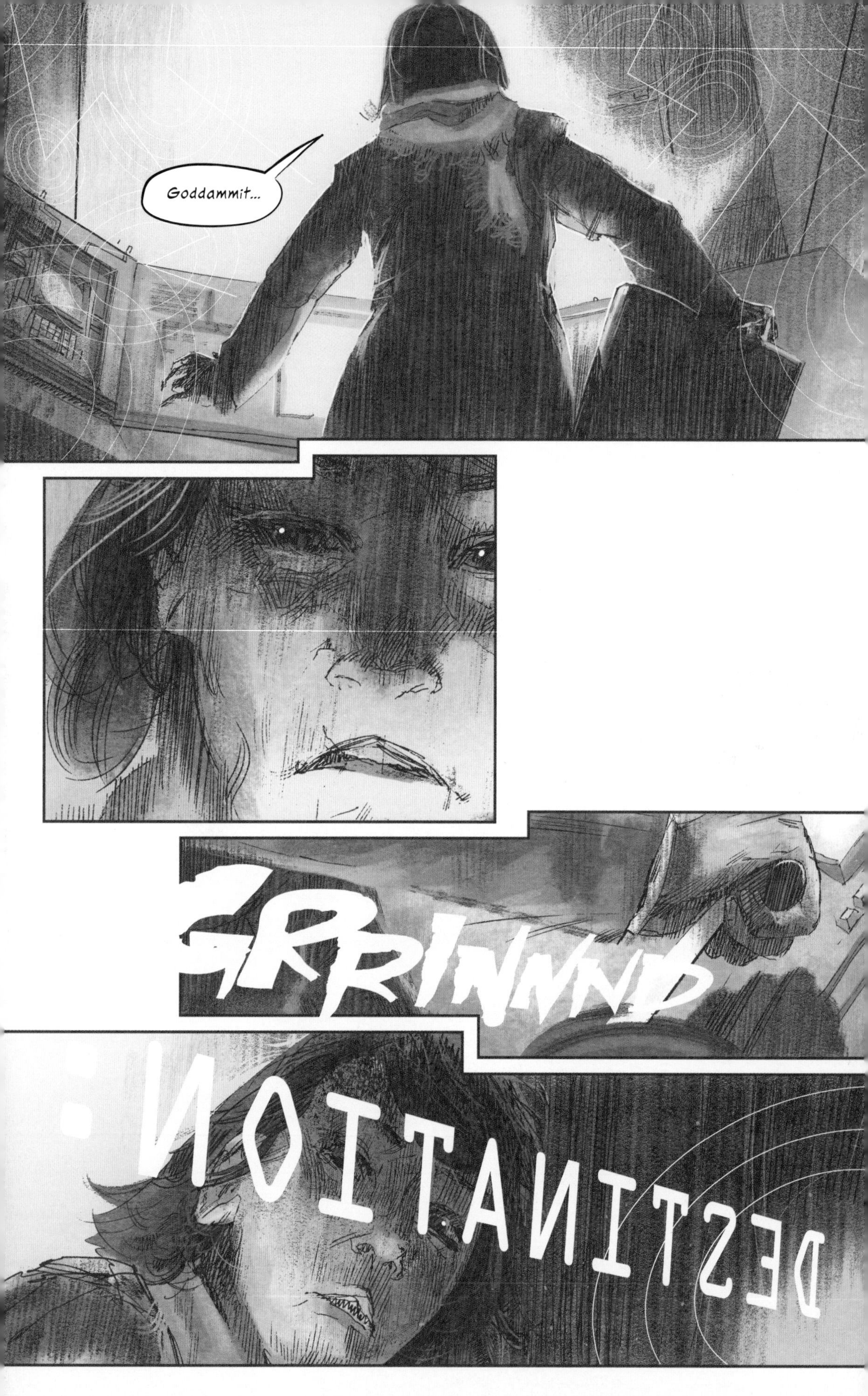
Goddammit...
GRRINNND
DESTINATION:

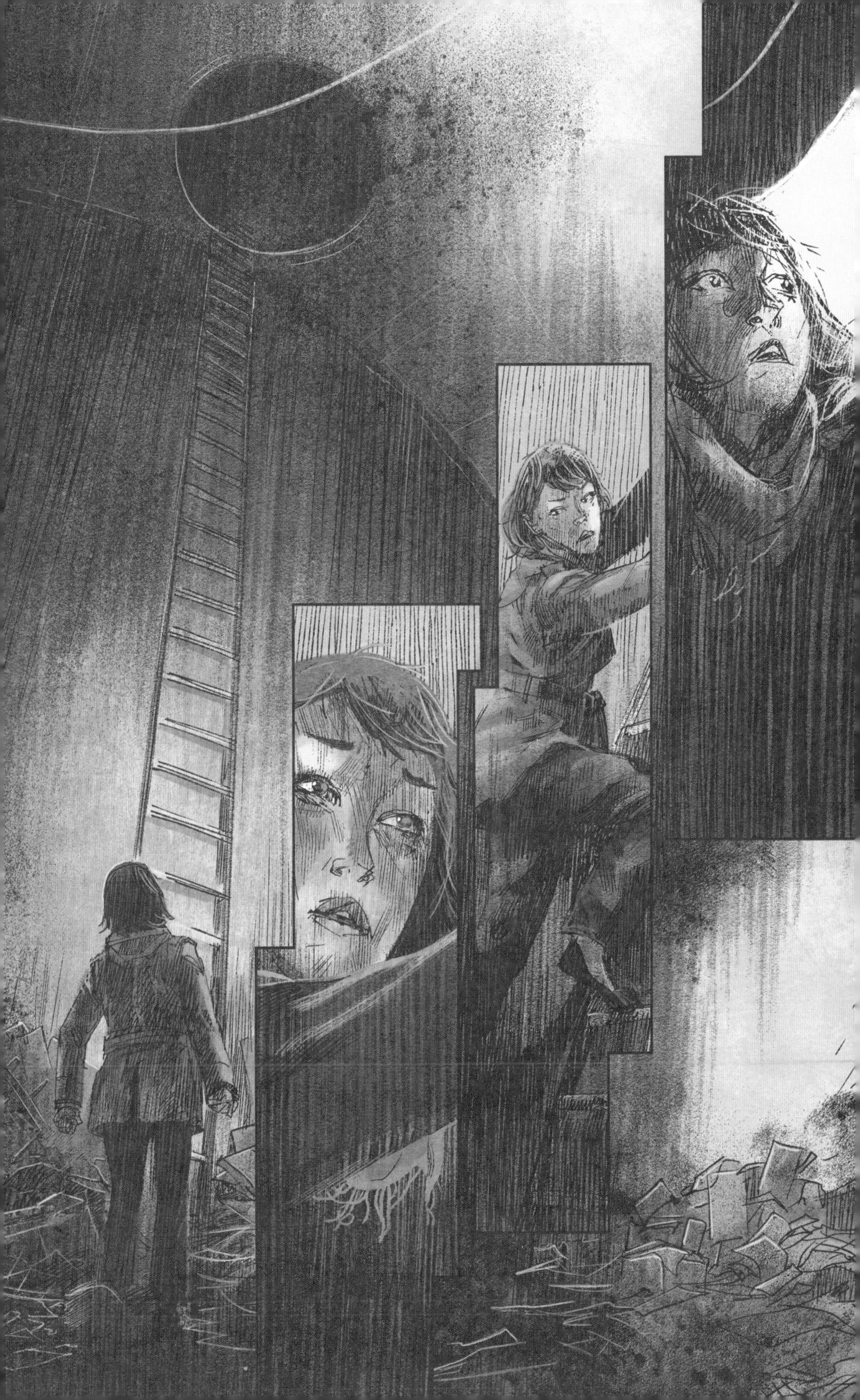

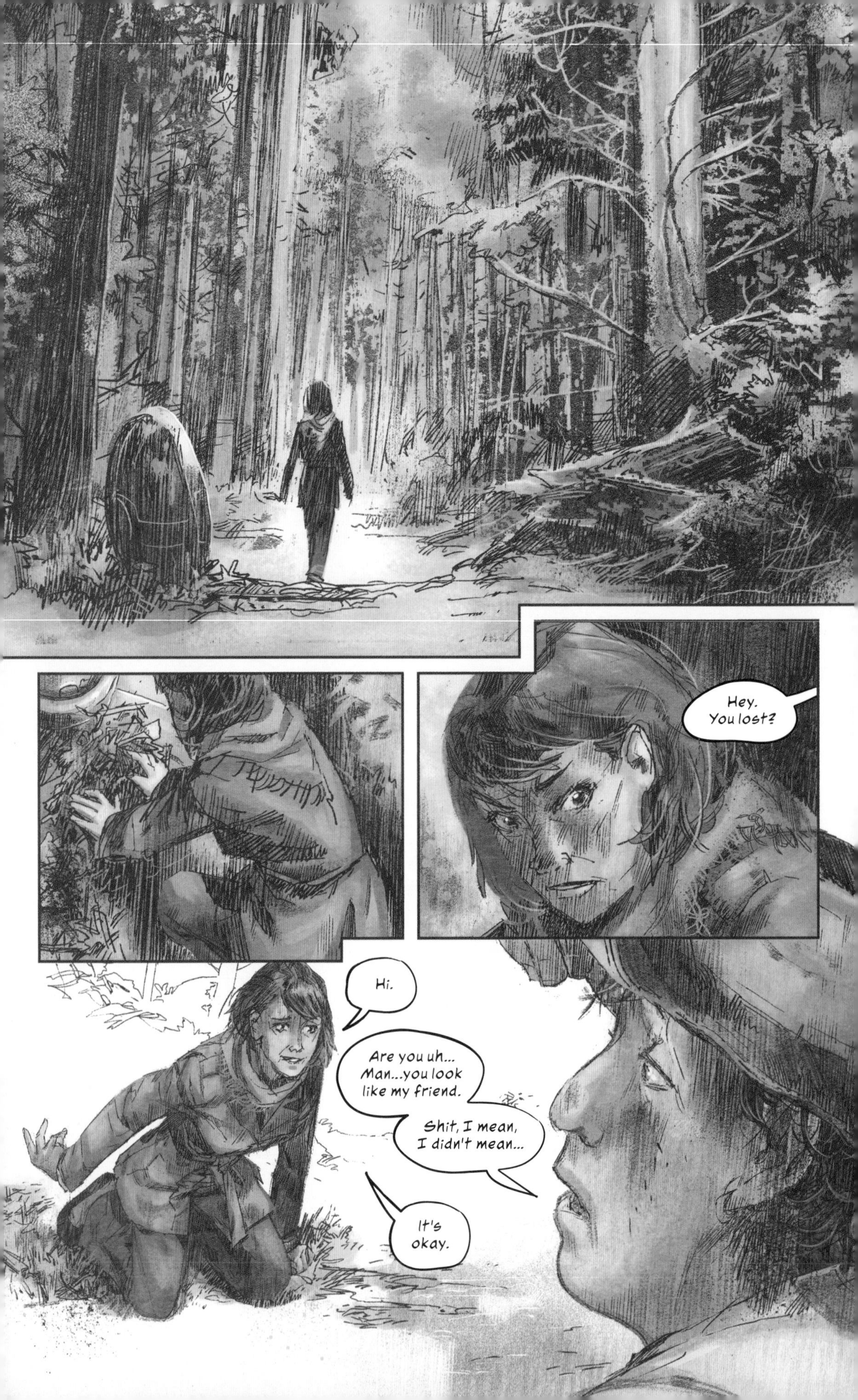
Hey.
You lost?
Hi.
Are you uh...
Man...you look
like my friend.
Shit, I mean,
I didn't mean...
It's
okay.

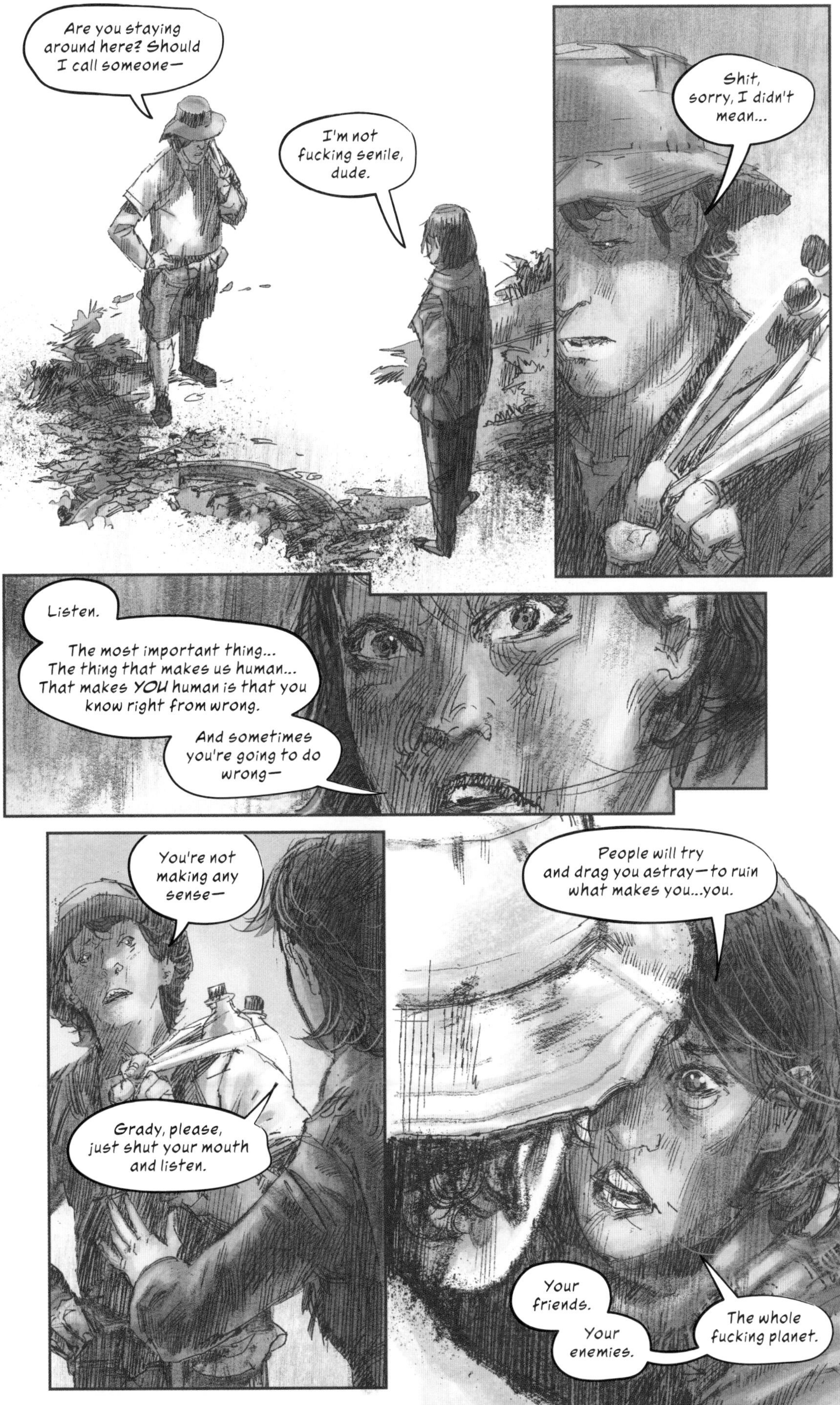
Are you staying around here? Should I call someone—
I'm not fucking senile, dude.
Shit, sorry, I didn't mean...
Listen.
The most important thing... The thing that makes us human... That makes YOU human is that you know right from wrong.
And sometimes you're going to do wrong—
You're not making any sense—
Grady, please, just shut your mouth and listen.
People will try and drag you astray—to ruin what makes you...you.
Your friends.
Your enemies.
The whole fucking planet.

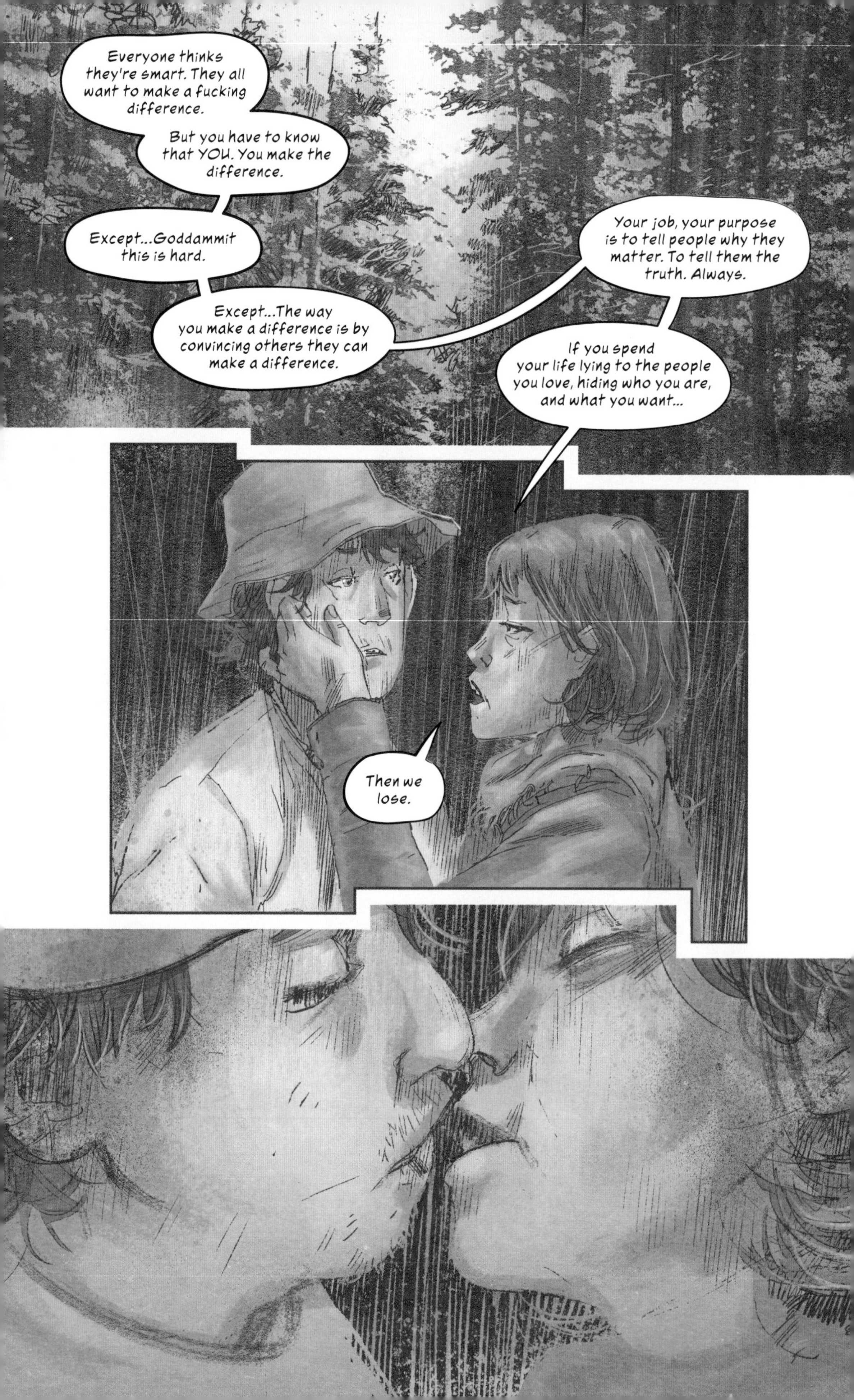
Everyone thinks they're smart. They all want to make a fucking difference.
But you have to know that YOU. You make the difference.
Except...Goddammit this is hard.
Except...The way you make a difference is by convincing others they can make a difference.
Your job, your purpose is to tell people why they matter. To tell them the truth. Always.
If you spend your life lying to the people you love, hiding who you are, and what you want...
Then we lose.

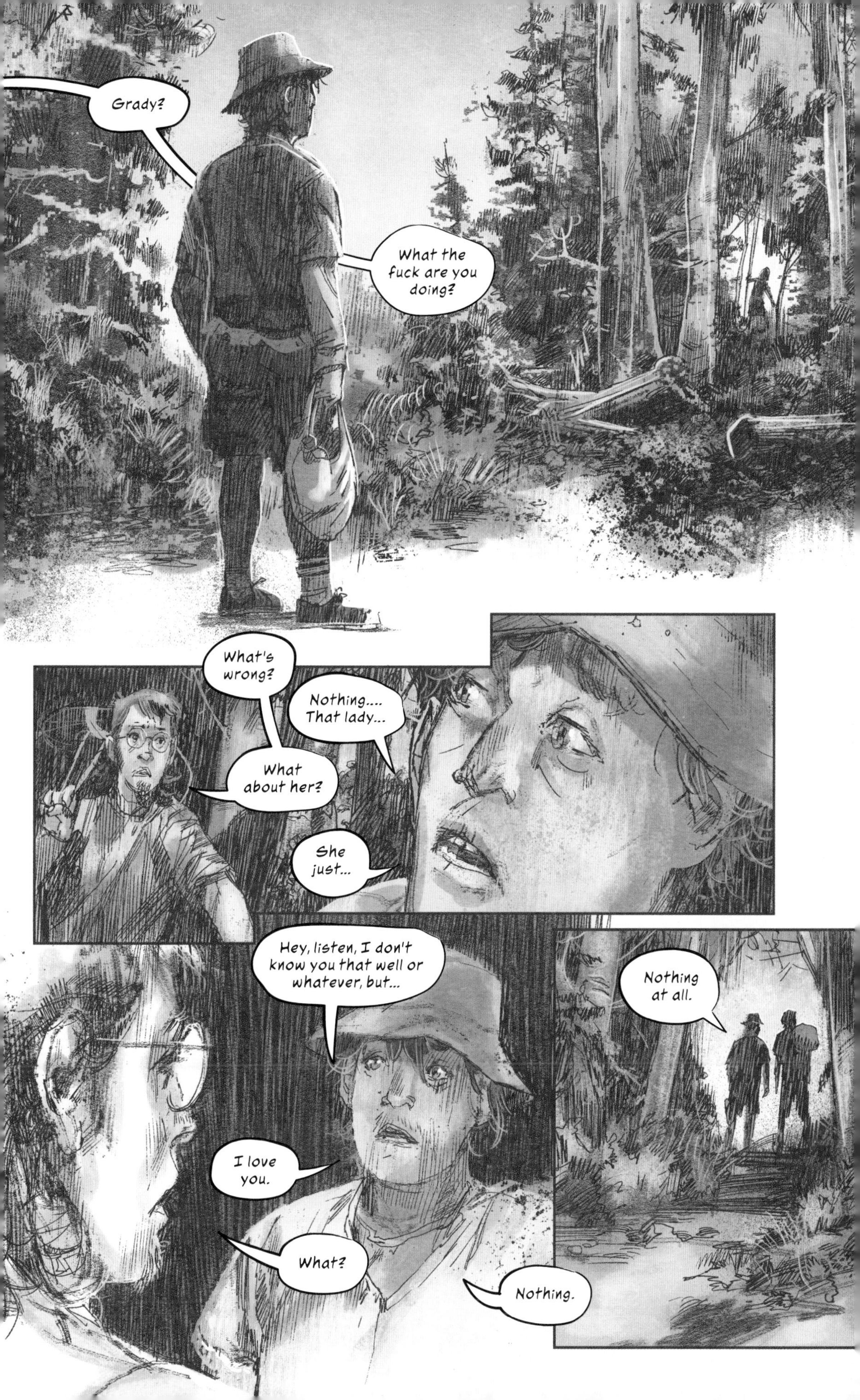

Grady?
What the fuck are you doing?
What's wrong?
Nothing.... That lady...
What about her?
She just...
Hey, listen, I don't know you that well or whatever, but...
I love you.
What?
Nothing.
Nothing at all.

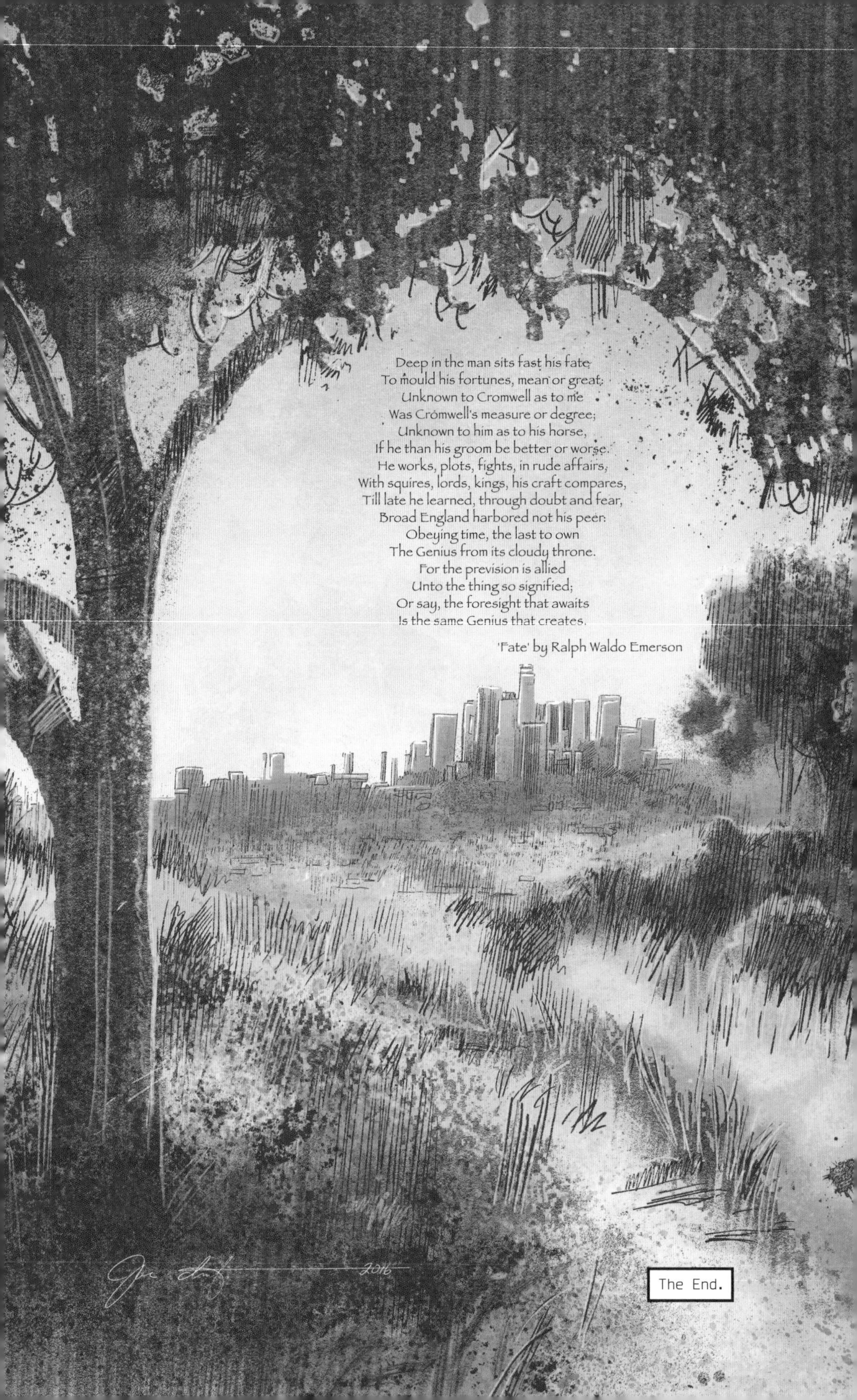
Deep in the man sits fast his fate
To mould his fortunes, mean or great:
Unknown to Cromwell as to me
Was Cromwell's measure or degree;
Unknown to him as to his horse,
If he than his groom be better or worse.
He works, plots, fights, in rude affairs,
With squires, lords, kings, his craft compares,
Till late he learned, through doubt and fear,
Broad England harbored not his peer:
Obeying time, the last to own
The Genius from its cloudy throne.
For the prevision is allied
Unto the thing so signified;
Or say, the foresight that awaits
Is the same Genius that creates.
'Fate' by Ralph Waldo Emerson
2016
The End.

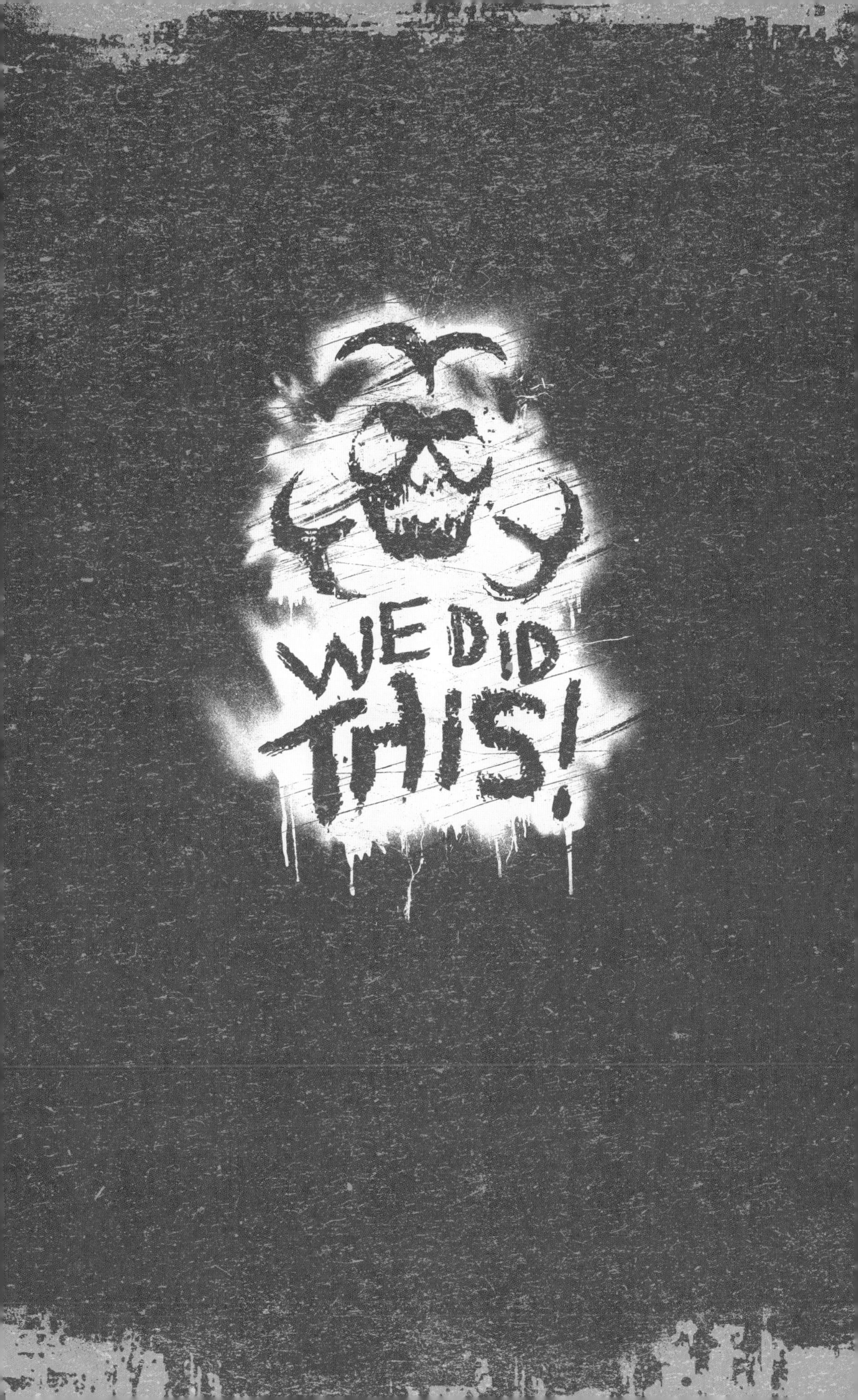
WE DID
THIS!

COVER GALLERY

THE
BUNKER
15
JOSHUA HALE FIALKOV / JOE INFURNARI / GONZALO DUARTE
2015

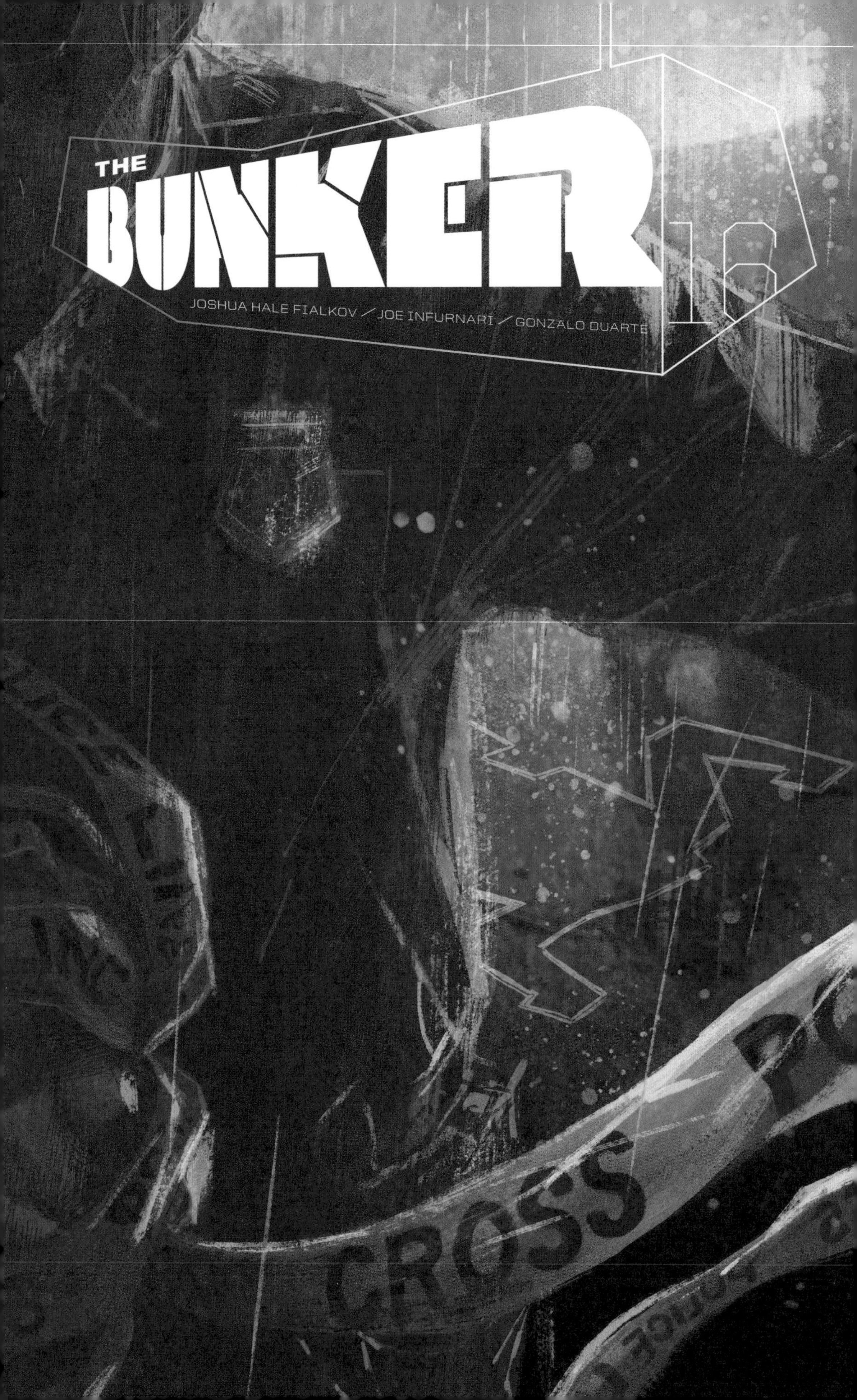
THE
BUNKER
16
JOSHUA HALE FIALKOV / JOE INFURNARI / GONZALO DUARTE
CROSS

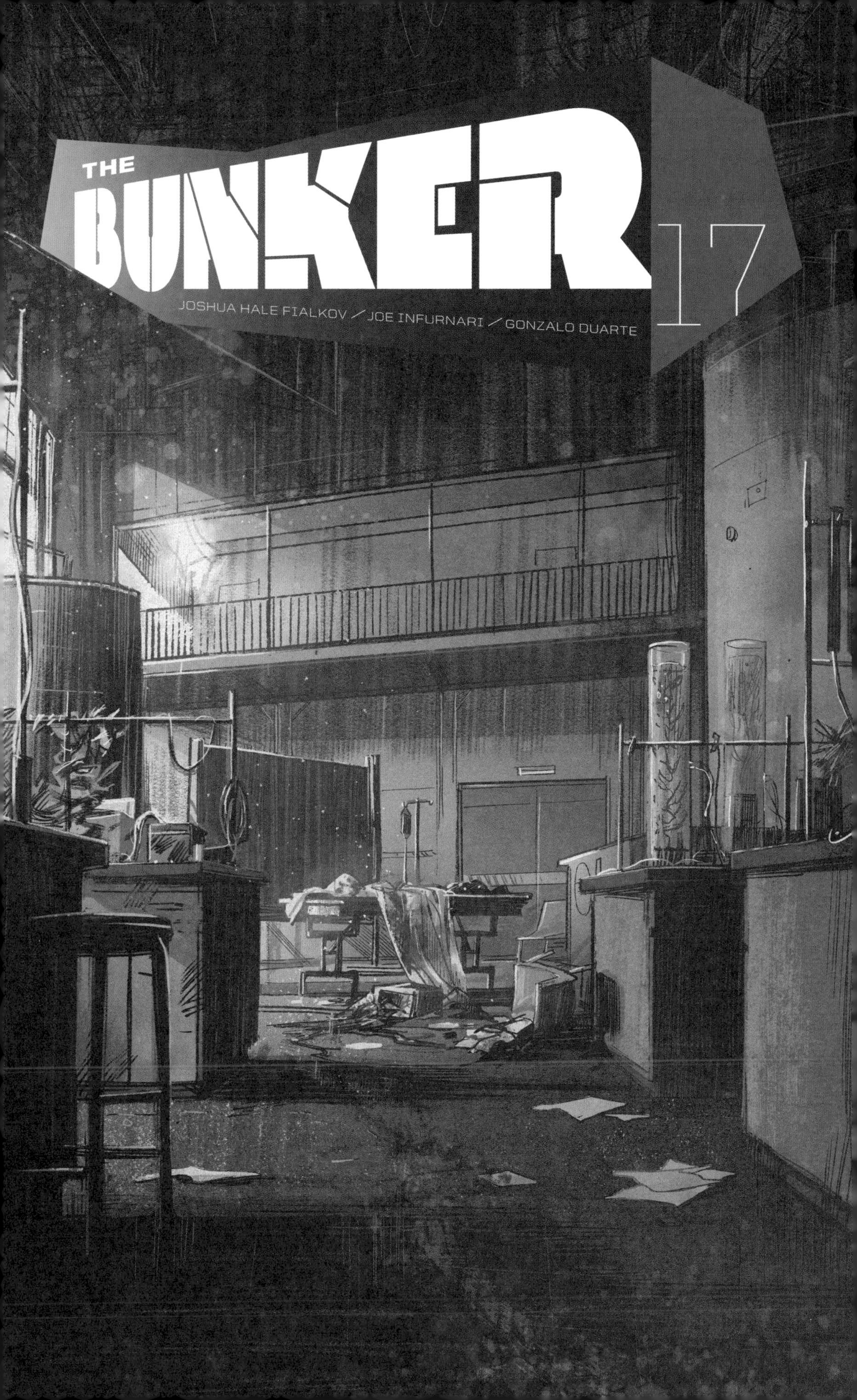
THE
BUNKER
17
JOSHUA HALE FIALKOV / JOE INFURNARI / GONZALO DUARTE

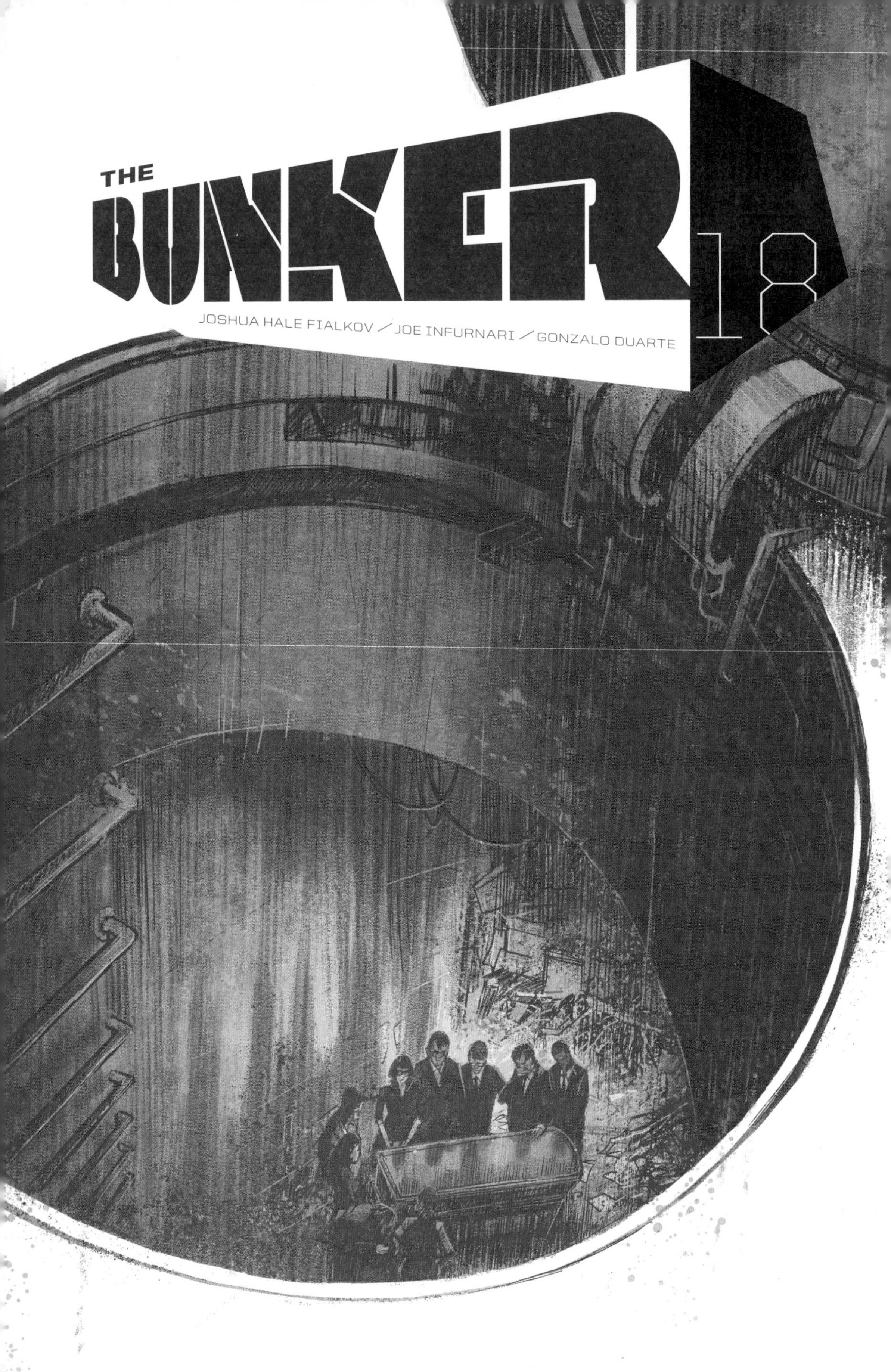
THE BUNKER
18
JOSHUA HALE FIALKOV / JOE INFURNARI / GONZALO DUARTE

THE
BUNKER
19
JOSHUA HALE FIALKOV / JOE INFURNARI / GONZALO DUARTE

Photo by Heidi Ryder

Joshua Hale Fialkov is the writer and co-creator of graphic novels including *Elk's Run*, *Tumor*, *The Life After*, *Punks*, and *Echoes*. He has written *The Ultimates* for Marvel and *I, Vampire* for DC Comics. He lives in Los Angeles with his wife, author Christina Rice, their daughter, who will be running the planet fairly soon.

Photo by Seth Kushner

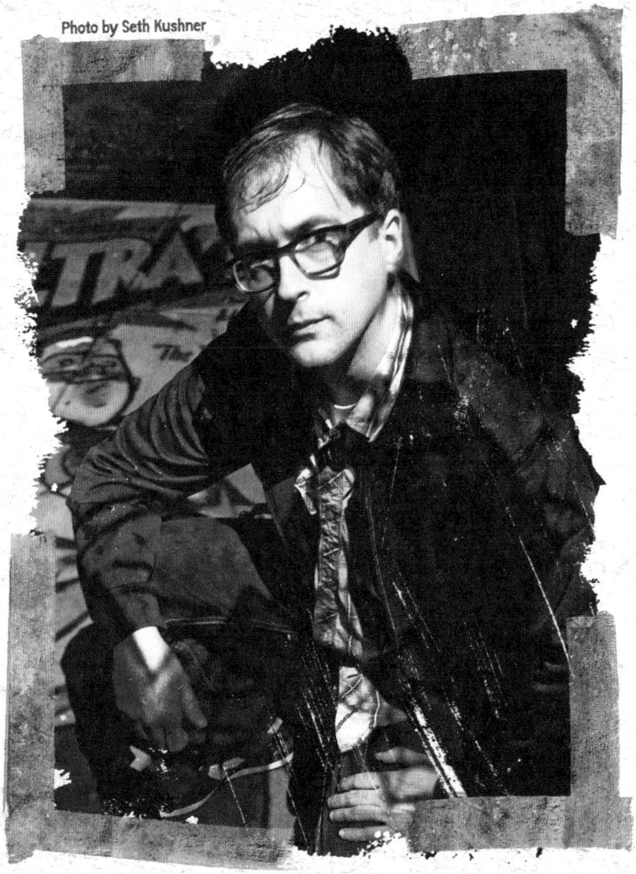

Being the singular genius behind the infamous *Time F#©ker*, Joe Infurnari's talents are uniquely suited to the vagaries of illustrating a time travel story. Whether tracing deadbeat dad DNA back to Paleolithic times or propping up a drawing pad in the midst of the apocalypse, Joe's upper lip remains stiff and his focus resolute. It's not all work and no play for Joe 'The Towering' Infurnari! Leisure time is lovingly spent with his new bride and their four crazy cats in a bunker of his own design.

Gonzalo Duarte was born in Buenos Aires, Argentina, in 1986. After a couple of years working in the animation industry he made the jump to comic books, his lifelong passion. He's been working since 2009 as a writer in the Argentine comics scene on magazines such as *Terminus* and *Proxima*, and as a colorist on titles such as Boom! Studios' *Big Trouble in Little China* and Oni Press' *Hellbreak* and *Brik*.

MORE FROM JOSHUA HALE FIALKOV AND ONI PRESS!

THE BUNKER VOL. 1:

By Joshua Hale Fialkov & Joe Infurnari

136 pages, softcover, full color interiors

ISBN 978-1-62010-164-3

THE BUNKER
JOSHUA HALE FIALKOV JOE INFURNARI
VOLUME 1

THE BUNKER
VOLUME 2

THE BUNKER VOL. 2:

By Joshua Hale Fialkov & Joe Infurnari

136 pages, softcover, full color interiors

ISBN 978-1-62010-210-7

THE BUNKER
JOSHUA HALE FIALKOV JOE INFURNARI

THE LIFE AFTER
JOSHUA HALE FIALKOV • GABO
1
10/10

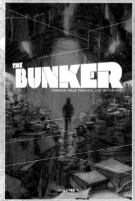

THE BUNKER VOL. 3:

By Joshua Hale Fialkov, Joe Infurnari, Brahm Revel, & Jason Fischer

144 pages, softcover, full color interiors

ISBN 978-1-62010-274-9

THE LIFE AFTER VOL. 1:

By Joshua Hale Fialkov & Gabo

136 pages, softcover, full color interiors

ISBN 978-1-62010-214-5

ELK'S RUN
A TALE OF SMALL TOWN HORROR
New York Times Best-Selling Authors
JOSHUA HALE FIALKOV
NOEL TUAZON
SCOTT KEATING

TUMOR
JOSHUA HALE FIALKOV & NOEL TUAZON

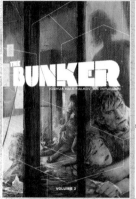

ELK'S RUN: 10TH ANNIVERSARY EDITION

By Joshua Hale Fialkov & Noel Tuazon

248 pages, hardcover, full color interiors

ISBN 978-1-62010-279-4

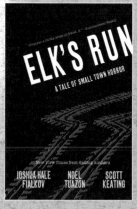

TUMOR

By Joshua Hale Fialkov & Noel Tuazon

248 pages, hardcover, black & white interiors

ISBN 978-1-62010-326-5

ONI PRESS
www.onipress.com

For more information on these and other fine Oni Press comic books and graphic novels visit onipress.com.
To find a comic specialty store in your area visit comicsphops.us.